THE ENGLISH ABIGAIL

THE MORNING GOSSIP

From *The Greatest Plague in Life*, by the brothers Mayhew, 1847

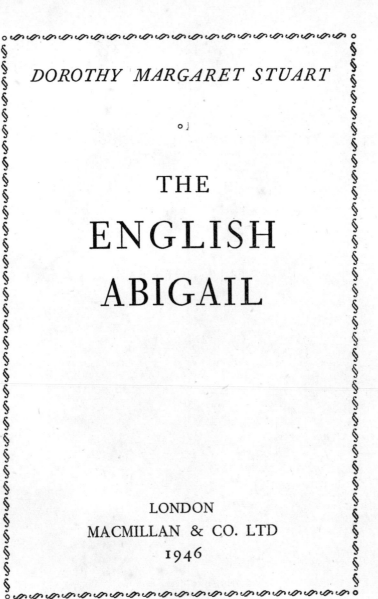

DOROTHY MARGARET STUART

THE
ENGLISH
ABIGAIL

LONDON
MACMILLAN & CO. LTD
1946

For

ELLA COLTMAN

Delightful friend

PRINTED IN GREAT BRITAIN
BY R. & R. CLARK, LIMITED, EDINBURGH

FOREWORD

THIS book is not a History of Domestic Service in England ; it is nothing so ambitious — or so controversial. Such a History, heavy with ethics and stiff with economics, will no doubt be written some day — but not by the present writer. Here will be found neither Indictment nor Apologia : all that I have done is to study the English Abigail through six centuries of history and literature, and to try to set her often interesting and entertaining figure more clearly against the background with which it has for so long been slightly confounded. Incidentally it may be that I have thrown a little light from a fresh angle upon several aspects of a bygone or obsolescent social system : but this has been only by the way, and the emphasis is upon the type and the individual, upon character, colour and comedy.

Some of my Abigails are those whom most of my readers will expect to meet : Lady Verney's Luce, Dorothy Osborne's Jane Wright, Samuel Pepys's Deb. Willett, Dr. Johnson's mother's Kitty Chambers, Byron's Mrs. Mule, Lady Byron's Mrs. Clermont, Mrs. Browning's Wilson, Miss Martineau's " Apocalyptic Housemaid ", Jane ; others, such as Charles II's pensioner, Cath. Mason, " a painfull old servant in the scullery ", are not so well known. In the field of literature immortals like Pamela, Mincing, Mrs. Slipslop, the Marchioness and Polly Perkins were bound to appear: but here again I have been fortunate in coming across a good deal of material both unhackneyed and amusing, while in old Wills I have found a valuable and vivid source of information as to the relations between mistress and maid in earlier times.

To many people, friendly strangers as well as friends, I owe much gratitude for much help and encouragement. Particularly I should like to thank the following, whose various acts of courtesy and kindness (some involving considerable exertion) the paper shortage forbids me to rehearse here: Alice, Lady Hylton, Lady Winifred Gore, Lady Craik, Sir Frederick and Lady Hopkinson, Dr. and Mrs. Arundell Esdaile, Mrs. Edmund

Fellowes, Miss M. G. Hart Dyke, Commander Bayntun Hippisley, Major A. G. Wade, M.C., and Mrs. Wade, the Rev. J. J. Antrobus, Mr. W. H. Godfrey, F.S.A., of the National Buildings Record, Mr. F. Algar, Mr. H. Clifford Smith, Mr. E. V. Davenport, Miss Draper, Mr. Joseph B. Rivlin of the New York Public Library, Miss Vera Douie of the Women's Service Library, Oxford, Mr. H. M. Sherry of the South Western Area Regional Library System, and — as always — the Librarian and Staff of the London Library. My thanks are also due to Miss V. Sackville-West and Messrs. Heinemann for permission to quote from the *Diary of Lady Anne Clifford*; to Mr. Arthur Bryant and the Cambridge University Press for permission to quote from *Samuel Pepys, the Man in the Making* and *Pepys, the Saviour of the Navy*; and to Miss G. Scott-Thomson and Messrs. Jonathan Cape for permission to quote from *The Russells in Bloomsbury* and *Letters of a Grandmother*.

D. M. S.

HOLT HATCH COTTAGE
ALTON, HANTS
1944–45

CONTENTS

ILLUSTRATIONS

CHAPTER 1

Brief Plantagenet Prologue

FOR a very early glimpse of an English Abigail we are indebted to a certain Friar Minor who flourished in the first half of the thirteenth century — Bartholomaeus Anglicus, Bartholomew the Englishman. In the choicest medieval Latin he compiled a vast, encyclopaedic treatise ' upon the properties of things ', including within his terms of reference subjects as far asunder as the nature of the angels and the habits of fleas. Somewhere between those two orders of creation he found a place for a woman-servant.

De Proprietaribus Rerum enjoyed great and long-persisting popularity. It was copied, quoted, copied again, and finally, towards the close of the succeeding century, turned into English by that industrious Cornish priest, John Trevisa. Beneath his quill many of Bartholomew's ideas and images gain much in vigour while losing something in dignity. In the description of " the servaunt-woman " we are told, for example, that she " is ordeyned for to lerne the wyve's rule, and is put to office and werke of traveylle, toylynge and slubberynge ". She is nourished upon " grosse mete and symple " — the coarsest bread and beer, says another authority, and beef baked or boiled on Sunday served cold for the rest of the week. She is " kepte lowe under the yoeke of thraldom and of servage ", beaten with rods, scarcely suffered to rest or take breath by day or night.

Against the medieval background, an arras-cloth woven with skyey towers and fretted pinnacles, with hawthorn-hedged plots where the fairest of maidens tarry, and forests where the most debonair of horsemen ride, or — to alter the metaphor — a page from a psalter wrought upon the margin with narrow-flanked ladies trailing embroidered heraldry behind them, and with monsters at once gruesome and gay, that stooping, monochrome figure makes a joyless patch indeed. Yet Bartholomew himself proceeds to show by implication that the " servaunt-woman "

did not invariably spend her days bowed down beneath the
" yoeke ". He quotes with marked approval the opinion of
Rabanus, a ninth-century Archbishop of Mainz, that when such
women are not kept in subjection by " drede " their hearts swell
and wax stout and proud ; for, most unfortunately, " goodly
love " and gentle treatment make bondfolk unbiddable.

From this it is clear that the lot of the Abigail in Plantagenet
England was not uniformly bleak, and that she was sometimes
treated with an indulgence of which the results were scarcely
encouraging. John Gower noted this with a gloomy eye : the
poor folk, he perceived, were becoming more haughty than their
lords, and trouble could hardly fail to follow. Thus early do
the two sharply-contrasted types detach themselves from the
mass — to be encountered again in life and in literature as the
centuries unfold : the " pampered menial " and the down-trodden
drudge.

The " servaunt-woman's " best chance of happiness was in
the household of some noble family. Bartholomew himself
conducts us into the great hall when a feast is in progress, when
the guests, having washed their hands, sit down beside the lord
upon the dais ; when " chyldren ben sette in theyr place and
servauntes at a table by them selfe ", while the " household
servaunts besyly helpe eche other to everythinge diligently, and
talke merily togider ". In such an environment she would
certainly fare better than if she were hired to serve the wife of
some yeoman-farmer, some town-dwelling merchant or crafts-
man, less far removed in station from herself.

To understand exactly how heavily or how lightly the yoke
of servitude pressed upon the shoulders of the medieval Abigail,
it is necessary to imagine in what sort of surroundings and under
what kind of conditions her childhood had been spent. Her
birth-place was one of those dim huts of wicker and clay described
cheerfully enough by Chaucer and by Langland with unmitigated
gloom. Sturdy fellow though the English villein might be,
stubbornly though he contended for his rights, heartily though he
savoured his infrequent pleasures, it cannot be denied that his
children began life burdened with a variety of handicaps, both
spiritual and material. Under the low roof of thatch, breathing

the acrid smoke to which no chimney gave any vent, they lay in their narrow cradles, rocked by the weary foot of their mother as she sat spinning with her distaff, or peeling rushes for rush-lights, or patching the rough homespun of her own and her husband's daily wear. Sometimes there was sharp dearth of even such fare as dusky-coloured bread made of beans and bran, and the children would weep for hunger. To such folk, says Lang-land, a farthing's worth of mussels would be a feast, and a farthing's worth of cockles, " these were almes to helpe ". Characteristic-ally he does not relieve the grim picture with any hint of any possible delights of mind or body ; it is winter in the hut ; no cherries redden in its small garden, no trestles are set up for a miracle play upon the village green. Yet even Chaucer has little to say that is cheerful about the life of a villein's daughter : his Griseldis, " povrelich y-fostred ", with a distaff in her childish hand or a bunch of wild herbs to be shredded and seethed for dinner, may stand as typical of them all.

Can it be doubted that when such a girl became a servant in some castle or manor-house the change in her way of living would be on balance a change for the better ? Even if she slept with the other maids on the rushes bestrewing the floor of the great hall, the atmosphere would be less smoky on account of the higher pitch of the roof ; and even if her supper had been " grosse mete and symple ", she would at least not lie wakeful for lack of food. In the later Plantagenet period it happened quite frequently that planking was fixed under the rafters of the hall to make sleeping quarters for the servants, and for any chance wayfarer who might tarry for the night ; and every time that it happened a forward step was taken towards more tolerable living conditions for the humbler units in the household.

What she looked like and what she wore, this maidservant in a medieval manor, we may guess well enough from the Luttrell Psalter and other illuminated manuscripts of the period. Not for her were the peaked and horned, the purfled and jewelled head-dresses against which Holy Church inveighed so vehemently when they were worn by ladies of high degree : a close white coif covered her head and concealed her hair. The " dark stuff gown " so often to be mentioned in later times is already her recognized uniform ; but, oddly enough, she is hardly ever depicted wearing one of those bibless aprons, adorned with stitchery or smocking, which are so frequently shown girding the bodies of peasant-women labouring in the fields.

We see her kneeling by a young lady and holding up a round hand-mirror so that the effect of the elaborate head-dress may be seen : we see her helping to make a bed, and stretching out sheets which fall into symmetrical, angular convolutions as she does so; and in one illumination we see her in attendance upon a lady who is taking a bath in a high, cask-like tub out of which the bather certainly could not have climbed without assistance.

In any medieval household the scouring of pots, pans and platters, candlesticks, tankards and bowls occupied much of the servants' time. Most of these things were made of metal, pewter, latten, brass, copper or bronze ; but those that were of wood demanded no less vigorous cleansing. Where a man-cook ruled the kitchen a scullion (or more than one) would be responsible for his numerous and sometimes complicated utensils ; in a more modest establishment Cecily and Gille would be constantly busy with fine sand, sifted ashes and linseed oil. The results of their industry are suggested in Chaucer's comparison of a lady's bright yellow hair to

any bason skouréd newe.

Small mops of heather, big besoms of osier or birch, and high, narrow pitchers of green or tawny earthenware, were in constant requisition ; and from time to time special rods were used to beat the fleas out of the bed-hangings and bedding : the bed-bug (*Cimex lectularius*) appears not to have been known in England before the sixteenth century. Whether the mistress were of high or middle degree she could hardly fail to busy herself with distaff and loom, and her damsels were expected to do like-wise. Surely one of the loveliest visual rhythms of that vanished way of life must have been the movement of the distaffs in the flicker of the firelight when the lady and her attendants sat " *dévidant et filant* " after the manner of Ronsard's Hélène : and the spinning-wheel was hardly less pleasing to the eye.

It was not only the nobly or the gently born who kept maidservants. Sometimes when it became necessary to fix a person's age legally by the sworn recollections of a neighbour there was an incidental allusion to that neighbour's household : for example, Geoffrey le White of Eton, testifying as to the age of a certain Isabel de Wolynton, deponed that sixteen years before, to wit, on the morrow of the Purification in the tenth year of King Edward II, he had an oast-house and three quarters of malt burnt, "through the fault of Cecily his maid". Her carelessness seems to have rankled in her master's memory both deeply and long. In Chaucer's *Miller's Tale* the household of John, the foolish carpenter of Oxford, consists of a maid called Gille and a youth, Robyn. When the unscrupulous lodger, Nicolas the Clerk, invented the story of an imminent flood and persuaded his host to plant three kneading-troughs upon the roof of his house so that they two and John's unfaithful young wife should be saved, he expressly excluded the servants from his plan. They must not be warned ; neither could they be spared : there were not enough tubs to go round. Their master was forbidden to ask why they should be doomed ; that was a secret between the Clerk and his Creator.

Poor John believed this, and many other things hardly more credible; but he was loth to see the lad and the wench perish, and upon the eve of the fatal day named by Nicolas he dispatched Robyn and Gille upon errands to London. He cannot have thought that the folk in the city would escape the deluge, for he did not suggest flight thither as an alternative to a roof-top tub; so one may imagine the departure of the unwitting pair along the London road, happy to have a mission that was also a holiday, and wondering why their master should take leave of them so gravely. That jovial shrew, the Wyf of Bath, had a maid whom she seems to have used upon occasion as a rod wherewith to chastise her husband — any husband of the five. In her inimitable instructions to other married women she suggests invoking the testimony of the maidservant if it should be necessary to hoodwink the master ; she counsels asking him angrily why he whispered in the girl's ear — as a means of keeping him up to the mark, whether the implied charge were well-founded or no ; and finally he should be told that, under pain of vague but alarming penalties, he must pay honour to his wife's old nurse and to her personal attendant or " chamberere ".

In the *Shipman's Tale* we catch a brief glimpse of such a " chamberere " in the making. The gay monk, Dan John, comes to visit his kinswoman, the old merchant's wanton young wife, and finds her walking in her garden :

> A mayde child çam in her compaignye
> Which as her list she may governe and gye,[1]
> For yet under the yerde [2] was the mayde.

The presence of this young person was not necessary to the plot, and it certainly imposed no restraint upon the behaviour of her elders. Perhaps Chaucer had intended to introduce her again, even to give her some lines to speak, and then had abandoned the idea. If so, he showed the same fine instinct as that which prompted Shakespeare to eliminate the figure of the child who plays a part in the original tale of *Othello*. His own wife, Philippa Roet, by virtue of her post in the household of Queen Philippa of Hainault, may perhaps be classed as a Plantagenet Abigail of the higher rank.

These higher ranks were sometimes recruited from families well above the villein class. Mrs. Geoffrey Chaucer, though her duties as " damoiselle of the Queen's Chamber " were very similar to those of her husband as " valettus " to the King, may have been a knight's daughter : and in certain cities (and circumstances) single women were liable to be ' impressed ' for domestic work. There is an intriguing entry in the fifteenth-century Leet Book of Coventry which illustrates this point. Spinsters under the age of fifty, of sound health, and " myghty in body to labour ", are forbidden " forthensforth " to take or keep houses or rooms by themselves, or with any other person, and enjoined to go into service until they marry. The penalty for the first default was " vis viiid ", but for a second lapse delinquents would be " comyted to prison there to abyde till they fynde suerte to go to service ".

Preoccupation with the city's morals is easily discernible behind these regulations ; yet none of these austere burghers

---

[1] guide, direct.   [2] rod.

seems to have boggled at the thought that his wife might thereafter have Doll Tearsheet for an auxiliary.

One of the anecdotes compiled by the Knight of La Tour
Landry for the benefit of his daughters in the fourteenth century,
and 'Englished' in the fifteenth, takes us into a bourgeois household where relations between mistress and maid tend to follow
the lines laid down by the Wyf of Bath. It tells how there was
a woman who kept a talking magpie in a cage ; and how her
husband kept a fat eel in a little pond in the garden, intending to
kill and cook it for the entertainment of some of his friends. But
one day, when he was out, the wife said to her maid, " Let us
eat the great eel, and I will say to my husband that the otter has
eaten him." And so it was done. And when the good man
returned, the magpie began to tell him what had happened to the
eel ; so he hastened to the pond, and seeing that the eel was not
there, began to question his wife. She would have made excuses,
but he said, " Excuse you not, for I wot welle ye have etyn yt, for
the pye hath told me " — and so " ther was gret noyse betwene
the man and hys wiff for the etynge of the ele ".

But after he had departed the wife and her maid came to the
magpie " and plucked off all the fedres on the pye's hede, crying,
' Thou has discovered us of the ele ' — and thus was the poor
magpie plucked. And ever after if she saw a man with a bald
head or a woman with a high forehead she was wont to say to
them, ' Ye spak of the ele.' "

Though the original, both text and provenance, of Caxton's
Dialogues (1488) was Franco-Flemish of the previous century,
the work may be accepted as giving a fairly faithful picture of
domestic life in England under the last Plantagenet and the first
Tudor. The background is hearty and homely, the typical
burgher background in northern Europe about that time. The
maids are by no means ignorant ; they can name all the great
feasts and seasons of the year ; nor are they down-trodden ;
when one of them, politely addressed as " Damyselle ", is
requested to show off this accomplishment, she roundly refuses
to do so. " I shall not, so God me helpe," she retorts ; " Agace
shall name them." This Agace proceeds to do at great length,
reeling off an interminable list of feast days and solemn seasons,

some of them sounding quaint in modern ears : " Our Lady in Harvest " — Lammas-tide, " the Paynful Week " — Holy Week. " Hye days " might be impressed on the memory of these maidens by the circumstance that, in honour of them, all the metal-work in the house had to be burnished and made to shine.

Later we are introduced to a maid at an inn. To her the hostess calls urgently as three travellers appear :

> Jennette, lyghte the candell ;
> And lede them ther above
> In the solar tofore ;
> And bere them hoot watre
> For to washe their feet ;
> And covere them with quysshuns.
> Se that the stable
> Be well shette.

Such must have been the duties of St. Joan when she was a maid-servant in the inn at Domrémy.

Less arduous, if more monotonous, was the daily round of those lay-women who were permitted to wait upon certain privileged nuns and to serve ladies who had retired into the cloister as ' parlour-boarders '. Obviously a gentlewoman who was allowed by custom, though not always by episcopal authority, to amuse herself with pet dogs, birds and apes, to listen to minstrels and to play chess, would not deny herself the additional solace of a personal attendant. In 1308 Bishop Stapledon of Exeter had something to say upon this subject when sending an episcopal remonstrance to Polsloe Priory :

> *Item*, seeing that certain Ladies of your Religion [*i.e.* Order] have, at certain times, had their own several serving-maids to prepare their meals apart from the rest, therefore we ordain, will and decree that all these maids be utterly expelled from the kitchen, and that a competent man-cook with a page [*i.e.* scullion] to help him be set to serve the whole convent.

It is not difficult to imagine the confusion, controversy and acrimony that might result from the culinary arrangements condemned by the good bishop ; but the remedy prescribed by him may have been quite acceptable to the maids — for more reasons than one.

Good service was often remembered and rewarded by the

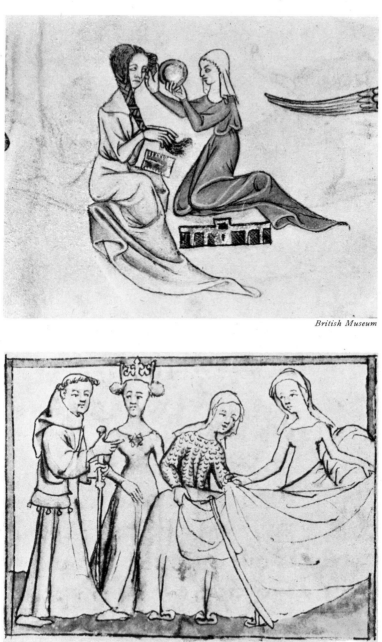

PLANTAGENET ABIGAILS

great ones of the earth, and when the tawny death-candles flared round the dark-palled catafalque the women-servants of the household, kneeling indistinguishable in their mourning hoods, were almost always comforted by the knowledge that the dead lord or lady had named them, generally or severally, when inditing a last Will and Testament. An early example is the Will of Agnes de Clifford, in the first quarter of the thirteenth century. She leaves ten marks to her servant Matilda, a scarlet robe, " *et unam Gulecem punctatum, et unam coöptorium* ".[1] Elizabeth de Burgh, Lady Clare, a granddaughter of Edward I, expressed her wishes in the most crabbed of English-French, but their benevolent tenor is not to be mistaken. After the settlement of all her debts, she dictates the distribution of various legacies, some of them very splendid-sounding, among the women of her household. Suzanne de Neketon is to have twelve silver porringers, two new cruets of silver, a horse's bit of silver, enamelled with the arms of the testatrix ; and to Anne de Lexeden are allotted twenty-two pounds sterling, and " my black robe with all its appurtenances ". These appurtenances (*garnements*) included the côte-hardy, a long close-fitting bodice, a sleeveless jacket or over-tunic, and a mantle ; for the ' robe ' of a Plantagenet lady was what a modern dressmaker would describe as a ' four-piece costume '. To Elizabeth Torel Lady Clare bequeathed a covered cup of silver, two enamelled silver bowls with spouts, and her second-best robe, with *garnements* : to Margarete Bauchon, four silver ewers and her third-best robe, with *garnements* ; to Agnes, wife of John de Southam, the three *garnements* of the fifth-best robe — nothing is said about the robe itself, and the fourth-best is passed over in silence. Other women of her household shared the rest of their lady's wardrobe between them, some of the items being rather curiously apportioned — as when Alison de Wodeham receives the sixth-best robe, but its *garnements* go to Jehane de Horselee. Two robes of ' tyrtene ', a rough sort of fabric from which the battle-dress of foot-soldiers was sometimes made, were divided between " the said Alison " and Johanette Drueys, who became the richer by six silver plates and eleven silver *quillers* — rendered ' bells ' by the editor of *Royal and Noble*

[1] An embroidered collar and a bedspread.

Wills, but more probably meaning ' platters ', as the use of small bells to decorate dresses did not become fashionable until the end of the century.

One year after Alison, Johanette and their fellow-servants had reaped the reward of their service there died an unusual character in the Plantagenet chronicle-play — a noble bachelor. He was Humphrey de Bohun, Earl of Hereford and Essex, Knight of the Garter, son of Elizabeth Plantagenet, daughter of Edward III. How he contrived to die a bachelor at the age of fifty must ever remain a minor historical mystery. Was he a misogynist ? Had he taken a lifelong vow of chastity ? Had he been cruelly crossed in love ? We shall never know ; but the terms of his Will suggest a kind master well served by faithful men and women. His household affairs seem to have been in the care of two trusted servitors, Walter and Marion Blunt, and to them he bequeathed his best robe furred with miniver. Marion was charged to deliver her master's jewels to his executors, and to divide among the women-servants of his household all the linen, kerchiefs and other stuffs in her keeping, to the end that they might pray for his soul. Three of these women are mentioned by name : Letice de Massendon, who was to have twenty pounds ; Helen Smyth, ten marks ; and Thomasine Belle, eleven marks for a marriage portion.

In 1427 Elizabeth, Lady Fitzhugh, bequeathed gowns and kirtles to her women-servants, but there is more personal feeling in the Will of Anne, Countess of Stafford, who died twelve years later. Judged by modern standards the attitude of the mighty to the meek left something to be desired in the Middle Ages, and for long after, though, according to their own code, these lords and ladies were usually benevolent and often bountiful. Seldom, however, did any of them feel such a prick of conscience as that which troubled Lady Stafford on her death-bed. This daughter of Prince Thomas of Woodstock showed singular scrupulosity in settling her own affairs, for after enjoining her executors to pay not only her debts but also her wrongs and extortions, she declares :

> I wole yat my seyde executors, havyng tendir consideracioun of souche of my servants, as well of women as of men, as have lengist

don most trewe and diligent servise to me and litil veleuid by me or nought, yat yey, after theyr wel avised discrecions, rewarde eche of hem aftir yeire degre and desertes, competently for their help and relyf as ferfurth as ye power of my seid executors wole stretche in that partie.

"Little veleuid by me or nought" — it is a tardy twinge, maybe the result of death-bed meditations or ghostly counsel, but it does honour both the lady and her servitors. Another great Plantagenet dame who remembered the women of her household was Elizabeth, Lady Latymer, who, on her demise in 1480, left a hundred marks to Joice Sheldon "in reward for her good service", and to Anne Sheldon, for *her* good service, a hundred marks "to her marriage". This sum was the average price of a really handsome tomb.

By her Will dated March 25, 1487, Dame Agnes Scott, widow of Sir John Scott of Scot's Hall, Brabourne, Kent, bequeathed to Thomasyne her servant "a ffederbedde wt a bolster, a paire of blanketts, a coveryng of blewe for a bedde, a playne table-cloth, a large playne towell, and v marc in sterlyng money for her mariage". To Margerie Pantu (Margerie of the Pantry?) she left "a matas wt a bolster, a pair of blankets, a paire of shetis and a covering for a bedde". A third dependent, Joys or Joise Barry, whose wedding portion of five marks had been the bequest of Sir John Scott two years before, was to receive "a goode ffederbedd, wt a bolster, a payre of blankettis, a coverlitt of tapestrie of xxx^{ti} flemyssh elles, a payre of gentilmen shetes, ij payre of yeomen shettis, and a flatte pece of silver".

Students of the Paston letters will remember Sir John Paston's poetical correspondent, John Pympe, a good-natured fellow, constantly in difficulties and in debt. He was a connection of the Scotts of Scot's Hall, in whose privately-printed *Memorials* his Will is given. It contains this revealing and at the same time endearing clause :

Item, I bequeith to Margarete Norton which som tyme was servant to my Fader and Moder in recompence of money to me at dyverse tymes lente bothe in my Childehode and syne and for mony other kindenes to me shewd, iiijli in gold so that she make a clere discharge to myn executours of all manner other demaundes, safe that I will that she have delivered ij salte of silver covered waing by estimacion xi^{te} and a standing cuppe covered parcell gilte and vii spons of silver, which all I borowed of her and have occupied hit be long space.

So early did John Pympe's difficulties begin, and so long did they endure — even to the end of his days, for another clause in his Will leaves " vjs viiid to the high auter " of his parish church at Nettlestead for " tithes and offringe forgoten, etc.". Testators of his time were often anxious to put things right with Heaven " while the lamp held on to burn ", but it is a rare and touching thing to find one thus mindful of early kindness from a humble friend.

The Plantagenet period and — in a sense — the Plantagenet line may be said to have ended in the diminutive person of Margaret Beaufort, great-granddaughter of John of Gaunt and mother of Henry VII. She grew up in an England almost untouched either by the glow of the Renaissance or the gloom of the Reformation ; America was as yet undiscovered, Caxton had not set up his printing-press at the sign of the red pale, and it seemed as if the Plantagenet dynasty in direct male descent from Edward III would continue to occupy the English throne. It is true that the rise of Lollardy and the decay of the feudal system already gave indications of great changes to come ; there were cracks in the social and religious fabric and rumblings in the foundations, but these as yet were marked only by a few anxious observers. When the Lady Margaret reached her journey's end in 1509 everything was altered. Two new worlds were being explored, one geographical, the other intellectual : the background was perceptibly less Gothic and definitely less gay. On the physical plane, people's faces and hands and feet were seen to be broadening and coarsening, and to the lank, ascetic medieval angles succeeded the gross and cumbersome Tudor curves.

A remarkable woman was Lady Margaret, " modre of the most Christian prince, king Henrie the VIIth ". She was the mother also of pious foundations, the patroness of holy and learned men, and, as might have been expected, a wise, watchful and merciful mistress to her household, for whom, says her confessor, St. John Fisher, Bishop of Rochester, she provided reasonable statutes and ordinances, which she commanded to be read aloud to them by her officers four times a year : " and often-times," he adds, " by her self she wolde so lovyngly courage every of them to do well ".

She outlived her son the King by two months, and while the Abbey was ringing with the anthems and the plaudits of her grandson's coronation, she lay dying not far away, racked with pain and crying aloud, " O blessyd Jhesu, helpe me ! O blessyd Lady, sucoure me ! "

In her funeral sermon, preached at Westminster in the presence of her sorrowing household, Fisher described the final scene :

> Lyke a spere it perced the hertes of all her true servaunts that was about her, and made them cry alsoe of Jhesu for helpe and sucoure, with grete haboundance of teares. But specyally when they saw the dethe so hast upon her, and that she must nedes depart from them, and they sholde forgoe so gentyll a maistris, so tender a lady, then wept they mervaylously, wept her ladys and kyneswomen, to whom she was full kinde, wept her poore gentyl-women, whom she loved so tenderly before, wept her chamberers, to whom she was full deare.

By her last Will she left £200 to buy black cloth for mourning for her executors and servants, men and women, and of this sum £34 : 0 : 4 in the currency of the period was expended upon " dyvers Mantells " for the female part of the household " ageynst the berying ". To delay the dispersal of her attendants she had inserted this clause :

> *Item* : we will that our executors give to every of our household servants viiid. for every day for their costs, to bring them from Westminster unto the place where our household shall be kepte after our decesse by the space of quarter of a yere. . . . And we will that our said executors cause all our household servaunts to be kept togider, and household kepte in all things convenyent for theym at and in such convenyent place as shal be thought by our executors most necessarye for the same from the tyme of our decesse by the space of quarter of a yeer at the leste.

They were to be provided with " mete, drynke, and other thing convenyent for household, as they have used and accustomed to have had heretofore in oure household " ; and every servant was to have half a year's wages, whether they wished to depart within the first three months following her death or elected to " tarry and abide togedir " during that space. By a codicil she further desired that her " old and serviceable household servants " should be rewarded at the discretion of Bishop Fox of Winchester, and when the executors rendered their accounts two years later a payment of " iiijli. iijs. iiijd " is noted " to divers of my lady's servaunts . . . for divers consyderacions ".

CHAPTER II

Tudor Background—Elizabethan Stage

THE changes, outward and inward, which marked the Tudor period affected almost every aspect of English social life and every class of the community. Among those who felt the pressure of these strange and powerful influences was the English Abigail. Though many serving-wenches still trod the old, arduous Plantagenet round, new demarcations became visible, and new subdivisions were made. Now appears the privileged waiting-woman, who toils not neither does she ' slubber ' ; and now appears the poor relation who, with no nunnery to go to, ranks little if at all above the servants, and is expected to make herself useful in any way that her prosperous kinsfolk may demand. Take the example of Dorythe Plympton, whose father, a Yorkshire knight of some substance, did not scruple to place her in a semi-menial position in the household of his second wife's mother : " wherefor ", she wrote to him, " yt is thought in these partes by those persones that list better to say ill than good that ye have little favour unto me ; the which error ye may now quench yf yt will like you to be so good and kynd father unto me ".

Whether the error was ' quenched ', whether, indeed, it was an error, we shall never know; but it is certain that poor Dorythe was only one of many gently-born girls of her time who had perforce to play the part of an Abigail.

Seldom can the part have been so merrily played as it was by Margaret Giggs, humble kinswoman to Thomas More's second wife, Mistress Middleton, in the More household, first at Bucklersbury and afterwards at Chelsea. For her companions she had the three daughters and the only son of the family : Margaret, Elizabeth, Cecily and John : for her occupation, in addition to attendance upon all the ladies of a preponderantly feminine circle, the study of Greek, Latin and music ; for her disport, a garden where grew

Privet and whitethorn, filbert-tree and peach ;

15

for her edification the frequent apparition of learned, famous, and even royal personages ; and for her mirth the antics of innumerable pets — dogs, rabbits, weasels, foxes, monkeys.

It is true that her principal patroness, Lady More, was brusque in manner, worldly in mind, loquacious in speech ; but these defects of hers could not avail to mar the gracious atmosphere ; and More's golden sweetness always obliterated the occasional acerbity of his lady. Margaret Giggs " used to relate that sometimes she would deliberately commit some fault " that she might enjoy his " sweet and loving reproof ". He encouraged her in her favourite study of medicine, and alludes to her medical skill in his *Dialogue of Comfort against Tribulation* ; but even in that other Eden, demi-Paradise of Chelsea, she was obviously not regarded as the equal of the daughters of the family. They were married off to men of rank and property ; their companion-attendant became the wife of John Clements, More's servant, secretary and pupil, whose duties included the care of his master's horses if he went on a journey, and such general valeting as a notoriously careless dresser could be persuaded to tolerate. His successor, John Harris, subsequently married one of Margaret Roper's maidservants, Dorothy Colley, of whom more anon.

A common interest in medicine drew the two dependents together, and after their marriage John Clements, having qualified, began to practise as a physician in the City, where he and his wife lived for a time in More's former house in Bucklersbury, that street of herbmongers proverbially fragrant " in simple-time ". On Sunday, April 12, 1534, their old master listened to a sermon from the open-air pulpit outside St. Paul's and later, instead of taking boat home to Chelsea, elected to pay them a visit. He was followed by one of the King's officers, who then and there cited him to appear the next day at Lambeth for the purpose of taking the new oath — which in the event he firmly refused to take.

The large and loving humanity in which Thomas More stood practically alone in his day and generation found a place within its compass for two of the maidservants of Margaret Roper, his " derlyng Megg ". These were Dorothy Colley and Joan Aleyn. When, on the Eve of St. Thomas, the Apostle's namesake (and

future fellow-saint) wrote with a fragment of coal the last of all
his letters to the dearest of all his children, he characteristically
interpolated this passage :

> I like speciall well Dorothy Colley, I pray you be good to her.
> I would wit whether this be she that you wrote me of. If not, I
> pray you be good to the other as you may in her affliction, and to
> my good daughter Joan Aleyn too. Give her I pray you some kind
> answer, for she sued hither to me this day to pray you be good to
> her.

Dorothy Colley was in constant attendance upon Margaret
Roper during those last tragic and heart-haunting days ; she
went with her and Mrs. Clements to the church of St. Peter-ad-
Vincula on the evening of the execution, to pray by the rough,
blood-smeared chest in which the headless body of More had
been thrust : and it seems not improbable that she was with her
mistress in a wherry on the Thames when the blackened head of
the martyr fell from its spike on London Bridge into the waiting
arms of his best-loved child.

In 1526, the year after More was appointed Chancellor of the
Duchy of Lancaster, there was issued a " Declaration of Bouche
of Court ", setting forth the allowances of food, drink and fuel
to which each member of the royal household was entitled. Her
Majesty's " mayde-servants " — it was still Katharine of Aragon
— received among them " for their Bouch in the morning, i
chet[1] lofe, i manchet,[2] one gallon of ale ; for afternoon, one
manchett, one gallon of ale ; for after supper, i chet lofe, one
manchett, two gallons of ale, dim' pitcher of wyne ; and from the
last day of October unto the first day of Aprill, three lynckes by
the weeks, by the day six sisies,[3] one pound white lights, six
faggots — amounting by the yeare to the sume of xxiiil
xixs ".

Among the maids thus frugally regaled must have been some
— if not all — of those who were in attendance on their royal
mistress when she lay dying at Kimbolton and on whose behalf
she pleaded so pathetically in her last letter to the King her " lord
and dear husband ". The three upon whom she begged him to

---

[1] Wheaten bread made of flour more coarsely sifted than [2], which was a small roll
of finest bread, tapering at either end.   [3] Wax tapers.

bestow marriage portions were, of course, her ladies-in-waiting ; but the " little maidens ", number not specified, to each of whom she willed £10, were her " chamberers ". Her prayer that the King would give them " a year's pay, more than their due ", was not granted.

Very different were the conditions in the household of Agnes, Duchess-Dowager of Norfolk, and very different were the characters and habits of her unruly waiting-women among whom her youthful step-grandchild, Katharine Howard, was left disregarded — to her undoing. These wantons slept in a sort of dormitory, where musicians and other male hangers-on paid them clandestine visits ; and in that place perilous Katharine was allowed to sleep also. The name of one of them — Mary Lassels — stinks in the nostrils, for it was she who, after encouraging and abetting the unhappy child in her folly, turned King's Evidence when scandal detonated and royal disillusionment cut deep, and she who glibly gave the information that helped to send the twenty-year-old Queen to the block. Her reward — and her brother's, who acted with her — was exemption from the indictment of Misprision of Treason, directed against every person of whatsoever degree who had been involved in Katharine's early escapades.

These women, the maids and waiting-women of Katharine of Aragon and the old Duchess of Norfolk, and those of the More circle, have their place, honourable or otherwise, in the history of the early Tudor period : but we can extract from Wills ranging through all the years from the accession of Henry VII to the death of Elizabeth brief fragments of domestic homespun to complete the tapestry.

Sir Henry Colet, Knight, citizen and Alderman of London, father of the famous Dean of that name, set aside a sum of £100 for marriage portions for poor maidens of good name and fame, and then added : " I will that every of my maidservants which shall happen to be in household service with me at the time of my decease have to her marriage a portion of the said C₁ after the discretion of my executors, and besides that a gown of cloth of black cloth ". John Cornwallis of Brome, Suffolk, bequeathed " to Ellyn Barker, my servant, vis viiid " at his death in 1505.

Many of the bequests were not in money but in kind — as when in 1511 John Middleton left seven quarts of malt to his daughter Joan and "another quarter of Malt" to his servant, Agness Brown. Ten years later Robert Frevyll of Ely made the following dispositions of movable property : "To Jane Colyne, my servant, a quarter of barley ; to Jane Barker, my servant, three quarters of barley, four sheep, and a pair of sheets".

Near the end of the century we find Francis Drake providing in his Will for the large retinue which he maintained at once to gratify his love of splendour and to support his dignity as the Queen's General at Sea. To four of his men-servants and to "Dorothy, the wife of Richard Lane", he left £20 apiece ; to the residue of his servants, "beinge of the better sorte, tenne poundes of lawfull English monie" ; to others, "being of the second sorte", £5 ; and "to the residue of all my common servantes, both men and women, which shalbe serveing in my house at the time of my death and departure, to each of them the sum of fortie shillings".

As the Tudor age climbed to its peak in the reign of Queen Elizabeth many forces were at work which made the lot of the serving-maid less bleak. Some of the contrasts between that age and the ages that went before were viewed without any enthusiasm by some austere persons. Parson Harrison, in his oft-quoted *Description of England*, remarks that "of old time" bran bread was baked for the servants, the "worst and weakest" of all the other sorts of brown bread, with "little or no flour left therein at all" ; but now, "because it is drie and brickle in the making", some people add a portion of rye meal "whereby the rough drieness thereof is somewhat qualified" — a truly Sybarite innovation. Morose ancients in Harrison's own parish of Rad-winter in Essex were inclined — after the manner of such ancients in all places and periods — to deprecate even those changes which were manifest improvements. Their fathers, yea, and they themselves, had been wont to lie upon pallets or mats of straw, covered only with a sheet, under coverlets made of dagswain or hop-harlots ("I use their owne termes", says their parson, in parenthesis), with a good round log under their heads ; pillows were thought meet "onelie for women in childbed" ; and as for servants, " if they had anie sheet above them, it was well, for seldom had they anie under their bodies, to keep them from the pricking straws that ran oft through the canvas and razed their hardened hides ". Now, it seems, pillows and bolsters, mattresses and sacks of chaff were found not only in the bedchambers of the well-to-do but also in cottages and in servants' quarters.

The waiting-woman, as distinct from the serving-woman, might have known in her own home such comforts and elegances as her grandparents had never recked of ; for a farmer would no longer be content with platters, spoons and candlesticks of wood, but must have pewter, and perhaps even a silver salt-cellar ; he must have tapestry hangings on his wooden bed, and " naperie " upon his table. " Inferiour artificers " also lived more delicately than their betters had lived in earlier reigns.

Harrison seems to have felt some sympathy with the growling of his aged parishioners, and his contemporary, Philip Stubbes, in *The Anatomie of Abuses*, is shocked to record that " every poore cottager's daughter " has her hat of " taffatie ", or else " of wooll at least, well lined with silke, velvet or taffatie ". Never was a time when sumptuary laws were so obviously needed or so brazenly disregarded. The personal attendant of a London merchant's wife might well spend two or three hours of every day in making her mistress ready to walk abroad. Even if the worthy dame did not, in the words of Mr. Stubbes, defile her face with " painting and slibbersauces ", the " trimming and tricking " of her head, with its false hair, " underpropped with forks, wiers and I cannot tell what ", was in itself a formidable task, for over these " boulstered " locks were fixed wreaths of gold and silver, " bugles (I dare not say baubles),' ouches, ryngs, gold, silver, glasses and such other childish gewgaws and foolish trinkets ". Then when the triple tier of ruffs had been adjusted, each filmy peak and whorl starched as stiffly as if fretted out of stone, there was the pomander to be filled with fresh civet or musk : and on muddy days there were the chopines, the high wooden clogs, to be fitted over the shimmering neats'-leather shoes.

In the *Colloquies* written by Claude Desainliens, the Huguenot schoolmaster of St. Paul's Churchyard, we get an incidental but lively glimpse of the maid in a London merchant's house of the middle sort. She rouses the son of the house betimes, telling him that she has brought him a clean shirt and a clean towel and a pitcher of water to wash in — the water-carrier had just been round, but if his wares were drawn from the river rather than the Cornhill conduit the chances were that neither the colour nor the odour would be agreeable. This Abigail is on the friendliest terms with her master's son, who begs her to pour the water over his hands, and to pour high, so that it makes a splash. She reminds him not to button his shirt-cuffs until he has washed his hands, bids him not tug too hard at the sleeves, which it will be her task to mend if he tears them, and finally tells him to truss up his points and go down and beg his father's blessing.

A maidservant in London City had a more amusing if not a less arduous life than her sister in the country. There were processions to watch, and marchings of trained bands, and the barges of the Lord Mayor and the City Companies moving in crimson and gold along the grey curve of the Thames, and it might even be the coming of the Queen's Grace herself to St. Paul's, in a blur of white, withered face, red-brown wig and bejewelled raiment. There were days when coloured tapestries hung from the Cheapside casements and the conduits ran with wine : and in all of these exciting events the 'prentices and the servant wenches had their share. We shall see an example of this presently, in *The Shoemakers' Holiday*.

In the country a completely different set of tasks and duties would be added to the normal daily round of the maidservant. Every housewife, whether of high or middling degree, had her herb-garden, her still-room and her book of infallible receipts handed down from her grandam and showing a considerable variety of scripts, from the angular old English to the smoothly curving Italian hand. To aid her mistress in the preparation of medicines, cosmetics and dyes must have been one of the most absorbing of the rural handmaiden's occupations. It is to be hoped that if she suffered from any of the discomforts for which the remedies were intended, whether " rednes in ye face " or " wind in ye belly ", she would be permitted to test their efficacy in her own person.

For " pimples in the face, be they never so greate " one treatment recommended about this period was rather drastic. The
patient was to be purged two or three days in advance, and
blooded as well, if she pleased ; then every night for fifteen nights
she was to anoint her face with a mixture compounded of rose
ointment, a halfpennyworth of the best brimstone, and a pennyworth of the best ginger, letting no water touch her face during
the whole of that time. " Queen Elizabeth's posset for winde "
sounds promising if rather sharp on the tongue. It consisted of
half an ounce each of ginger, cinnamon, galingale, aniseed,
carraway seed, fennel seed, and two drams each of mace and
nutmegs, to be reduced to powder and taken before or after meat.
Some of the formulae for green ointment and plague-water read
almost like Perdita's flower-speech or like Ophelia's sweeter
ravings.

Small beer makes an unexpected appearance in the receipt for
liquid blacking — a compound which the rural Abigail might
one day help her mistress to mix and the next day apply to her
mistress's shoes. Dyes often had attractive names — a fair
scarlet, purple in grain, popinjay green — and the ingredients
ranged from green grass to chamber-lye.

Thomas Churchyard, the Elizabethan versemonger, in his
Fayned Fancye betweene the Spider and the Gowte, turns aside to
draw a lifelike picture of the maid who was the Spider's most
active enemy. A charming person,

> She wanne the love of all the house,
> And pranckt it like a pretty mouse ;
> And sure at every word she spake
> A goodly curtchie would she make.
>
> . . . .
>
> She sweeped under every bench
> And shaekt the coshens in their kinde.
> When out of order did she finde
> A rushe, a straw, or little stick,
> She could it mend, she was so quicke
> About her business every houre :
> This maide was cald her mistres' floure.

Her outfit consisted of two fair new kirtles, one blue, one black ;
a gown for " holydays " of which every yard cost a crown " and

22

more by xviii pence " ; three smocks, four " raylls " [1] and five
fair kerchiefs. Hose and shoes being " dere ", she had but one
pair of each, and saved them by going barefoot. When we come
to her fairings the analogy with Mopsa and Dorcas in *The Winter's
Tale* is complete :

> She went to toune but ones a yere,
> At Easter or some other day
> When she had licens for to play.
>
> . . . .
>
> And as for gloves and knives full bright
> She lackèd not, nor trifles slight,
> And pins and laces of small cost.

The perfect Elizabethan housewife watched over her household in all its branches with a vigilance that would have charmed
King Solomon. In 1600 we hear of my Lady Cholmeley who,
having ordered the day's duties in the morning and instructed
her numerous daughters in a variety of arts, elegant and domestic,
would go round her whole domain " from hop-garth to hen-
yard, from linen-closet to lardour ", prying, tasting and admonishing until the family and the servants were summoned to dine
at " xi of the clocke ".

What the tastes and acquirements of Elizabethan rustic
servants would be is amusingly revealed in the conversation
between Autolycus, the Clown, Dorcas and Mopsa in *The
Winter's Tale*, Act IV, Scene iii. The two Bohemian wenches
bearing Greek names are styled ' shepherdesses ', but they may
be taken as representing typical maids in a Warwickshire farmhouse of the period. Mopsa's aspirations at fair-time include a
pair of sweet (*i.e.* scented) gloves and a " tawdry lace " — one
of those gay, flimsy gauds originally sold at St. Audrey's fair
and borrowing their name from it — and from her. Both girls
betray that round-eyed credulity and that avid appetite for marvels
characteristic of the peasant in every period, and when Autolycus
unstraps his wallet and brings forth his blackletter broadsheets
full of monsters and prodigies they vie with each other in urging
the Clown to buy. Mopsa's comment, " I love a ballad in print,
a-life, for then we are sure they are true ", suggests that she was

---

[1] A sort of linen neckerchief.

able to read ; and, like a considerable portion of the population of England in that tuneful time, she understood part-singing. Upon Autolycus naming the tune of one of his " merry Ballads ", she says promptly, " We can both sing it ; if thou'lt bear a part thou shalt hear ; 'tis in three parts," and Dorcas adds, perhaps disdainfully, " We had the tune on't a month ago." And so to their sheep-shearing feast, graced by warden pear pies coloured with saffron and flavoured with nutmeg and mace ; by raisins, dates and currants, and — if the farmer's wife were of Perdita's mind — the even rarer luxury of rice into the bargain.

It is a little curious that Shakespeare's crowded gallery of contemporary portraits should contain only one lady's-maid and only one woman-servant in a middle-class household such as his own must have been. Lucetta in *The Two Gentlemen of Verona* is the quintessence of a score in that kind — high in her mistress's confidence and favour, pert in speech, prompt in action, but presenting no unmistakable or unforgettable touches of character. Mrs. Quickly in *The Merry Wives of Windsor* is another story altogether : she is instinct with lusty life. In spite of her declaration, " I wash, wring, brew, bake, scour, dress meat and drink, make the beds, and do all myself," it is clear that she is Dr. Caius's housekeeper rather than his serving-wench. She has abundant leisure for activities unconnected with her normal domestic duties, and one hazards a guess that John Rugby was called upon to give what modern advertisements define as " help for rough ", whether he would or no. Mrs. Ford had a maid, and so no doubt had Mrs. Page ; but we never see or hear the niece of Mrs. Prat, the Fat Woman of Brainford, she whose gown, muffler and thrummed hat, left in the attic of Mrs. Ford's house at Windsor, were used to disguise Sir John Falstaff on a certain celebrated occasion. Maria in *Twelfth Night*, like Margaret and Ursula in *Much Ado about Nothing*, is a waiting-gentlewoman, probably enjoying a status slightly superior to that of Margaret Giggs in the More household. We should be surprised to see her pairing off either with Fabian or with Feste ; and no astonishment seems to have been felt when she blossomed into Dame Belch.

To many people one of the most pathetic of Shakespeare's minor characters is one who never appears on the stage at all, and

who exists only by sorrowful analogy in the mind of Desdemona
as she sighs :

> My mother had a maid called Barbara ;
> She was in love, and he she loved proved mad
> And did forsake her ; she had a song of ' willow ' ;
> An old thing 'twas, but it expressed her fortune,
> And she died singing it.   That song to-night
> Will not go from my mind ; I have much to do,
> But to go hang my head all at one side,
> And sing it like poor Barbara.

Shakespeare's contemporaries were fond of introducing confidential maids, and wherever the scene of a play may be laid it
is certain that these characters — like all the rest — are authentic
Elizabethan from lawn coif to cork heel.   Some of them are
important to the unfolding of the plot, but most of them vanish
disregarded before the close of the final scene.   In Part I
of Christopher Marlowe's *Tamburlaine the Great*, Zenocrate,
daughter of the Soldan of Egypt, has a maid called Anippe ;
Zabina, wife of Bajazeth, Emperor of the Turks, also has one,
Ebea by name.   Anippe appears but does not utter in Act III,
Scene ii, when Zenocrate confesses to Agydas her love for the
Scythian conqueror ; she has, however, a great deal to say for
herself in the succeeding scene, when the two royal ladies bandy
insults with a vigour that would have done credit to a couple of
Billingsgate fishwives similarly employed.

Zabina informs Zenocrate,

> Thou shalt be laundress to my waiting-maid ;

and adds,

> How lik'st thou her, Ebea ?   Will she serve ?
> *Ebea* : Madam, she thinks perhaps she is too fine,
> But I shall turn her into other weeds
> And make her dainty fingers fall to work.

Zenocrate, not to be outdone, swings round to *her* handmaid :

> Hear'st thou, Anippe, how thy drudge doth talk ?
> And how my slave, her mistress, menaceth ?
> Both for their sauciness shall be employed
> To dress the common soldiers' meat and drink.
> For we will scorn they should come near ourselves.
> *Anippe* : Yet sometimes let your highness send for them
> To do the work my chamber-maid disdains.

C

On the stage as in real life, the waiting-woman had her own attendant who, in her turn, relegated the humbler and harder tasks to the servant on the ladder-rung beneath her.

After the rapid and complete defeat of Bajazeth ' off ', Tamburlaine, having celebrated his triumph in a characteristic speech of gorgeous bombast, concludes :

> Come, bind them both, and one lead in the Turk ;
> The Turkess let my love's maid lead away.

In Act IV, Scene ii, Bajazeth is hauled on to the stage in a cage on wheels, the unfortunate Zabina trailing behind. He is dragged forth and flung down at the conqueror's feet to serve as his footstool ; and, as always with Marlowe, a crude and violent episode is veiled and garlanded with magnificent rhetoric. Zabina upbraids Tamburlaine in language as ornate as his own, and he says angrily :

> Zenocrate, look better to your slave.

Zenocrate corrects him :

> She is my handmaid's slave, and *she* shall look
> That these abuses flow not from her tongue ;
> Chide her, Anippe.

And this, nothing loth, Anippe proceeds to do. The shrill voices of the boy-actors who played the women's parts on the Elizabethan stage must have been singularly well adapted to such passages of railing and recrimination. Both Anippe and her mistress, however, show signs of compunction when Tamburlaine's cruelty rises to fresh heights — with results likely to appal even the most apathetic of the groundlings. Bajazeth and his wife dash out their brains against the bars of the cage, he from within, she from without ; and Zenocrate, whose eyes are now " glutted with these grievous objects ", cries :

> See, see, Anippe, if they live or not.
> *Anippe* : No breath, nor sense, nor motion in them both ;
> Ah, madam, this their slavery has enforced,
> And ruthless cruelty of Tamburlaine.

Zenocrate then importunes " mighty Jove and holy Mahomet " not to punish her beloved, and Anippe, recovering her poise, offers consolation :

Madam, content yourself, and be resolved
Your love hath fortune so at his command
That she shall stay and turn her wheel no more
As long as life maintains his mighty arm
That fights for honour to adorn your head.

The handmaid does not appear in Part II of this magnificent, preposterous tragedy, though her presence would have been appropriate enough in the last scene, where Zenocrate is " discovered lying in her bed of estate with Tamburlaine sitting by her ", and about her bed " three Physicians tempering potions ".

Equally lurid but of much poorer substance is Thomas Kyd's immensely popular *Spanish Tragedy*, and here there is a character described merely as " Maid to Isabella " whose function is to act as a foil to that unhappy lady's wild-witted laments over her murdered son, Horatio. She is a well-read young damsel, for she tries to console her mistress with the reminder that the boy

Sleeps in quiet in the Elysian fields.

Another bookish maid is Pero, waiting-woman to Tamyra, Countess of Montsurrey, in George Chapman's lurid and complicated tragedy of *Bussy d'Ambois*. Tamyra, on the evening when the hero is to pay her a clandestine (but blameless) visit in her room, borrows a book from Pero, and adds :

. . . I'll this night trouble
None of your services. Make sure the doors
And call your other fellows to their rest.

" I will," responds Pero, meekly, only to say to herself (and the audience), " yet I will watch to know why *you* watch." She is the typical unscrupulous waiting-woman, pert, free-spoken, resourceful : but there comes a moment when she rallies to her lady's defence almost as vehemently as Paulina did to Hermione's. Montsurrey accuses his Countess — " she seems to swound " — and Pero turns upon him, crying,

. . . sweet lord, clear up those eyes,
Unbend that masking forehead. Whence is it
You rush upon her with these Irish wars
More full of sound than hurt ?

In *The Duchess of Malfi*, that sombre tragedy which haunted and enchanted Swinburne, the Duchess's maid, Cariola, has a not inconsiderable part to play. She is in the secret of the lady's undivulged marriage with her faithful steward, Antonio — a marriage to be concealed at all costs from her two ruthless brothers, Ferdinand, Duke of Calabria, and the Cardinal : from behind the arras she is the witness of their contract *per verba di presenti*, and, left alone on the stage, she makes this grim comment :

> Whether the spirit of greatness or of woman
> Reign most in her I know not : but it shows
> A fearful madness. I owe her much of pity.

In a later scene it is incidentally revealed that — Antonio not daring to share his wife's room for fear of discovery — Cariola is often the Duchess's bedfellow. The three of them are on terms of easy playfulness, and Antonio combats Cariola's avowed intention never to marry by citing the examples of Daphnis, Syrinx and Anaxarete—

> whereas those
> That married or proved gracious to their friends
> Were by a gracious influence trans-shaped
> Into the olive, pomegranate, mulberry,
> Became flowers, precious stones, or eminent stars.

The waiting-woman's brief retort is characteristic — " This is vain poetry ". When Antonio has embroidered further on the theme, he suddenly changes the subject :

> Now I look on both your faces so well formed,
> It puts me in mind of a question I would ask.
> *Cariola* : What is it ?
> *Antonio* : I do wonder why hard-favoured ladies
> For the most part keep worse-favoured waiting-women
> To attend them, and cannot endure fair ones.

The Duchess supplies the obvious answer :

> Did you ever in your life know an ill painter
> Desire to have his dwelling next door to the shop
> Of an excellent picture-maker ?

and with unconscious irony — for the sinister turn of the plot is close at hand — she asks,

> I prithee
> When were we so merry ?

Duke Ferdinand discovers the secret, and Antonio for a moment suspects Cariola of having disclosed it. He threatens to pistol her, and she retorts,

> Pray, sir, do ; and when
> That you have cleft my heart you shall read there
> Mine innocence.

The rest of the play is largely taken up with the persecution and final assassination of the Duchess, her husband and her children. The instrument used by the cruel kinsman is a soldier of fortune called Bosola, first cousin to Iago, but unlike him in that he feels faint, fugitive twinges of compunction. At first the unhappy pair, with their young children, are banished, and the faithful Cariola is seen sharing their exile at Loretto and carrying the youngest child in her arms. To them enters Bosola, bearing a letter from Ferdinand in which he offers " a noble and free league of amity and love ", but in such ambiguous terms that his sister could hardly have been deceived. She urges Antonio to take their eldest child and " fly towards Milan ", and in his valediction to her and the other children there is interpolated an aside to the waiting-woman :

> Do not weep.
> Heaven fashioned us of nothing, and we strive
> To bring ourselves to nothing.   Farewell, Cariola,
> And thy sweet armful.

In the sequel, the Duchess is held prisoner by her unnatural brothers in her own castle of Amalfi, where Ferdinand institutes a sequence of cruel stratagems by which he hopes to drive her to madness or self-murder. Cariola, though still in attendance on her, is not with her mistress in the first scene of the fourth Act, otherwise one hazards the guess that her sturdy common sense might have convinced the Duchess that the waxen images of her dead children were merely waxen images, not the children them-selves, and also that the severed hand was not necessarily Antonio's because upon one of the cold fingers shone the troth-ring she had given him. In the next scene she enters with her mistress, to the sound of wild tumult ' off '. The Duke, in pursuance of his plan, has introduced " a consort of madmen " into his sister's lodging. Like most Elizabethan villains, he has a pretext ready for each deed of villainy : when the Pope was ill, the antics of such unfortunate creatures " forced him to laugh, and so the imposthume broke ".

Cariola tries to comfort the Duchess by assuring her that she " shall live to shake this durance off ", but she is reminded that " the robin redbreast and the nightingale never live long in cages ", and a little later she is asked the question,

> Dost thou think we shall know one-another
> In th' other world ?
> *Cariola* :   Yes, out of question.
> *Duchess* :   O, that it were possible we might
> But hold some two days' conference with the dead
> From them I should learn somewhat I am sure
> I never shall know here.

After descanting most poetically upon her sorrows, she asks abruptly, with one of those natural touches that redeem the play,

> . . . Who do I look like now ?

and Cariola answers,

> Like to your picture in the gallery,
> A deal of life in show, but none in practice ;
> Or rather like some reverend monument
> Whose ruins even are pitied.

The end of their ordeal is now very near, though not the end of the tragedy itself. At the close of the madmen's ballet Bosola enters, announcing, " I am come to make thy tomb " : he is followed by executioners bearing " a coffin, cords and a bell ". " This ", he tells the Duchess, " is your last presence-chamber." Cariola utters a cry, " O my sweet lady ! " — she tries to chide the doomful figures forth ; in the same breath she pants, " Call for help ! " All is in vain : she is bustled off the stage before her mistress, unfaltering, meets her death, but not before our hearts are wrung by one last poignant colloquy between them :

> *Duchess* :   Farewell, Cariola.
> In my last will I have not much to give ;
> A many hungry guests have fed upon me ;
> Thine will be a poor reversion.
> *Cariola* :   I will die with thee.
> *Duchess* :   I pray thee, look thou giv'st my little boy
> Some syrup for his cold, and let the girl
> Say her prayers ere she sleep.

Cariola shows a singular lack of dignity and fortitude when she is dragged back and sees the Duchess lying in her coffin. It may be that the omission to provide a second coffin gave her a gleam of hope concerning her own fate, for she asks not altogether despondently,

> . . . . my turn is next,
> Is't not so ordered ?

but when Bosola answers " Yes ", and adds darkly that he is glad she is so well prepared, she soon shows that her declaration that she would die with her mistress has no further meaning. She demands a trial : she offers to reveal treason to the Duke : she is " contracted to a young gentleman ", she is " quick with child ". Unsoftened, Bosola bids the executioners dispatch, saying, no doubt with an eloquent movement of eye or hand,

> You kept *her* counsel : now you shall keep ours.

The men, having done their work, bear Cariola off the scene. Webster, for all his wildness, was too good an artist to let a second lifeless form distract the attention of the audience at the supreme moment of the play — the moment when Duke Ferdinand looks down at his dead sister and mutters,

> Cover her face : mine eyes dazzle : she died young.

The strong Elizabethan appetite for ghosts and madmen on the stage was tickled by Middleton and Rowley in their play *The Changeling*, of which the plot is described by Saintsbury as " intricate and not over savoury " ; and here again we have a villain not unlike Iago and a waiting-woman of the Cariola-Emilia type. Diaphanta is the chaste handmaid of the wanton Beatrice, her chastity being tested by means of a truly remarkable drug which causes virgins to gape, sneeze and laugh in the order named, while the unvirtuous woman remains " dull, heavy and lumpish ". Beatrice, knowing that her future husband will apply this test and knowing also that the result will be her undoing, bribes Diaphanta with the sum of one thousand ducats to take her place on the wedding night — and arranges for her to be neatly and conveniently murdered immediately after. Several incidental remarks in the course of the play touch upon the character and habits of these attendants.

> These women are the ladies' cabinets,
> Things of most precious trust are locked into 'em,

says Alsemero : " Who ", asks the villain, de Flores, cynically, " would trust a waiting-woman ? " and two lines further on he expresses the opinion that they are " termagants ". Diaphanta's death having been so contrived that she seems to have been accidentally burnt, her mistress says hypocritically,

> As good a soul as ever lady countenanced,
> But in her chamber negligent and heavy ;

and Beatrice's old father, Vermandero, says not unreasonably,

> Those sleepy sluts are dangerous in a house
> An' they be ne'er so good.

A more famous play, constantly revived, is Massinger's *A New Way to Pay Old Debts*, with its classical miser-villain, Sir Giles Overreach. Its heroine, the well-dowered, widowed Lady Allworth, has a chamber-maid and a waiting-woman who enter together in Act I, Scene i, and in a very pointed manner express their disgust at the ragged and malodorous Wellborn, reduced to misery by his own imprudence and the wickedness of his uncle, Sir Giles. The miser engages a reduced gentlewoman to wait upon his daughter, Margaret, and expounds his ideas to his creature, Marrall :

> I'll have her well attended ; there are ladies
> Of errant knights, decayed and brought so low
> That for cast clothes and meat will gladly serve her.
> And 'tis my glory, though I come from the city,
> To have their issue whom I have undone
> To kneel to mine as bondslaves.
> *Marrall* : 'Tis a fit state, sir.
> *Sir Giles* : And therefore I'll not have a chambermaid
> That ties her shoes, or any meaner office,
> But such whose fathers were right worshipful.

The post is filled by a certain Lady Downfallen, whose husband has been thrown into a debtors' prison by Overreach. We do not see her in the flesh, but she is cleverly projected upon our consciousness in a brief dialogue between Margaret and her father. The girl, who is a nice girl, confesses that she blushes to find herself giving orders to her

> that was once attended
> By persons not inferior to myself
> In birth :

Sir Giles, with characteristic brutality, boasts how he " took her up in an old tamin [1] gown ", starving even " for want of tuppeny chops ", to serve his daughter. There must have been only too many poor souls in that predicament at a time when fortunes were so lightly and so suddenly won and lost.

Young Allworth is an object of much solicitude to his step-mother's maids, who flutter round him when he visits her and press upon him quince-cakes and marmalade of their own pre-serving. They have a part to play in the stratagem by which Overreach is first deluded and then undone : but Massinger forgets them long before everyone who deserves to be happy has been made so. Incidental light is thrown upon the comforts of a Tudor servant's life when another of Overreach's tools, Greedy, is crowded out from the high table and laments losing " his dumpling, and buttered toast and woodcock ", only to be assured by Marrall that if he sits with the waiting-women all these delicacies will come his way at last.

To match the racy and truly English character of Mrs. Quickly we must turn to Dekker's city comedy, *The Shoemaker's Holiday*, where we find the very atmosphere of homely good-will mixed with civic pageantry which we might have expected to breathe in the plays of Shakespeare, himself an Alderman's son. He fails us here who so seldom fails us anywhere, but Dekker almost makes amends with his attractive picture of London life, nominally in the reign of some vague Plantagenet but manifestly in the reign of the last Tudor.

Rose, the well-favoured daughter of Sir Roger Oakely, Lord Mayor of London, has a maid called Sybil, who finds her weaving a garland of pinks, roses, marigolds, violets and gillyflowers for her noble lover, Rowland Lacy, nephew of the Earl of Leicester. To separate her from him Rose has been banished to her father's

---

[1] A thin worsted fabric with a shiny surface : French, *étamine* : cf. the " thrummed hat " of Mother Prat in *The Merry Wives of Windsor*.

house at Old Ford, and she importunes Sybil for news from the
City. Has she seen Lacy ? Has he " sent kind greetings to his
love " ? Sybil has seen him, but he has avoided speaking to her.
" I scarce knew him," says she. " Here 'a wore a scarf, and here
a scarf and here a bunch of feathers, and here precious stones and
jewels, and a pair of garters — O ! monstrous — like one of
our yellow silk curtains at home here in Old Ford. . . . I stood
at our door in Cornhill and looked at him, he at me indeed, spake
to him but he not to me, not a word ; marry, go up, thought I,
with a wanion ! He passed me by as proud — marry, foh ! are
you grown humorous, thought I : and so shut the door and in
I came." Rose protests that Sybil does Lacy wrong.

> No dove was ever half as mild as he.

" Mild ? " echoes the Abigail, " Yes, as a bushel of stamp-crabs "
— crushed crab-apples. She is evidently a theatre-goer, for she
quotes a phrase from Kyd's *Spanish Tragedy* : " if I were as
you," she declares, " I'd cry ' Go by, Jeronimo, go by ! ' "

Meanwhile Lacy, whose noble uncle supposes him to be
fighting in France, has disguised himself as a Dutch shoemaker,
and has found work with Simon Eyre, among whose merry
'prentice lads Sybil has an admirer, Firk by name. Their master,
boisterous, whimsical Simon, asks the two English workmen
what they are doing.

> *Hodge* : I am making a pair of shoes for my lord Mayor's daughter,
> Mistress Rose.
> *Firk* : And I a pair of shoes for Sybil, my lord's maid.
> *Eyre* : Sybil ? Fie, defile not thy fine workmanly fingers with the feet
> of kitchen-stuff and basting-ladles. Ladies of the court, fine ladies,
> my lads, commit their feet to our apparelling : put gross work to
> Hans.

The irony of this last injunction would be fully appreciated by
the audience, who were in the secret of Lacy's disguise.

In Act III, Scene v, we are at Old Ford again, where Sir Roger
entertains Simon Eyre and his wife Margery, and the shoemaker
apprentices amuse the company with a morris-dance. Sybil is
sent to fetch drink for them, and after they have all gone dancing
out, followed more soberly by Sir Roger, Simon Eyre and Dame
Margery, Rose cries desperately to her, " Sybil, what shall I do ? "

She has recognized Lacy, and is at her wits' end. Sybil, nothing daunted, swears an oath which suggests close affinity with Juliet's nurse, that "Hans, the Dutchman, when we come to London shall not only see and speak with you, but in spite of all your father's policies steal you away and marry you".

It is doubtless her idea that Hans should be summoned from the shop to "pull on" the shoes he had made for Mistress Rose: its execution gives her an opportunity to visit the shoemakers at their work and to bandy strong-flavoured quips with them. It was doubtless she who unbolted the door and admitted the noble youth to Sir Roger's house in the City; and it was certainly she who interrupted their loving colloquy with shrill cries announcing the imminent arrival of the master of that house. Hardly has Hans knelt down to go through the motions of trying on Rose's shoe when the approach of the Earl of Lincoln is announced, and the handmaid is hastily bidden to "make things handsome" in his honour. Later she repeats her previous performance of a truly catastrophic entry by rushing in with the news that her young mistress has "fled out of doors with Hans the shoe-maker"; and she is present later when Firk gives misleading information to the Earl and Sir Roger as to the proposed scene of the clandestine wedding of the lovers; but her last utterance is "I am glad she is 'scapt", and we are reminded of her presence only when the fickle Firk, pointing at her, observes that he "has no stomach as yet to a red petticoat", or when he says, even more ungallantly, "send simpering Syb away". "Housewife, get you in," commands Oakely, and, with a curious meekness, Sybil makes her final exit. We hear no more of her, not even when royal intervention reconciles father and daughter, uncle and nephew, in one unanimous and miraculous harmony.

Reginald Scot, in his *Discoverie of Witchcraft*, gives an interesting example of that association between maidservants and 'manifestations'[1] (genuine or otherwise) which has frequently been noted since his time and has been known to occur in our own. On October 13, 1574, "Mildred, the base daughter of Alice

---

[1] Another sixteenth century example was "the white bird" or "the voice in the wall", when, in March 1554, a servant-maid called Elizabeth Croft carried out a clever imposture to make it appear that supernatural powers condemned the proposed marriage between Mary I and Philip of Spain.

Norrington, servant to William Spooner, of Westwell in Kent, being of the age of seventeen years, was possessed with Satan in the night and day aforesaid ". To visit her and to wrestle with the foul Fiend for her soul came two Preachers of God's Word, four substantial Yeomen, and three women of good fame and reputation. Satan in her person " roared and cryed mightily ", oftentimes repeated " He comes, he comes " and " He goes, he goes " with " striving and gnashing of teeth, and otherwise with mowing and terrible countenances ".

Though the sixteenth century investigators could not discern it, the complex at the root of the girl's behaviour is plainly revealed to the modern observer by " Satan's " answers in the course of the following interrogation :

> We said, Who sent thee ? He said, Old Alice, Old Alice. Which old Alice ? said we : Old Alice, said he : Where dwelleth she ? said we : In Westwell Street, said he. . . . What did she bid thee do ? said we : he said, kill her maid : wherefore did she bid thee kill her ? said we : Because she did not love her, said he.

" Satan's voice ", the investigators noted, " did differ much from the maid's voice." They departed, convinced that they had had speech with the Evil One and that by their prayers he had been driven away, and signed a joint statement to that effect.

" How ", asks Reginald Scot, " could Mother Alice escape condemnation and hanging, being arraigned upon this evidence ? " How, indeed ? Fortunately for her, the tricks of " the Pythonist of Westwell " came to light, and the girl was forced to confess that " all her diabolicall speech was but Ventriloquie and plain cozenage ". After she had been searchingly questioned by two Justices of the Peace, " not through extremity of tortures nor yet by guile and flattery ", she not only acknowledged her fraud but gave a demonstration of ventriloquism, feigned trances and illusions " in the presence of divers Gentlemen and Gentlewomen of great worship and credit ".

Scot's purpose in writing his book was to show that " the compacts and contracts of Witches with Devils and all Infernal Spirits and Familiars are but Erroneous Novelties and Imaginary Conceptions " ; but he was far in advance of his age in England, and even farther in Scotland, where King James not only had

By courtesy of the Warburg Institute

BLANCH PARRY, "HANDMAIDE TO A QUEENE"

The Discoverie of Witchcraft burned by the common hangman but himself penned a learned refutation. What Queen Elizabeth thought of the book — if ever it engaged her royal attention — has not, apparently, been recorded : but her traffickings with the astrologer, John Dee, suggest that she was in her own way as credulous as her kinsman and successor.

Miss Strickland is severe on Dr. Dee, whom she unjustly calls " a disreputable quack " ; and she seems to find it difficult to understand how a woman of Elizabeth's intellectual calibre could show him so much favour. With obvious disapproval she adds, " Her confidential maid, too, Blanch Parry (who was in all the secrets of her royal mistress both before and after her accession), was an avowed disciple of Dr. Dee, and his pupil in alchemy and astrology ".

Whether Blanch was related to Thomas Parry, cofferer to the Princess and later Comptroller to the Queen, is not known, but it was probably more than a coincidence that two members of the small, harassed household at Hatfield, at Chelsea, and elsewhere should have borne the same surname, and should have hailed from the Welsh marches. Her epitaph in St. Margaret's, Westminster, tells us that she served Elizabeth faithfully, " from Her Highnes birth ", and that she " died a maide in the eighte two years of her age, the twelfe of February, 1589 ". Though she is there described as " Gentlewoman of Queen Elizabeth's most honourable bedchamber and Keeper of her Matie's juells ", the rhymed epitaph in Bacton Church, Herefordshire (where, at her desire, her heart was buried), gives a definition which makes it possible to include her among the Abigails of England " of the better sorte " :

> I lyvde always as handmaide to a Queene,
>   In chamber chief my tyme dyd overpasse,
> Uncarefull of my welthe then was I sene,
>   Whylst I abode the runnynge of my glasse.
> Not doubtying wante whylst that my mystresse lyvde
>   In woman's state whose cradell sawe I rockte,
> Her servant then as when her crown atcheeved
>   And so remaynde till death he my doore had knockte.

Elizabeth is often accused of parsimony, but let it be set down to her credit that her ancient handmaid did not die a poor woman.

Blanch Parry by her Will left a sum of money sufficient to ensure that " seaven score bushells of wheat and rye " should be given yearly to the poor of Bacton, her birthplace ; she also provided for two handsome monuments, one over her heart in Herefordshire, the other over the rest of her in St. Margaret's, Westminster. In addition to a kneeling figure of Blanch herself, an effigy of her royal mistress, complete with sceptre and orb, adorns the Bacton memorial.

Writing to the Earl of Shrewsbury on February 17, 1589, Thomas Markham observed : " on Thursdaye last Mrs. Blanshe a Parry dep'ted : blynd she was here on earth, but I hope the joyes in heven she shall se ". He also reported that the Queen was in good health, so if Her Majesty grieved for her friend and servant she did not allow her grief to upset either her nerves or her digestion.

CHAPTER III

Stuart Scene

IF we include the rather shabby epilogue of William and Mary, it will be found that the Stuart pageant follows almost exactly the course of the seventeenth century — for with Queen Anne's accession, ninety-nine years after James I and VI ambled eagerly south, a new play begins. Across the middle of the old one broods the double gloom of civil war and dictatorship, but in the earlier and later scenes there is brightness enough, by turns coloured and clear. It is in the purer light that we can see Charles I with his Queen and his children, presenting for the imitation of his lieges an incomparable family piece : and the same light falls upon Verneys and Osbornes and other delightful people, all of them attended by devoted Abigails.

That indomitable woman, Lady Anne Clifford, Countess of Dorset, affords an excellent example of the Stuart housewife of high degree, vigilant and despotic, but a generous rewarder of faithful service. The catalogue of her household at Knole between 1613 and 1624 shows that large numerical preponderance of men- over women-servants which continued far into the next century. From the chaplain at one end of the scale to " John Morockoe, a Blackamoor ", the men number ninety-three : the women, ranging from two housekeepers sitting at the " parlour table " to " Goodwife Small " and " Grace Robinson, a Blackamoor " sitting with nine others at " the laundrymaids' table ", number only twenty-one.

Judith Simpton, whose name is the first in the latter list, must have stood high in her mistress's favour, for in Lady Anne's diary we read how she spent a day " walking in the Park with Judith ", carrying her Bible with her and meditating upon her various tribulations. A month later — in April 1617 — when her Lord " was very ill and could not sleep ", she records, " This night I went into Judith's chamber, where I mean to continue until my Lord is better " ; but two days later she notes that she

39

was " so ill with lying in Judith's chamber " that she had " a plain fit of fever ", complicated by a swelled face ; so she moved into " the green cloth-of-gold bed " in the room formerly occupied by herself when her husband was in France.

Henrietta Maria's household included six chamberers, an unspecified number of under-chamberers, and certain function-aries known as " the Queen's Women " — the forerunners of the Necessary Woman, the Starcher and other female satellites whom we meet in the service of the later Stuart Queens. They had to share with many other Abigails the privilege of contem-plating royalty at close range, for most of the ladies whom loyalty, curiosity or a kingly summons brought to the rambling old palace of Whitehall seem to have been attended by their personal maids. In the regulations made for their guidance it is laid down that " ladies of the nobility and gentlewomen of good rank and fashion had liberty to pass through the privy gallery ", but only the ladies might be followed by their maids : the maids of the gentlewomen had to " goe downe by the Councill-chamber staires ".

The *Memoirs of the Verney Family* open a wide window upon the daily doings of an ancient and loyal house. Dame Margaret Verney, making her Will in 1631, remembered by name the women-servants of her household and left £10 to provide a situation for one of them called Betty or Bess Coleman, " and ", she added, " pray take som care to see her plased with it ". Ten years elapsed between the making of the Will and the death of the testatrix, but when Dame Margaret died all the maids men-tioned were still at Claydon, the Verneys' ancestral manor, Bess Coleman among them : and all of them remained in attendance upon the five motherless Verney daughters, even when the altered fortunes of the family had made service there much less comfortable and rewarding than it had formerly been.

Susan, the eldest of the five, went to stay with kinsfolk not far away, but Pen, Pegge, Molly and Betty lived on in the beauti-ful, sombre old house under the care of Mrs. Alcock the house-keeper and their venerable nurse, Nan Fudd. Various aunts and uncles kept an eye upon the sisterhood, and one aunt, Mrs. Isham, took it upon herself to suggest that Pegge's " mayd might sarve both her and Pen ". Pegge, a wilful young person, repudiated the idea with scorn. Her maid's duties already included the care of Baby Betty, to " dress hur and heare hur hur booke, and teach her work " — that is, needlework. " Pegge's mayd " was not illiterate, even if her education had not gone far beyond the first two R's.

While life went a little bleakly on in the motherless house, its head, Sir Edmund Verney, was far away, fighting for the King whose standard-bearer he had the honour to be. Presently word came that he had fallen in the battle of Edgehill. His body was never recovered, but according to tradition his severed hand was found on the field, locked round the staff of the standard. His son and successor, Sir Ralph Verney, was no such fanatical royalist : yet later he suffered exile for conscience' sake — thereby, one hopes, propitiating the paternal *manes*.

The new Lady Verney, his wife, had two handmaidens, Luce and Bess. Concerning them he wrote to her : " you say chamber-maides will have 4 or 5 pounds wages and neither wash nor starch ; that is to say they will doe nothing but dresse you, for I do not vallew their needlework at a groate a moneth ". Luce, as a matter of fact, received only £3 a year, but this modest sum would probably be supplemented by the annual gift of " a dark stuff gown ". Both maids went with the family to France, and Luce was in attendance upon Lady Verney when she visited England " to look after her husband's affairs ". Her — Luce's — brother demurred at the idea of her going abroad again, and Lady Verney records that she had sent " a pare of gloves trimed " to his wife, " to make them willing she should stay with mee ". She adds, not quite fairly, as the sequel showed, " but to tell the truth methinks the wench is nott soe much troubled to part with me as I am to part with her, which has taken off the edge of my sorrow to part with her ".

Bess, who had declared her willingness to stay with the Verneys even if they should be constrained to live abroad " for halfe-a-dozen years ", remained in France, and learned to speak enough French " to buy anything ". She, too, received a gift of " trimed gloves ", embroidered, fringed, perhaps perfumed as well. They were a token of her master's regard, and they cost him no less a sum than £1 : 5s.

Though she was not behind Sir Ralph in her appreciation of Bess's solid virtues, Lady Verney could not promote her to be her personal maid, to replace the supposedly half-hearted Luce, because she knew she could not starch, and could never learn to dress her. One of the most important branches of a chamber-maid's duty was washing " fine linnen ", and starching " Tiffanies, Lawns, Points and Laces ", and even in exile and comparative poverty gentle Mary Verney does not seem to have thought of abating any of these elegances. She was troubled, however, by the idea that Bess's feelings might be hurt if Luce's successor were ' put over her '. " I am ", she wrote to Sir Ralph, " in a great straite."

At last she found someone who seemed suitable, a good-natured young person whose father was a gentleman " of £400 a yeare ", and who, though wearing " a gentlewoman's habitt ", promised that she would not refuse to do anything. But the sight of a stranger in attendance upon her mistress wrought a change of heart in Luce, and she told Lady Verney that if she would permit her to go down for one week to her brother's in the country, to " settle her buseness with him ", she would remain at least for a month or two, until her ladyship could find a woman " fitting to her mind ". " Soe ", wrote Lady Verney to her husband, " I will putt of this made againe though truly I think 'tis a very good wench butt she is nott at all hansom, which I know would not please thee." From this remark we may infer that Luce and Bess were well-favoured, and that Sir Ralph did not suffer from the sight of such ugly " maze " as Lady Castle-wood's jealousy inflicted upon her lord.

During Lady Verney's absence from her exiled family her little daughter Margaret — another ' Pegge ' — died at Blois. " Had you but seene ", wrote Sir Ralph, ". . . with what discretion and affection she disposed of all her wearing clothes to her maid that tended her."

Luce's " month or two " expanded into a term of many years. After her lady's death she remained with the family as something between housekeeper and *dame de compagnie*, carrying out a variety of duties in addition to supervising the motherless children. She negotiated the sale of a house for Sir Ralph, and another time she arranged for the repair of his shabby old periwig. Two more little Cavalier girls were added to her flock, Mary and Margaret Eure, cousins of the Verneys, and to visit them all, especially if Sir Ralph were absent, came worthy Mr. Cordell, who acted as a sort of informal tutor to bandy-legged little Jack Verney and the rest of the small exiles. A wild rumour reached the head of the house that a romance was dawning between Mr. Cordell and Luce, a rumour which he received with a scepticism which was hardly complimentary to the poor woman, whose early charms had faded, and whose own thoughts do not seem to have turned seriously towards matrimony. " I am not maryed to Mr. Cordell," she wrote to Sir Ralph, " nor have I any intention to mary him or any other " : she hints that her " deare littall gentill-women " will always come first : and she adds, " neither can I devyne how this coms about unlesse it be because wee entertaine a civill corispondance one with the other, and if that be dangerous I cannot tell then how to behave myselfe in the world ".

We hear nothing more of this phantom flicker of a love-story, and the life of the Verneys went forward under Luce's quiet direction against the background of Blois, its ornate château crawling with the salamander of François I, its gaunt Gothic church of St. Nicholas and St. Laumer, its soft-tinted perspectives of river and poplar and vineyard along the Loire valley. She was particularly devoted to sickly, merry-hearted, deformed Jack Verney, for whom she contrived a new set of clothes out of an old scarlet cloak, and concerning whose unlucky nether limbs she sent reassuring reports to Sir Ralph : " truly, sir, they are not much seene now his stocking is wrinkled downe over them ".

When the King enjoyed his own again and English exiles began to win back to England from Spain, the Low Countries and France, Luce received instructions to dispatch all the most valuable Verney movables to Claydon and to dispose of the remainder in Blois. " I shall ", she wrote, " sell the old fether bedds with all the expedition I can but I feare att very low rates, because the tickes are old and the feathers but hens and capons fethers." Among the items she sent home were the belongings of her late mistress, her guitar, her travelling-trunks marked M. V.

in brass nails, together with " fringes, cordes of stooles, cushions and such-like ". She was also commissioned to buy French seeds, shrubs and vegetables for the garden at Claydon.

At a later date we find the invaluable Luce installed at Bur- leigh, in attendance upon the " littill gentillwemen " of Lord Exeter's family, but she did not desert the Verneys, and it was she whom Mrs. Palmer, *née* Mary Eure, called to her aid when the first Palmer baby was born. She, too, it was who was charged with the responsibility of procuring fish and foreign fruit against the return to Claydon of Edmund Verney, the eldest son, and his well-dowered bride, Mary Abell. Thanks to her activities, they found themselves supplied with oysters, sturgeons for pickling, " lemonds at an exelent cheap rate ", and oranges at " twel- pence " apiece.

The Edmund Verneys had a maid whose name was Bess King and who would appear to have been neither diligent nor discreet. She went with her master and mistress on two occasions when they visited their kinswoman, Lady Hobart, in London, the idea being that she should cleanse Edmund's chamber " and doe all ", while other " mayds ", in attendance on his wife, should shoulder the rest of the extra work. To them Lady Hobart promised a " very good Login to thar selfs whar hur truncks shall stand ", but Bess King was to be told that " she must Leve tiling storys ". In spite of this sad propensity on Bess's part, and the dread felt by Lady Hobart's servants of the mischief she was likely to cause, her ladyship was fain to confess that her coming would be " very convenant ", and she added thoughtfully, " she may wash all thar clos hear ". Her own maid would " ly in all the beds, and all shall be well ayred ". Bess gave her no reason to revise her early bad opinion, and was ultimately stigmatized as " the greatest slut " that she had ever known.

Poor Mrs. Edmund Verney had what would now be called ' a nervous breakdown ', and it became necessary to look for a companion-attendant who would not make matters worse by being afraid of her. In his perplexity the young husband turned to that unfailing stand-by, Luce, and she came for a time, straight from the Palmers and their new baby. After Mrs. Verney's partial recovery a housekeeper had to be found to assist her, and

Edmund's troubles began all over again. There was one candidate called Mrs. Felton, but she was alarmingly exacting about the amount of waiting-upon to be allowed her, and her salary of £12 a year seemed exorbitant in a period when £4 was considered at least adequate. So she was rejected, and so likewise — though for other reasons — was a certain Mrs. Major, concerning whom old Sir Ralph wrote words of wisdom to his son. "I beleeve her", said he, "to bee very honest and modest because all the Brood have been soe": but he adds the warning that many of them were very slow and "softly" persons, "and being behinde hand in the world have not had any Breeding, and if this be soe she cannot bee fit for your purpose".

Though Luce's romance was still-born — if ever, indeed, it grew beyond the embryonic stage — other Abigails connected with the Verney circle were more fortunate. A painter named Harris, employed at the White House, East Claydon, where Edmund lived during Sir Ralph's lifetime, fell in love with Jane Avery, Mrs. Edmund's favourite maid. He had a rival in the person of his own brother, a joiner by profession, who had been wainscoting the lady's chamber : "the Party", it is recorded, "hath no love for either of the brothers, but they are both unfeignedly in love with the party". The painter brother was skilful enough to make copies of some of the "Peeces" on the walls of Claydon House, and it was he to whom Jane Avery's heart finally inclined. They were married, and a year later, being not yet twenty, she died, probably in child-bed. Old Sir Ralph had been rather disposed to disparage Luce's charms when he heard the rumour that Mr. Cordell was their slave, but at least he never compared her to Charybdis — the comparison which occurred to Edmund Verney when writing to *his* son at Oxford in 1688. "My cosen, Ann Hobart's maid, Nan Rogers," he wrote, "is to be married to one Berger, a french Barber, an unfortunate Protestant, to avoid Sulla [*sic*] in his own country [he] comes Heare into ours and is like to ffal very suddenly into Charibdis [*sic*] thro' so ffoolish a choise."

Before we part from the Verneys we may note two instances in the Claydon circle of that system under which — in certain circumstances — a gently-born girl might be compelled to perform the duties and even to accept the status of a waiting-woman. Old Lady Osborne, *née* Penelope Verney, whose daughters had died in infancy, wrote : " After driving up and down the streets in my Coach by 6 or 7 of ye clocke I am at home, and do find ye nights so long. Had God blest me with a Dau^r I had not kept a maid." What the life of a spinster " Dau^r " of hers might have been like we may guess from the experience of her niece and namesake, Penelope Stewkeley, who, when on a visit to her, was kept busy washing " her old crape and such-like work ".

Ancient blood was not an antidote to poverty and its hardships. Poor Ruth Lloyd, a Verney on the mother's side, was fain in 1704 to take a situation as waiting-woman but, noted a compassionate relative, " she has hir health so ill in sarves " that unless her two brothers will come to her aid, " she cannot tell how to live ". Too much depended in such cases upon the character of the mistress : if she were anything of a petty tyrant her opportunities might be too numerous and her temptations too strong. There was none the less a standard set up for her guidance in such matters in one of the manuals of the period, under the heading, *Behaviour to Servants*. " If ", says this authority, " the Gentlewoman finds through inspection that she has a faithful servant, she should give her to understand that she is not insensible thereof by her loving carriage and kind acknowledgment of her fidelity, and frequently find occasions to give her some little encouragement to engage her continuance therein." If the maids affect " bravery " too much, " and presume to wear what misbecomes their present condition ", the lady should " rebuke them mildly into a moderation " for their future advantage and the credit of the family wherein they are. And if she finds that she has a bad or unfaithful servant — " as nowadays there are too many — more than ever " — whom she cannot " either by fair means or foul reclaim ", she must make her sensible of her errors and give her fair warning. " Do not ", says this monitor, " give her too bad a character ; it will raise you little benefit though it may lay the basis of her utter ruin."

The work of the household — as we shall see later — was not apportioned rigidly among the several domestics composing it, and the chamber-maid was expected to deputise for the waiting-woman, who in her turn might be called upon to carry out at least some of the functions of the cook. In the ideal establishment the servants " should so relieve one another in the performance of their duties that they may be sometimes hearers of a good sermon ". We shall find a similar injunction in a similar book almost exactly two centuries later.

The passages quoted above come from *The Compleat Gentlewoman*, an immensely popular and frequently-reprinted treatise written in the second half of the seventeenth century by that remarkable person, Hannah Woolley. Left an orphan at the age of fourteen, she ran a small school for a couple of years ; later she acted as governess, first in one noble family and then in another ; later still she soared higher, becoming " acquainted with the Court " and " with the deportment suitable thereunto " ; and all the time she was adding to the list of her accomplishments, which included moss-work, shell-work, bugle-work, the " setting out of Banquets ", the compounding of sweet powders " for the Hair, or to lay among Linnen ", and the healing of " any wounds not desperately dangerous ". Having viewed life, high and low, from several angles and at close range, she was well equipped to lay down the law, and her precepts were received with appropriate piety by a large circle of female readers.

Though her name does not appear on the title-page and the book is not mentioned in the *D.N.B.* list of her published works, Hannah Woolley was almost certainly the writer of *The Compleat Serving-Maid*, 1677, considerable excerpts from which are to be found incorporated in *The Compleat Gentlewoman* as late as the edition of 1711. From the less ambitious book a great deal of valuable information may be gleaned, particularly regarding the duties of the chamber-maid, waiting-woman, housekeeper and other feminine members of the household staff — she has little to say about men-servants, except a few disparaging or admonitory interpolations. As if to reassure her humble readers, she begins the Preface to *The Compleat Serving-Maid* with the encouraging apostrophe, " Sweethearts ".

We soon learn that the young damsel who aspires to be a waiting-woman to a person of honour or quality must learn to dress (her mistress) well ; to preserve well ; write " a legible hand, good language and good English ; have some skill in arithmetic ; carve well ". The first and last clauses are rather unexpected, for one would hardly have thought that the sphere of such a servant would extend beyond the bedchamber and the parlour. She should be sober in her countenance and discourse, not using any wanton gesture which might give gentlemen any occasion to suspect her of levity, and so court her to debauchery, " and by that means lose a reputation irrecoverable ".

Hannah kindly furnishes the neophyte with full instructions on a variety of subjects, from making a quill pen to carving swans and bustards.

The chamber-maid also must be able to dress her lady, so that she may fill the place of an absent or ailing waiting-woman. She must, as we have already seen, know how to wash " fine linnen " and to starch tiffanies, lawns, points and laces. She must wash black and white sarsenets, " with such like things ", and mend then all neatly. Then she must learn to make her lady's bed " well, soft and easie ", lay up her night-clothes, see that her room be kept neat and clean, " and that nothing be wanting which she desires or requires to be done ". To her lady she must be modest in deportment and behaviour, endeavouring to mitigate her anger — even if unjust — with " pacifying words ". To her fellow-servants she should be loving and courteous, " not gigling or idling out her time, or wantoning in the society of men ". " All sorts of needlework and plain work " come within her province, and she must further be able to " make all manner of spoon-meats, to raise Paste, to dress meat well (though not often required thereunto), to make sauces both for fish and flesh, to garnish dishes, to make all sorts of pickles, to see that everything be served in well and handsomely to the table in due time, and to wait with a graceful decorum at table if need should require ".

" Spoon-meat " seems to have meant broth, flummery, caudle, jelly, etc., and these may have been prepared in the still-room : but it is difficult to see how this versatile Abigail could have " raised Paste " or " dressed " (*i.e.* cooked) meat without invading the realm of the cook. The lines of demarcation between one household department and another must at this time have been irregular and indistinct.

The tale of the chambermaid's responsibilities is not yet complete. She must be skilful in marketing, and it is she who should " see that all things are decent and fitting in the parlour and the dining-room ". If she masters all these branches of her calling she " will deserve a good salary and a great deal of respect ". She may also look forward to being promoted to the honourable post of housekeeper.

Those who aspire to be housekeepers " should carry themselves grave, solid and serious " In addition to their more obvious duties, they had to have " a competent knowledge of physick and chyrurgery, that they may be able to help their maimed, sick and indigent neighbours, for commonly all good and charitable ladies make this a part of their Housekeeper's business ". Directions are then given how to prepare specifics for a variety of ills, ranging from corns to colic.

A constant source of interest and an occasional source of evil in the servants' quarters was the coming and going of charwomen, pedlars and a variety of nondescript female hangers-on, many of them of doubtful honesty, and most of them ready to purvey gossip, convey messages and tell fortunes, if nothing worse. Maids in general are warned to beware of such persons, whose more sinister activities are hinted at in the following admonition : " beware of gossips and chairwomen [*sic*] for they will misadvise you ; take heed of the sollicitations of the flesh, for they will undo you ; and though you may have mean thoughts of yourself, and think none will meddle with such as you, it is a mistake, for sometimes brave gallants will fall foul upon the Wench in the scullery ". Mrs. Woolley reverts to this question — though from another angle — in *The Compleat Gentlewoman*, where she remarks, " let there be a competent allowance for the servants that they may have no just cause to complain, nor so much superfluity as that they may entertain a sort of loose gossips in corners, the very bane and spoil of servants ".

In spite of the danger that she might thereby render herself more attractive to the " brave gallant ", the scullery wench is exhorted to be sweet and clean in her person, remembering always that as soon as she has made an end of her dirty work she should wash and dress herself " neatly, titely, and cleanly ".

One of the most insidious of the back-door visitors was the woman — you see her in a seventeenth-century ' Cries of London ' print — who went round calling, " Kitchen stuff ha' ye, maids ? " The temptation must sometimes have proved irresistible to sell or barter more kitchen stuff than the maid had honestly at her disposal, and this evil endured and expanded well into the nineteenth century. Another regular comer was the woman who sold that indispensable cleansing and burnishing agent, sand. She is met with in the delightful old folk-song where her supposed happy lot, and that of the broom-seller, the chimney-sweeper and the cobbler, are contrasted with the precarious or penurious fate of the husbandman, the merchant and the serving-man :

> Who liveth so merry in all this land
> As doth the poor widow that selleth the sand ?
> And ever she singeth as I can guess,
> " Will you buy any sand, any sand, mistress ? "

There are some interesting counsels offered in *The Compleat Gentlewoman* to " all Gentlewomen who, though well born, are notwithstanding by indigency necessitated to serve some Person of Quality ". Parents who neglect their daughters' education, " vainly imagining that poverty will never approach their gates ", often expose them to great hardship, for it many times happens that they have to serve as chambermaids, " because they have not the accomplishments of a waiting-woman or a housekeeper ". But for this " they might have inclined Ladies to covet their company, might have sat at Table, had a command in the House, respect from the rest of the Servants, worn good clothes and received a considerable sallary. Instead thereof the meanness of their qualifications renders them only fit for companions of Grooms and Foot-boys." If her father had once large revenues and could talk loudly of his birth, such a young woman may think life in service beneath her : but she should thank God that she can do something for an honest livelihood, " and be never the less submissive ; for ", she is reminded, " if you are a servant you must do what becomes a servant ". All maids of whatsoever degree are earnestly exhorted not to waste their money upon " over-gaudy clothes ", since " to see a maid finely trickt up, having a fine show without and not one good qualification within, is like a joynted Bartholomew baby,[1] bought for no other use than to be looked upon ".

Mrs. Woolley's careful enumeration of the duties of a waiting-woman helps us to understand the position and imagine the duties of Dorothy Osborne's faithful, outspoken Jane. G. C. Moore-Smith, in his edition of Dorothy's letters to William Temple, follows Judge Parry in identifying this Jane with the Jane Wright mentioned on the tombstone of her brother-in-law, Parson Goldsmith, for sixty-three years Rector of Campton, Bedfordshire, the nearest village to the Osbornes' house, Chicksands Priory. She and Mrs. Goldsmith seem to have been the daughters of Thomas Wright, the trusted bailiff of Dorothy's father, Sir Peter Osborne, in Jersey, and his accredited agent there during the siege of Castle Cornet by the Parliamentarians in 1645.

Writing to her good-looking, witty young suitor, Dorothy not infrequently borrowed his whimsy of describing Jane as his " fellow servant " : for example, in March 1652, when she was taking an infusion of steel as a remedy for the spleen — a *régime* necessitating constant exercise. " Your fellow-servant has a blessed time on't ", she told him : " I make her play at shuttlecock with mee and she is the veryest bungler at it that ever you saw, then am I ready to beat her with the Battledore and grow soe peevish as I grow sick that I'le undertake she wishes there were noe steel in England " : but Dorothy was in a good humour all the day after, for joy that she was well again.

Soon after this letter was written Jane went to visit her relations in Guernsey, where she saw Temple, and alarmed him with her talk of his lady-love's melancholy. Dorothy wrote to reassure him, pointing out that the wench thought nobody in a good humour " unlesse they Laugh perpetually as she and Nan do's " — Nan (Stacy) being a young woman of Jane's own age and class, probably employed for a time at Chicksands, and

---

[1] A doll with movable limbs, dressed in spangles and tinsel, such as used to be sold at the famous Bartholomew Fair in West Smithfield, not abolished till 1855.

certainly by Temple himself in London.

In spite of this excessive mirthfulness Dorothy liked and valued Jane, whom she declared that she would part with only for her own advantage ; and when asked if she had missed her, she replied : " I cannot say but what I have missed Jane, but it has bin rather to have someone to talk with of you than that I needed anybody to put me in mind of you ". Later, when Jane had failed to find Temple in London and had had to leave with Nan Stacy the letter of which she was the bearer, her mistress wrote : " I was in hopes that she would bring me one from you, and because she did not I was resolved to punish her, and kept her up till one a clock telling mee all her Storrys. Sure if there be any truth in the old observation your cheeks glowed notably."

When, in September 1653, the waiting-woman ventured to send the young gentleman a pot of quince marmalade of her own making, Dorothy affected to think that she had taken " a pritty freedom " ; but she told Temple that he had himself to thank : " shee thinks because you called her ffellow-Servant she may use you accordingly. I bred her better, but you have spoyled her." It will be remembered that quince-cakes were among the dainties pressed upon young Allworth by his stepmother's maids in *A New Way to Pay Old Debts.*

Even more of a " freedom " was the message she dictated to her lady : " You must promise her to bee merry and not take colde when you are at ye Tennis Court for there shee hears you were found ".

Bold-tongued, merry-hearted Jane Wright served both the lovers faithfully, and lacking her intervention their long-drawn-out courtship would have been even more tedious and difficult than it was. In October 1653 she was badgering or, as Dorothy called it, ' baiting ' her mistress every day to persuade her to take pity on Temple and leave Chicksands for London. " When I urge, (as 'tis true) that there is a necessity of my stay heer, she grows furious, say's you will dye with melancholy, and confounds mee so with storrys of your ill-humour that i'le swear I think I should goe meerly to be at quiett." On another occasion Jane aroused Temple's anxiety by revealing to him that Dorothy stayed up late at night, reading — to the peril of those eyes of which he himself had said that they could " dispell all mellancholy clouded humours ". Again the charming creature feigned wrath : " I shall be even with her ", she swears, " some time or other ".

While Temple corresponded with her maid Jane, she corresponded with his maid Nan, whom she commissioned to cut and send her a lock of his hair, the dark brown, naturally-curling hair of which his sister, Lady Giffard, wrote that " while that was esteem'd a beauty nobody had it in more perfection ". Nan apparently showed her master Dorothy's letter of thanks describing how carefully she had put the lock away — and got called a " vile wench " for her pains.

The Osborne-Temple correspondence, witty, tender, gallant and gay, makes a patch of light and colour upon the grey surface of Commonwealth England. How would their square-toed neighbours have gloomed and growled if they had guessed that on St. Valentine's Day, 1654, Mistress Dorothy, Mrs. Goldsmith and Jane Wright had drawn lots for sweethearts in the time-honoured manner — by writing their names upon three slips of paper and the names of three gentlemen upon three precisely similar slips. It was by pure hazard that Dorothy drew Temple : " you cannot imagin ", she wrote to him, " how delighted I was by this little accident " ; but she does not mention whether Jane drew Mr. Fish or James B. — the names on the other two slips.

This faithful friend and servant remained with William and Dorothy Temple after their marriage, and we get a last glimpse of her in 1655 at Reading, where Mrs. Temple was then expecting her first child. " Your horses ", wrote the lady to her husband, " shall be looked to, too, as well as William and I and Jane and Mrs. Goldsmith can doe it, for wee understand it much alike mee-thinks."

Country maidservants, and those in households where neither man nor boy was kept, spent a good deal of their working time struggling with sticks and logs, pokers, tongs and bellows, to make and maintain good fires in parlour and hall. Thomas Fuller grants us a delightful glimpse of such a maid in a passage illustrating the axiom that " an estate suddenly gotten is not so lasting to the owner thereof as what is duly got by industry ",

and the text that " the substance of the diligent is precious "
(*Proverbs* xii, 27) :

> I saw a servant-maid, at the command of her mistress, make,
> kindle, and blow a fire. Which done, she was posted away about
> other business, whilst her mistress enjoyed the benefit of the fire.
> Yet I observed that this servant, whilst industriously employed in
> the kindling thereof, got a more general, kindly, and continuing
> heat than her mistress herself. *Her* heat was only by her, and not in
> her, staying with her no longer that she stayed by the chimney ;
> Whilst the warmth of the maid was inlaid, and equally diffused
> through the whole body.

In the old ballad of *The Wife of Usher's Well* it will be
remembered that the young man says

> And fare ye well, thou bonnie lass
> That kindles my mother's fire.

One section of the Abigail community suffered sad things
under the Puritan dispensation. Of the multitude of Anglican
clergymen ejected from their livings the majority were married
men, with wives and families, and one maidservant apiece, or
more than one. Even bachelors like Robert Herrick had some
sort of domestic assistance in their vicarages and rectories. When
these loyal churchmen and their families were being harried like
rogues and vagabonds there can have been little worldly induce-
ment to their humble friends to stand by them : yet it is clear
that in many instances these dependents elected to share their
hardships and even their perils.

When the Dean of Bristol was driven from his Deanery, his
wife, " poor gentlewoman, pitied by all though not holpen by
any ", was reduced to sending her sole remaining maid to the
market-place, selling posies of rosemary and bay " to buy
bread ". Even greater fortitude was demanded of Prudence
Baldwin, Herrick's Prue, who, with the local squire and his lady,
formed the whole congregation of Dean Prior Church on Mid-
summer Day, 1647, when the Reverend Robert did " seditiously,
defiantly and for the last time read evening service from the
Book of Common Prayer, including the collect for the Feast of
St. John the Baptist ". On the morrow he was ejected from his
living.

Prudence has been granted her little portion of immortality in four lines of *His Grange or Private Wealth* :

> I have
> A maid, my Prue, by good luck sent
> To save
> That little Fates me gave or lent.

Elsewhere Herrick alludes to the belief — touched upon by Mercutio in his Queen Mab speech — that the Queen of the Fairies may actively make known her dislike of sluttishness :

> If ye will with Mab find grace
> Set each platter in his place ;
> Rake the fire up, and get
> Water in, ere sun be set.
> Wash your pails and cleanse your dairies,
> Sluts are loathsome to the fairies :
> Sweep your house : who doth not so
> Mab will pinch her by the toe.

By one of those agreeable paradoxes that seem peculiar to the English story, Bishop Corbet's poems, including the delightful *Farewell to Fairies*, were published in that same grim year — 1647 :

> Farewell, rewards and fairies,
> Good housewives now may say,
> For now foul sluts in dairies
> Do fare as well as they ;
> And though they sweep their hearths no less
> Than maids were wont to do,
> Yet who of late for cleanliness
> Finds sixpence in her shoe ?

Before Milton's poetical arteries were incurably hardened by his political opinions, he, too, condescended to sing of the English rural divinities, of Mab, eating the junket and pinching the maid, of the lubbar-fiend, lob-lie-by-the-Fire, who earned his " cream-bowl duly set " by making himself miraculously useful about the house and the farm : but it is Herrick who gives us the most vivid picture of that England which died with the second Stuart and somehow failed to come to life under the third. He shows us the village girls, milkmaids or serving-maids or both at once, enjoying the simple delights of the year,

> Tripping the comely country round
> With daffadils and daisies crowned,

the Maypole, the morris-dance, the Christmas mummeries, the fireside chatter, with its

> . . . talk of brides, and who shall make
> The wedding-smock, the bridal cake.

Herrick's country maid is less idealized than Sir Thomas Overbury's, all of whose care was that she might " die in the springtime, to have store of flowers stuck upon her winding sheet ", but of each it could probably with equal truth have been said, " she is never alone, but is still accompanied with old songs, honest thoughts, and prayers, but short ones ". " The garden and bee-hive ", remarks Sir Thomas approvingly, " are all her physic and surgery, and she lives the longer for it " ; no doubt she did, for the nostrums compounded by the city apothecary were then only a little less horrible than those of his predecessor in Chaucer's day, though he might vary a solution of powdered woodlice with delicious concoctions of damask roses and lilies of the valley. That a good master was mindful of his maidservant in sickness as in health is shown from this extract from the diary of a Sussex parson towards the middle of the century : " my mayde being sicke, I paid for opening her veine, 4d. ; to the Widow Rugglesford for looking to her, I gave 1s. ; and to Old Bess for tending on her 3 days and 2 nights, I gave 1s.".

A diligent maid was not always left unrewarded, even when Queen Mab no longer encouraged her by dropping an occasional sixpence into her shoe. The Wills of this century contain many practical recognitions of faithful service. For example, the Will of Sir Hugh Middleton, the promoter of the New River scheme, who bequeathed to all his men-servants, " except the boy in the kitchin ", five pounds apiece, " and to the said boy and Elizabeth my maidservant, to each of them the sum of fortie shillings ". Even more famous in his day and generation was Mr. Speaker Lenthall, who had the agitating experience of presiding over that last session of the Long Parliament when it was violently dissolved by Cromwell in person. In 1662, two years after " the King enjoyed his own again ", Lenthall made his last Will and Testament in terms which throw a pleasing light upon his character and upon the household over which he and his wife had ruled. " I doe also," he wrote, " in respect of the great care and diligence of my servant, Elizabeth Hemmings, my wife's late servant, give her, in the remembrance of my deare wife, the summ of thirty pounds for a portion . . . and alsoe such wages as may be due to her at the time of my decease : her wages is six poundes by the yeare." In a codicil, having divided his wife's " cloths ", " velvett gownes " and " petty cotes " between his sister and his daughter-in-law, he added, " *Item,* I will that my servant Elizabeth shall have three other garments next, and that the rest of my wife's clothes shall be divided among servants ". Sir Henry de Vic, Chancellor of the Order of the Garter, dying in 1669, bequeathed £20 to his maidservant, Jane Taylor, and £10 to her sister June. He had already paid into " the hands and custodie " of his faithful housekeeper, Bridgett Wing, the £500 he had intended to bequeath to her by Will.

To encourage dutiful and steady conduct on the part of maid-servants John Cogan of Canterbury in the year 1657 had bequeathed the interest of his property in the parishes of St. Mildred and St. Mary Castle to give £5 apiece to any three such maid-servants as should without compulsion dwell with any master or mistress not being their own kindred, within the city of Canter-bury for six or seven years together, " without shifting their service ".

The curious recurrent association between maids and 'mani-festations' is illustrated about this period by the case of the young woman employed by Joseph Bennett, Puritan minister of the town of Brightling in 1659. The story is told by Increase Mather in his *Remarkable Providences.* Some kind of mischievous agency — the Poltergeist type — seemed to be haunting the house : several objects, including crabs (whether dead or alive, raw or dressed, is not stated), were flung about by an invisible hand, and the darkest conjectures were aroused, " yet ", says Mather, " there was a seeming blur cast, though not on the whole, yet upon some part of it, for their servant-girl was at last found throwing some things ". She averred that an old woman had bidden her to do so, saying that " her master and mistress were bewitched, and that they should hear a great fluttering about their house for two days ".

In a different category, and apparently beyond any suspicion of trickery, was the case recorded by Evelyn in his *Diary* for August 3, 1670. On that day a neighbour, aware of his interest in natural curiosities, sent to him a young servant-maid, " a plaine, ordinary, silent working wench, somewhat fat, short, and high-coloured ", to whom a very strange thing had happened as she sat sewing in the presence of her mistress one day in the previous month. She then felt a stroke on her arm, a little above the wrist, as if she had been struck by an unseen hand. The smart " caused her to hold her arme awhile till somewhat mitigated, but it put her into a kind of convulsion or hysteric fit. A gentleman coming casually in, looking on her arme found that part poudred with red crosses, set in most exact and wonderfull order, neither swelled nor depressed, about this shape : "

```
                    ×

             ×            ×

      ×            ×            ×

             ×            ×

                    ×
```

She gained nothing by it, had no religious fancies, was rather confounded than otherwise by the attention attracted to herself. The F.R.S. was solemnly interested, remembering " the impostorious Nuns of Loudun in France ", whose claim to have received the sacred stigmata was questioned even by some pious members of their own church. Unlike the nuns, " this poor wench was willing to submit to any trial ; so that I profess ", concludes Mr. Evelyn, " that I know not what to think of it, nor dare I pronounce it anything supernaturall ".

The number of advertisements offering rewards for the detection and apprehension of absconding and dishonest servants forms an eloquent commentary upon Hannah Woolley's remarks as to the scarcity of what she calls " faithful " ones. Some of these delinquents, women as well as men, were negroes, liable to be bought and sold like cattle, and wearing the name of their employer on a brass collar riveted round the neck. The following announcement from *Mercurius Politicus*, May 1658, is typical, though it is not clear whether the person concerned was a negress, a mulatto or merely an English girl with dark colouring.

A Black-haired maid, of a middle stature, thick set, with big breasts, having her face full marked with the smallpox, calling herself by the name of Nan or Agnes Hobson, did, upon Monday the 28 of May, about six o'clock in the morning, steal away from her ladies house in the Pall Mall a mingle-coloured wrought Tabby gown of Deer colour and white ; a black striped sattin Gown with four broad bone-black silk Laces, and a plain black watered French Tabby Gown ; Also one Scarlet-coloured and one other Pink-coloured Sarcenet Peticoat died, a white watered Tabby Waistcoat, plain ; several Sarcenet, Mode and thin black Hoods and Scarfs, several fine Holland Shirts, a laced pair of Cuffs, and Dressing, one pair of Pink-coloured Worsted Stockings, a Silver Spoon, a Leather bag, etc. She went away in a greyish Cloth Waistcoat, turned, and a Pink-coloured Paragon upper Peticoat with a Green Tammy under one. If any shall give notice of this person or things to one Hopkins, a Shoomaker's, next door to the Vine Tavern, near the Pal-Mall end, near Charing Cross, or at Mr. Ostler's, at the Bull Head in Cornhill, near the Old Exchange, they shall be rewarded for their pains.

There are several interesting features in this advertisement. The leather bag, one conjectures, was taken by Nan Hobson to facilitate the removal of the rest of her booty. From the circumstance that the sole article of plate in the list is a single silver spoon — probably a posset-ladle — it would appear that the black-haired maid was the personal attendant of the lady, and enjoyed unrestricted access to her chests and cupboards. The " greyish waistcoat, turned " and the pink petticoat sound as if they must have been cast-off garments bestowed upon this dishonest Abigail, but in the under-petticoat of humble green tammy she may have had an original possession of her own.

A more enterprising spirit marked the proceedings of a woman who was advertised for in the same news-sheet only two months later. She was Eleanor Parker, by birth Haddock, and she was a servant in the household of Mr. Frederick Houpert of Kentish Town — then a pleasant rural outskirt. Tall of stature, with a tawny reddish complexion and " a pretty long nose ", she ought not to have been hard to identify, even lacking any description of the clothes in which she ran away. Eleanor broke open her mistress's cabinet, and stole from it a number of valuables — two silver spoons ; " a sweet tent-work-bag with gold and silver lace about it and lined with satin " ; a bugle-work cushion very curiously wrought with all manner of slips and flowers ; a shell cup with a lion's face and a ring of silver in its mouth — besides many other objects " to the value of ten pounds and upwards ".

If Eleanor was caught, she was almost certainly hanged ; at a slightly later date her punishment would have been transportation and she might have ended up as a settler's wife in Maryland after the manner of Moll Flanders.

CHAPTER IV

Concerning Samuel Pepys, Deb. Willett
and Some Others

TOWARDS the middle of the seventeenth century the lines of social demarcation were much less deep and distinct in the lower and lower-middle classes than they were afterwards to become, and there was a good deal of ' infiltration '. Examples may be marked in the immediate family circle of Samuel Pepys, whose father, a tailor, married Margaret Kite, a simple ' wash-maid ' of Whitechapel, but whose maternal uncle was a butcher, while his maternal aunt married a fellmonger who rose to be an alderman. In the little house, half shop, half dwelling, abutting westwards into St. Bride's Churchyard, Margaret Pepys was herself the mistress of a maid, Barbara Williams by name : yet when her son Samuel was boarded out at Kingsland, near Stoke Newington, and played with his toy bow and arrow in the fields there, he could plainly see the large and fair house of one Mrs. Herbert, among whose maidservants was his mother's humble kinswoman, Ellen Kite. In after years, when God had prospered him beyond all expectation, Pepys's own Abigails were to range from Deb. Willett, the niece of a worthy merchant of Bristol, to Doll, a female ' blackamore '.

It is yet another instance of the infiltration referred to above that the Fleet Street tailor's son could claim kinship with Edward Montagu, afterwards Earl of Sandwich, a personage who on the other side could in his turn claim kinship with Drogo de Monta-cuto, one of Duke William's Norman adventurers ; and it was as a sort of secretary-steward to his already powerful kinsman that young Pepys, fresh from Magdalene College, Cambridge, began his career. With his even more youthful wife he lived in his master's lodgings in Whitehall ; they occupied cramped quarters in the turret over the gateway and as yet could afford no maid.

Two of Montagu's maids left on board-wages under Pepys's

supervision used to take their meals in one or other of the numerous little cookhouses in the warren of narrow streets round the Palace of Westminster. In this way they made some undesirable acquaintances : one of the foolish girls eloped, carrying some of Montagu's goods with her, and, not unnaturally, Mr. Pepys was called upon rather sharply to give an account of his stewardship. He denied with some warmth that there had been anything lax or indiscreet in his own conduct, but the pages of his Diary show only too plainly that he had dallied in a rather undignified manner with Sarah, the non-eloping maid. Anxiously he wrote to Montagu that he would see to it that the *next* maid should " diet on four shillings a week " with himself and his wife : in this way, he says, " the disrepute of a maid's going to a victualling house in neglect of your Honour's own doors will be prevented ". With the help of his master's sister-in-law, Mistress Ann Crewe, he sought about for another domestic, whose duties would include making fires, cleaning the rooms, washing clothes, scouring silver and pewter.

A year later Mr. and Mrs. Pepys quitted their Whitehall quarters for ever, and moved into a five-roomed house in Axe Yard, off King Street. The sun of prosperity was beginning to shine full and fair upon the little man, and in August 1658 Elizabeth also felt the warmth of its beams. No longer now would she have to do all the washing with her own hands, and ' dress ' all the meat, as she had been wont to do in her first home ; in that month Jane Wayneman became her servant-maid. Washing continued to fill a great part of many days, and even a small part of some of the nights. At one o'clock on a cold, frosty morning in January Mr. Pepys went to bed and left his wife and the maid " a-washing still " ; and on another occasion he recorded, " Home, and being washing-day, dined upon cold meat ". As Jane habitually rose at two o'clock in the morning on those days, it is to be hoped that her labours — even aided by her mistress — did not often extend through twenty-three hours. In addition to the regular work of the house her duties included washing her master's feet in herb-strewn water, knitting his stockings, putting him to bed, and lighting him with a lanthorn on his way to merry meetings after dusk. Her wages were £3 a year.

She was a dreamy, amiable wench, Jane Wayneman, too tender-hearted to kill a turkey, and so untidy that Pepys, a stickler for order in all things, was occasionally moved to beat her with a broom. She submitted so meekly that he afterwards felt sharp twinges of compunction. Yet her life compared favourably with that of many of her predecessors in the medieval and Tudor periods. She lived with the family she served, shared their amusements, went visiting with them unless they were calling upon ' quality ', gathered may-dew with Mrs. Pepys on mid-summer morning. On one occasion, after a Christmas party at Sir William Batten's, Mr. Pepys was taken so ill in the middle of the night that it was necessary to rouse Jane, who pleased him and his wife by " running up and down so innocently in her smock ".

Gentle though she was, Jane Wayneman had her moments of freakishness, as when she snipped off the moustache of a carpenter working at the house, thereby causing him to shed tears and getting him into sad trouble with his wife. Nor was she illiter-ate ; for she possessed a book (title not stated) and Pepys had to rebuke his disagreeable sister Pall for stealing it.

In August 1660 Samuel Pepys became Clerk of the Acts to the Navy and moved into his official residence in Seething Lane, a fine, brick-built house of eight or nine rooms. This rise in the world was marked by the introduction of a house-boy — first a transitory specimen called simply ' Will ', and then Jane Wayne-man's young brother. Perhaps because it was near the river, perhaps because the previous tenants had been negligent, the place was swarming with rats and mice ; so Pepys remembered the cat which he had left behind in Montagu's lodgings at White-hall, where the maid Sarah was still looking after it, and went and fetched it home.

About this time Elizabeth Pepys began to evince that desire for a sort of waiting-woman or maid-companion which was later to be fulfilled more than once, with varying results. The first choice of a person to fill the rôle was an unlucky one — her morose sister-in-law, Pall Pepys, who proved both idle and proud, and put the whole household out of gear. So, weeping bitterly, and fortified by a gift of twenty shillings and a great deal of fraternal admonition, Pall was packed off home. Then Sarah, sister to the maid at The Swan, temporarily replaced Jane Wayneman, and for a time pleased Mrs. Pepys so well that she took her with her to Brampton ; but the *entente* was of brief duration : mistress and maid fell out, and on their return Sarah was dismissed. She, too, wept ; and Pepys, kissing her goodbye, came near mingling his tears with hers.

In the meantime Jane had returned — first to take charge of the house in Seething Lane during the absence of Elizabeth, and then to be promoted to the status of chamber-maid, when a personable cook-maid called Susan joined the domestic staff.

And now Balthazar, otherwise Balty, St. Michel, the lady's gay, irresponsible brother, bestirred himself to find her the companion whom her soul desired. His choice fell upon a certain Miss Gosnell, one of two attractive sisters well skilled in singing and dancing, and he beguiled her with enchanting promises of daily visits to the playhouse and the court. When the young person discovered that the truth was quite otherwise, she departed — after a sojourn of only three days. Later she went on the stage, and appeared with some success at the Duke of York's theatre. To her succeeded Mary Ashwell, fresh from a boarding-school in the academic groves of Chelsea. First impressions were good : an unassuming, industrious girl, and skilful upon the harpsichord. But she was soon seen to be a " merry jade ", and though she introduced a note of gaiety into the house it became evident that she had a bad influence upon Elizabeth, sharpening her appetite for amusement — and not in its most simple or economical forms. Even Samuel was so far carried away as to purchase a new bass viol. She taught her master and mistress card games, and a new pack of cards had to be bought. With them she went on charming little jaunts, to gather cowslips at the Rotherhithe Halfway House and to hear the nightingales at Woolwich : and visits to Hyde Park and the Theatre Royal, Drury Lane, were only a degree less frequent than Balty had told Miss Gosnell that they would be.

Pepys concluded with alarm that Mary Ashwell was inciting his wife to be insubordinate as well as spendthrift and frivolous. Yet she had her merits, and so hungry a gossip as he must have been uncommonly obliged to her for the story she brought from Chelsea concerning his powerful kinsman, now Earl of Sandwich, who was dallying with a certain Mrs. Becke, a denizen of that riverside village, " carrying her abroad, and playing his lute under her window, and forty other poor, sordid things ". Finally, neither Ashwell's skill upon the harpsichord nor her value as a retailer of scandal outweighed in her master's eyes the deleterious influence she exercised upon her mistress. Cynically mindful of what had happened in the case of Sarah, he packed the two of them off to Brampton, where they did not fail to fall out. Mrs. Pepys boxed Ashwell's ears — the maid retorted with a hearty cuff — and the chapter was closed for ever. Hannah, Susan's successor as cook-maid, then went off in a huff, and the temporary return of Susan revealed the regrettable fact that she had taken to the drink. A ' daily ', Goody Taylor, filled the gap, after the unsatisfactory manner of such auxiliaries in all ages.

Pepys's brother Tom, hearing of the family's predicament, produced from the parish of St. Bride's a diminutive charity girl called Jinny, " of honest parents and recommended by the Churchwardens ". Personal cleanliness was not among Jinny's qualifications — though that, perhaps, the churchwardens did not know. As soon as Elizabeth had scrubbed her and clothed her in neat new clothes, she decamped. " We have ", noted Mr. Pepys sadly, " no luck in maids nowadays."

The Clerk of the Acts patronized a Westminster barber, Jarvis by name, who employed a pretty little maidservant, Jane Welsh. In the summer of 1664, yielding to the pressure of fashion, he acquired a periwig, and was thenceforth compelled to have recourse to Mr. Jarvis's assistance more frequently, in order to have the wig mended, cleaned and recurled. It was thus that he became increasingly conscious of Jane's youthful charm. Catching her alone one day, he implored her to meet him in Westminster Abbey " at sermon time " on the ensuing Sunday : but though he paced up and down the aisles till six o'clock in the evening she did not come. Nothing daunted, he renewed his pursuit the very next day. Having ascertained at what hour the barber and his wife would both be out and Jane alone in the house beneath the striped pole, he went and mooned about the

Abbey until the time came, and then — most reprehensibly — joined the little maid, with whom he spent a couple of hours, " kissing but nothing more ". All the sharper must his disappointment have been on the next Sunday after, when she again failed to keep tryst with him among the tombs. He called at the house on Monday, and found her cold, which he told himself was " no great matter " ; but, says Arthur Bryant, " there is no doubt that his heart was touched ". Later, after more evasions, he heard that she had chosen another sweetheart, " a sorry fellow and poor ".

After Ashwell's departure the constantly changing procession of Abigails went on : there was Bess, who infuriated Pepys by forgetting to set out his clothes in the morning, another Susan, who proved to be " a most admirable slut ", and Nell, who grew lazy and proud and took herself off. Of different stuff was Jane Birch, " a good-natured, quiet, well-meaning, honest servant ", whom we meet many years later as Mrs. Edwards, keeping house for Will Hewer. At the time of the Ashwell crisis the faithful Will was lodging with a family of the name of Mercer, one member of which, Mary Mercer, had a good voice and ear and played upon the harpsichord " passing well " : at his suggestion she was engaged to wait upon Mrs. Pepys. Like Ashwell, she went about with her master and mistress, shared in their cheerful jaunts by land and water, and bore a part in the music and dancing with which they entertained their friends — or were entertained by them.

The early summer of 1665 was rainless, breathless and charged with doom. In quest of the cooling breeze that failed to blow, Mr. and Mrs. Pepys would take to the river, attended by a boat-load of dependents — Will Hewer, Mercer, Mary the cook and others ; but presently, when the red crosses multiplied upon doors and the weekly Bills of Mortality began to rise, Pepys decided to send his mother, his wife, Mercer and Mary (" both good wenches ") to stay at Woolwich, in the house of William Sheldon, Clerk of the Cheque. He himself, with admirable fortitude, remained in Seething Lane, with two more maids, Susan and Alce, in charge. According to Defoe many unhappy servants, both men and women, were turned adrift by their

THE TEMPTRESS

A seventeenth-century woodcut illustrating the Cries of London

employers when the Plague was at its peak : but the Pepys house-hold, though it split up for the time being, knew no such dis-integration.

Sometimes when Susan was curling his hair on a Sunday morning, her master would behave in a manner at once indecorous and undignified, but not very dangerous. He could not go to church for fear of infection, and because of the deathly influence of the mounds of newly and hastily-dug graves, piling up every day ; but on week-days the pleasure gardens at Vauxhall were still open, and he did not hesitate to frequent them. It is by no means unlikely that Susan and Alce occasionally went there, too, and gathered cherries from the famous orchard : persons of their calling were — and remained — regular and enthusiastic patron-esses of the various London equivalents of the modern ' fun-fair '. Like their master and mistress, they escaped the visitation, and when the Plague at last abated they all met again in Seething Lane—the house now beautified with green serge curtains, pewter candle-sconces and chairs covered with gilded Spanish leather.

To keep his womankind occupied, and not unprofitably so, Mr. Pepys then set his wife and Mercer ruling paper for the Navy Office, — thereby augmenting their modest finances and bringing a whiff of sea-salt and a tang of tar into the room where they sat. Mercer was a merry creature, and a cause of mirth in others. There is no gayer entry in all the Diary than that of August 14, 1666, which relates how Pepys took his wife and her maid to the Bear-garden. "We had ", he notes, " a great many hectors in the box with us . . . where they drank wine, and drank Mercer's health first ; which I pledged with my hat off." After supping at home, they went round to the house of Mercer's mother and spent the best part of three hours letting off serpents and rockets in the street outside. Towards midnight they went into the house ; " and there mighty merry, smutting one another with candle-grease and soot, till most of us were as devils ". Thence they all streamed round to Seething Lane : " and there I made them drink, and upstairs we went, and then fell into dancing . . . and Mercer put on a suit of Tom's like a boy, and mighty mirth we had, and Mercer danced a jigg ". Elizabeth Pepys took part in these junketings, and she, with two of the other ladies present, put on masculine periwigs. But she had noted various occasions when her husband's wandering eye had wandered towards Mercer and then come to rest upon one or other of her excellences — among which a shapely leg must surely have been numbered. Less than a month later, on the morning of September 2, the Great Fire broke out which was destined to form a lurid and flickering background to their last broil and their temporary severance.

It was one of the maids — Jane Birch — who called them up about three o'clock in the morning with news of a glow in the sky over towards the City. Pepys, being, as he himself remarked, " unused to such fires as followed ", was not much perturbed, and went back to bed : but later in the day, moving to and fro in his usual eager, avid manner, he saw many lamentable sights, steeples flaming, long furrows of fire running along the water-front, and distracted householders trying to get their belongings away to safety. Among these last was Mercer's mother, to help whom Mercer herself, against the express orders of her mistress, had hastened. A distressing scene followed. Mrs. Pepys, hurrying round to the house in quest of Will Hewer, fell upon the truant maid and beat her soundly. Then up spake Mrs. Mercer, saying that her daughter was not a 'prentice girl to ask leave every time she went abroad — interesting incidental evidence that the status of a maidservant was regarded as superior to that of an apprentice, perhaps because the latter category was recruited so largely from charity children. Angry, and in her husband's opinion, rightly angry, Elizabeth waited till Mercer returned to Seething Lane, and then " bid her begone again ". Pepys's comment is characteristic : " and so she went away, which troubled me, but yet less than it would, because of the condition we are in, in fear of coming in a little time to be less able to keep one of her quality ". The break, however, was not to prove final, and the gay figure of Mercer reappears in the Diary, going with her old master and mistress to the playhouse, to Spring Garden and to Bartholomew Fair. In the meantime another figure, very different and far more engaging, had made its first entry : on September 24, 1667, Deborah Willett " came to serve my wife as woman ".

She was young, a very fledgling, fresh from a boarding-school at Bow — apparently a less lax and worldly school than the one attended by Ashwell at Chelsea. The orphan child of a Bristol merchant, she had been a pupil at Bow for eight years — about half of her whole life. In Jewen Street, not very far from Seething Lane, there lived an aunt of hers, Mrs. Hunt, who " kept her carriage " and was — in the immortal words of Mr. Boffin — " a high flyer at fashion ". The street was not unworthy of her aspirations, for it had been laid out and built some ten years earlier by the Goldsmiths' Company, and contained both fine houses and fine gardens. None the less, Aunt Hunt seems to have been quite well pleased that the shy and rather immature Deborah should be maid to the wife of the Clerk to the Acts.

" Grave beyond her bigness and age ", Pepys noted, and " exceeding well bred as to her deportment ". Even more gently he wrote of her at this time, " very pretty, and so grave as I never saw a little thing in my life ". He considered her too good for his household, and trusted, somewhat uneasily, that Elizabeth would treat her well. At first there was no great cause for un-easiness on that score. " Willett " was a favourite with them both : into their childless environment she brought something of the grace and freshness that might have been brought by a small daughter of their own. Presently Mr. Pepys began to spend more hours at home than it had been his wont to spend there : he walked in the garden with Elizabeth, and Deb. walked with them : in the cool of the evening they would all sit on the leads of the house, where a roof-garden had been contrived, looking out over a forest of dark-red chimney-pots. And Elizabeth was neither jealous nor suspicious — so far.

On October 7, 1667, a cheerful party of five set out for Cambridgeshire in a coach and four, hired for the occasion. It was Mr. and Mrs. Pepys, Deb. Willett, Will Hewer and a certain Mr. Murford, an old acquaintance from Pepys's Westminster Hall days. A halt was made at Audley End, where Pepys suffered that disillusionment often felt by people revisiting a place that has impressed them in their youth. " The house ", he wrote, " indeed do appear very fine, but not so fine as it hath heretofore to me ; particularly the ceilings are not so good as I always took them to be." It is not difficult to imagine the little party trailing through the beautiful old house, Pepys darting hither and thither, peering and peeping; Elizabeth, excitable, would-be-modish, with her high cheek-bones and her flexible, generous mouth ; Deb. stealing quietly beside her ; and, bringing up the rear, the rather indistinct figure of worthy Mr. Murford. They joined in noting that the staircase was " exceeding poor " ; and of the numerous pictures they thought none merited their attention except " Harry the Eighth done by Holben ". They marked the strange absence of " a single suit of good hangings " ; but nothing damped their spirits, and they were " mighty merry ". They went down into the cellars — there, at least, Pepys's memory had not betrayed him — they drank much good liquor, and Mr. and Mrs. Pepys sang a duet among echoing barrels and bins. If Deb. drank also, the liquor did not inspire her to sing, nor to utter any words thought remarkable enough to be recorded in her master's Diary. She was indeed a curiously inarticulate little person : pre-occupied with her as he was, and observant of her looks and ways, Pepys would surely have noted any words of hers that pleased or amused him. Yet this silence may have been part of her good breeding, or the result of a discretion that was, like her pretty gravity, beyond her years.

At Cambridge, the party put up at The Rose, and " the town musick did come and play : but Lord ! what sad musick they made ". And then away to Brampton, to the house of old Father Pepys, to carry out the main object of the expedition — nothing less than the disinterring from the garden there of the money buried by the diarist during the tumults of the Civil War. Neither of the womenfolk was called upon to help to dig up the treasure or to wash the dirt off the gold pieces with " several pails of water and besoms " : nor did Pepys think it necessary to take his wife and her attendant with him when he walked up to Hinchingbroke to pay his respects to Lady Sandwich.

On October 11 they set out for home, with the gold in a basket under one of the seats : but on the following day the anxious owner, fearing that the bottom of the coach might give way under the weight, divided the coins into three bags, of which he held one, his wife another and " the girle " the third. As the

months pass we see that "Willett" merges into "Deb.", and
"the girle" becomes "our girle". A short time after they all
returned to London Will Hewer escorted "my wife and girle"
to the playhouse to see *The Tempest* — a performance graced by
the presence of King Charles in person. "The most innocent
play that ever I saw", says Pepys, who went later with Sir
William Penn. Even in that Restoration travesty a sensitive
spectator acquainted with Deb. Willett might have been reminded
of her now by Miranda and now — though less vividly — by
Ariel : but such fancies were unlikely to germinate beneath the
periwig of Samuel Pepys.

Towards the close of the year 1667, Mrs. Hunt, Deb.'s
fashionable aunt, called upon Mrs. Pepys, whom she dazzled with
her flow of elegant conversation. She appears to have been well
pleased with her niece's position and prospects, and even better
pleased to notice that the child's breasts were growing, "she
being afeared before that she would have none".

At Deb.'s first coming Pepys had confessed himself afraid of
being too much charmed with her, and not without reason. He
was the most susceptible of men, emotional, demonstrative, and
yet weighted with an inner core of Puritan principle. It was this
which inhibited him for nearly two months after she became a
member of his household ; but at the end of that time he took
courage to give her "a little kiss" — she being, he adds, "a
very pretty-humoured girl, and one that I love mightily". It
was hardly to be expected that Elizabeth should remain deaf and
blind ; she became peevish and querulous, causing poor Deb. to
shed tears, which her master dried with much tenderness, accom-
panying his consolations with good counsel. All through the
winter his infatuation grew, fed by the fact that — in accordance
with the custom of that period and class — it was one of "the
girle's" duties to comb his hair every night, to brush his clothes,
and to help him to undress. This was common form, and Mrs.
Pepys could hardly object : but she must have noticed that the
hair-combing lasted for an hour at a time by the fireside in the
long, dark evenings, and she may have divined that Deb.'s
services to her husband would give him oppportunities which it
would have been most unlike him not to take. Presently he took

them, but the child repelled him so modestly that he "could scarcely bring himself to attempt more ".

In the spring of 1668 she was still their " girle ", and when she accompanied Elizabeth to Brampton the analogy of Sarah and Gosnell did not hold good, and no violent breach resulted. Pepys, seeing them off at the coach-office, slipped ten shillings into Deb.'s hand, and had difficulty in abstaining from kissing her goodbye.

The early summer of that year was marked by extensive journeyings, the party being the same as on the previous occasion, but with the addition of Mr. Murford's cousin, Betty Taylor. Westward-bound, to the no small content of both Mrs. Pepys and Deb., they halted at Salisbury where, not being able to hire coach-horses to carry them to Stonehenge and not feeling disposed to use their own, they got " saddle-horses, very dear ". Pepys rode solo, and " the three women ", as he calls them, rode pillion behind Will Hewer, Mr. Murford and the guide. They returned by way of Wilton, which failed to please, and when they reached Salisbury Pepys sent the women home to the inn while he inspected the tombs, " among the rest some very ancient of the Montagus ". The beds at the inn were the next morning pronounced to be " good but lousy ", whereat these most philosophical and light-hearted of travellers were " very merry ". On June 12 they reached " The Bath ", not yet a Palladian city of austere Augustan grace but just the sort of busy place, full of music, movement and fine folk, that would charm Pepys. On the first day of their stay the whole party rose at 4 A.M. and were borne in chairs to the Cross Bath, where they had designed to bathe " become company come " ; but they had not finished soaking when " much company come ". It does not seem to have detracted from their enjoyment. They all stayed above two hours in the gently-steaming water and were then carried home to their lodgings wrapped in sheets.

They next proceeded to Bristol — " in every respect another London " — and alighted at The Horseshoe. While Deb. went with Betty Taylor to call upon her uncle, Pepys characteristically gravitated to the quayside to contemplate the fine new ship under construction there. The sequel is best told in his own words :

Walked back to the *Sun,* where I find Deb. come back with her uncle, a sober merchant, very good company, and so like one of our wealthy London merchants as pleased me mightily. . . . Then walked with him and my wife and company round the quay and to the ship : and he showed me the Custom House and made me understand many things of the place and led us through Marsh Street, where our girle was born. But Lord ! the joy that was among the old poor people of the place to see Mrs. Willett's daughter, it seems her mother being a brave woman and mightily beloved ! And so brought us a back way by surprize to his house, and did give us good entertainment of strawberries, a whole venison pasty cold, and plenty of brave wine, and above all Bristol milk.

While they were thus regaling themselves, another poor woman, hearing that Deb. was there, came running in " with her eyes so full of tears and her heart so full of joy that she could not speak when she come in ", thereby causing Mr. Pepys to weep in sympathy. He was always at the mercy of any momentary emotion ; but if some recurrent memory of that little scene ever rose up to admonish him, it lacked the force to turn him aside from that course of conduct which was to separate him from Deb. for ever. Having put it on record that her aunt was " a good woman, and so sober and substantiall as ever I saw ", that he was " never more pleased anywhere ", and that he tipped the maid two shillings, he thus concludes the story of that summer day : " We back, and by moonshine to the Bath again about ten o'clock ; bad way ; and giving the coachman 1s., all of us to bed ".

It is tempting to dwell upon this last unchequered vision of Deb., and saddening to realize how within less than a year all things were altered. Pepys would be more forgivable in this regard if he had never seen her against the Bristol background, had never sat at the table of her " sober and substantiall " aunt and uncle, or shed facile tears when the poor woman came running in that had known her mother. If any member of the little party soon homeward bound had any doubts, misgivings or fears, it was he ; Elizabeth's suspicions were dormant, if indeed they had ever been wide awake.

By way of Avebury, Marlborough and Reading the travellers returned to London, and there for a time things went fairly smoothly and Pepys behaved pretty well. In July, Cooper, the famous miniaturist, was painting Elizabeth's portrait, and we hear of Will Hewer and Deb. escorting her to his studio and remaining with her during the sittings. They were all very merry, and the resurgent Mercer with them at the house of Mr. Batelier — the friend through whom they had first heard of Deb. — one evening in August, when their host's cousin, " a good-humoured, fat young gentleman ", Gambleton by name, won their admiration by his fine dancing. Indeed, they all danced throughout the night " with a noble supper : and about two o'clock in the morning the table spread again for a noble breakfast, beyond all moderation ".

Unfortunately the jaunt to the west country seemed to have unsettled Mrs. Pepys's nerves ; she was inclined to be now excitable, and now melancholy, and her oscillations of temperament bore rather hardly upon her husband. One night she rose, weeping wildly, from his side and fled to Deb.'s bed, where she remained till morning. The old hangings from the best bedroom had recently been transferred to Deb.'s room, new hangings of greater dignity having been bought for the chamber thus impetuously abandoned by its lawful mistress. Yet Elizabeth was soon willing to be gay again, and we often hear of " my wife, Mercer and Deb." going to the playhouse in an apparently harmonious trinity. On one occasion they had their fortunes told by gypsies, but the result was not divulged — at least, not to Mr. Pepys.

It was about this time that he determined to give a trial to a new kind of aid to sight sponsored by the Royal Society. This consisted of a pair of tubes or funnels, made of leather and cardboard of such simple construction that they could be manufactured at home. So the women of the Seething Lane household were soon busy upon a new task.

One August evening, as Deb. was helping him to undress, her master fondled her rather more freely than he had hitherto permitted himself to do, and Deb. resisted rather less firmly than she had done before. " The little creature ", as Arthur Bryant says, " was serving her first perilous apprenticeship in life." If Elizabeth perceived that Samuel's love for their " girle " was beginning to get out of control she made no sign — as yet : but she carried Deb. off with her on a visit to Cousin Roger Pepys at Impingham. Disaster had been averted — but not for long.

On October 10 they were all together again in the house on Tower Hill, where improvements were being planned in the blue chamber : " my wife and I ", says Pepys, " mighty busy laying out money in dressing up our best chamber, and thinking of a coach, and coachman, and horses, etc." He was also busy at the Navy Office, and such leisure as he could snatch was spent at court, at the playhouse or at meetings of the Royal Society. None of these interests and occupations was enough — all of them together were not enough — to distract his mind from the irresistible charm of Deb.

One Sunday evening — it was October 25 — Pepys called her as usual to come and comb his hair, " which ", he wrote sadly, " occasioned the greatest sorrow to me that ever I knew in this world, for my wife coming up suddenly did find me embracing the girl. . . . I was at a wonderful loss upon it, and the girl also." We know, for it is not a question upon which the *Diary* would mislead us, that he had not yielded to the worst of his regrettable impulses ; but Elizabeth may be forgiven for believing that he had. At first she was mute with fury : when she found her tongue, it had become a veritable whip of scorpions.

The weeks that followed must have been painful both to Deb. and to her master, but even more so to him than to her. He was not suffered to go and seek her in the blue chamber when she sat at work there with the upholsterer's men, and he saw her only when the three of them met in strained, unhappy silence at the supper table, Elizabeth's eye alert to see if Samuel's eyes would stray to Deb.'s, which, he acknowledged, " they could not but do, and to my grief did see the poor wretch look on me and see me look on her and then let drop a tear or two, which so make my heart relent at this minute that I am writing this with great trouble of mind " : for he had " no mind to part with the girle ", much less that she should be undone by his folly.

Yet part with her he must, as very soon appeared. Elizabeth had an interview with Mrs. Hunt, the elegant aunt in Jewen

Street, and " told her of her desire of parting with Deb. in kind terms ". It is a pity that the lady did not carry her niece off with her in the coach, together with all the gear she had brought with her to Seething Lane. This included a chest of drawers which will figure again in the sad, sordid little story.

The parting, when it did come, was anything but kind : for the tide of Elizabeth's anger continued to rise, and finally she compelled her husband to dismiss Deb. with bitter words — not one of which came from his heart. " Did, with tears in my eyes, which I could not help, discharge her and advise her to be gone as soon as she could, and never to see or let me see her more while she was in the house, which she took with tears, too, but I believe understands me to be her friend ", wrote Pepys ; but, so well had Mrs. Pepys wrought upon him already, he added, " I am apt to believe by what my wife hath of late told me [that she] is a cunning girle, if not a slut " — *i.e.* a wanton. In spite of these misgivings, he wrapped forty shillings in a twist of paper on the day of Deb.'s departure, trusting for an opportunity to slip it into her hand. None was vouchsafed to him, and he listened with the meekness of remorse to his Elizabeth railing at him, calling him a dog and a rogue, and telling him that he had a rotten heart. " And word being brought presently that she [Deb.] was gone away by coach with all her things, my wife was friends, and so all quiet, and I to the office with my heart sad, and find that I cannot forget the girle, and vexed I know not where to look for her."

It was perhaps not altogether to his discredit that he should have been anxious about poor Deb., and his anxiety mounted when a chance remark of Elizabeth's revealed that the girl was lodging in the house of a certain Dr. Allbone in an unsavoury, ambiguous district known as Whetstone's Park, between the north side of Lincoln's Inn Fields and the south side of Holborn, a place which it troubled him mightily she should be in. Enlisting the aid of the lad employed by Dumbleby, the flageolet-maker, he ascertained that Allbone was " a poor broken fellow that dared not reveal his whereabouts lest his creditors should find him ". Why Deb. should have sought shelter in his house is not clear.

Pepys, now determined to track Deb. down, betook himself

to Somerset House, where porters plied for hire, and began to make enquiries about the chest of drawers which had been removed from Seething Lane to Whetstone's Park. Dr. Allbone's difficulties seem to have been common knowledge, for when the porter who had carried the chest was identified, he resolutely refused to bear a message to the same address, fearing to get the Doctor into trouble. " At last ", says Pepys, " I told him that my business was not with him but with a little gentlewoman, one Mrs. Willett that is with him, and sent him to see how she did, from her friend in London, and no other token." The man brought word that she was well, and he might see her if he would, but no more. " So ", confesses Pepys, " I could not be commanded by my reason, but must go this very night, and so by coach, it being now dark, I to her, close to my tailor's, and she come into the coach to me, and je did baiser her." Characteristically, he gave her at the same time much good advice, exhorting her to have a care of her honour, and to fear God, and to suffer no man to do to her as he had done, " which she promised ". After that he gave her twenty shillings, and a note of an address where they might meet — at his bookseller's, Mr. Hemingway's " in the 'Change ". Next day the foolish fellow was full of joy, thinking " in what a safe condition all matters now stand between my wife and Deb. and me " : but returning at noon from the office he found that Elizabeth had somehow discovered — or guessed at — their clandestine meeting. More violent than ever, she threatened to slit Deb.'s nose, demanded £300 or £400 so that she might leave him for good, and let the whole world know his shame. In great distress he sent the faithful Will Hewer to Whetstone's Park to warn Deb. that he had confessed to having been with her, so that, if Mrs. Pepys should send to enquire, she might not make the matter worse by denying it : but when he went home his lady was " in a horrible rage afresh ", and could not refrain from striking him and pulling his hair. Once again Hewer intervened, but as the price of peace at home his master had to promise to " call Deb. whore " under his hand, to declare that he hated her, and that he would never see her again. It is true that he boggled at the word " whore ", but Elizabeth was adamant, and his sole consolation was a wink from Will Hewer which seemed to suggest that if he were the bearer the full text of that cruel letter would never be seen by Deb.

Next day he records that Will Hewer did " most honestly bring me back the part of my letter to Deb. wherein I called her whore, assuring me that he did not show it to her and that he did only give her to understand that wherein I did declare my desire never to see her, and did give her the best Christian counsel he could, which was mighty well done of him ". It was indeed, and it may have been thanks to his steadying influence that Pepys began to pray to God alone in his room every night to confirm him in his solemn resolve not to enquire after Deb. or think of her more.

One person besides himself mistrusted the strength of his good intentions, and that was Elizabeth. Her still smouldering fury flared up when she heard that Deb. had been seen going abroad in mighty fine clothes, wearing black patches, and that a friend had been giving her money. Even when persuaded that the " friend " was not her husband, she remained suspicious : and hearing Pepys cry out " Huzzy ! " in his sleep, hastily concluded that he must be dreaming of Deb.

In March 1669 one of their Janes — Jane Birch — got married. They gave a wedding feast for her in the Seething Lane house, and she and her husband, Tom Edwards, spent their wedding night in the blue chamber. Later Mrs. Pepys passed a whole day at her former Abigail's home, " helping her to cut out linen and other things suitable to her condition ". In the meantime Pepys had most unfortunately had an accidental but very upsetting encounter with Deb. It happened one April day in the courtyard at Whitehall, when Will Hewer was with him, that he spied the small, unforgotten figure, " which ", says he, " made my heart and head to work ". Will Hewer, too, saw her, but his master, uncertain whether he had noticed that *he* had seen her, sent him away on sudden wild errand " to look for Mr. Wren ", while he himself hurried after Deb. As he ran he noted with relief that she was wearing her old clothes, and that the people with her, two women and a man, were quite ordinary people. Here was no rich and powerful rival and protector !

Disregarding her efforts to avoid him, he spoke to her, and

prevailed upon her to tell him where she was living. She gave him an address in Jewen Street — apparently her aunt's house — and her promise to say nothing of having met him : it does not seem to have occurred to either of them that the three persons with her might be interested and might not be discreet. " So ", he writes, " with my heart full of surprise and disorder, I away, and meeting Sir H. Cholmley, walked into the Park with him and back again, looking to see if I could spy her again in the Park, but I could not." It was St. James's Park, where he had once stolen some apples off one of the primly-planted young trees and then hidden them guiltily in his large cuffs : forbidden fruit, whether literal or figurative, had always a fatal lure for the Clerk of the Acts. With characteristic self-deception, being determined to track Deb. down, he confided to his Diary, " My great pain is lest God Almighty should suffer me to find out this girl, whom indeed I love, and with a bad amour, but I will pray to God to give me grace to bear it ". Two days later Mr. Pepys was sitting anxiously in a coach in Aldgate Street while he sent the coachman to enquire whether Mrs. Hunt, Deb.'s aunt, were in town. The man brought word that she was not ; and his fare went away, troubled that he might do no more for the time being. It does not seem to have occurred to him that this failure to make contact with Deb. might have been a divinely-sent occasion to break off the search.

Then Deb. herself took a hand, and sent him a note by the wife of one Bagwell, at the Navy Office. In this note she suggested that they should meet in Moorfields that afternoon. Time and place were well chosen ; Mrs. Pepys had gone to dine at " Cozen Turner's " (can Deb. have been aware of this ?), and the great open space where Londoners skated in winter and wrestled, drilled and revelled in summer, was bound to be thronged with idlers on a fine spring day. Neither the book-stalls nor the ballad-mongers for which Moorfields was famous detained Pepys when he kept the tryst. He walked up and down by the equally famous windmills, and presently his peering eyes found Deb. They strolled to and fro in the crowd for a little while, leaving — or intending to leave — " further discourse and doing to another time " : and when they had parted, Pepys

made an unnecessary detour through Jewen Street, " my mind,
God knows, running that way, but stopped not ", he says.
Stopping would have availed him nothing, for Deb. had not gone
straight home. They were fated to meet again that day, for,
going down Holborn Lane by the Conduit, he saw her on foot,
going up the hill. She saw him also, but did not pause, and
seemed unwilling to speak to him. Mending his pace, he over-
took her at the end of Hosier Lane, by Smithfield, and they went
together into " a little blind ale-house within the walls ". There
for the last time he kissed and fondled Deb., " but she mighty
coy, and I hope modest ". He gave her " in a paper 20s." and
they agreed to meet in Westminster Hall on the following
Monday, her " carriage " giving him great hopes that she continued " honest and modest ". On the appointed day he walked
for two weary hours in the Hall and Deb. did not come : " but
whether ", he writes, " she had been there before and missing
me went away or is prevented coming, and hath no mind to come
to me (the last whereof as being most pleasing, as showing most
modesty, I should be most glad of) I know not ".

One last glimpse he had of her, and one only — just by the
Temple Gate he spied her with another gentlewoman, and she
smiled at him, but did not tarry. When, a week later, he took a
coach again to Jewen Street and again sent the coachman to
Mrs. Hunt's house, he was informed that her niece had gone to
Greenwich, to one Mary's, a tanner's, " at which ", adds the
diarist, throwing all his virtuous resolutions to the winds, " I
am glad, hoping to have an opportunity to find her out ".

Pepys's odd but perfectly genuine preoccupation with Deb.'s
" modesty " and " honour " (little though he had done to make
her careful of either) pleads for him against the most severe
verdict that could be passed upon his conduct. A dyed-in-grain
profligate would have felt no such qualms, and to the very end
the little creature retained in his eyes something of the quaint
and sweet aloofness that he had marked in her at the beginning.
Mrs. Pepys, however, had no doubts as to what Deb. was, what
she had become, and where and how she was likely to have found
employment. Driving round by Old Ford and Bow with her
husband three days after he had had that fleeting glimpse of her

by the Temple Gate, she unluckily noticed " some young gentle-women at the door of a house " — we can guess what sort of house — and, her old suspicions and present convictions flaring up together, she violently informed him that he knew well enough it was " that damned place where Deb. dwelt ". Conscious of innocence for once, Pepys acted boldly : he insisted on going back and proving to the agitated Elizabeth that she was wrong.

Some three weeks later the last page of the Diary was written, and Pepys betook himself to that course — having it kept by others in long-hand — which was almost as much as to see himself go into his grave. That touching epilogue contains a paren-thesis to the effect that there cannot be much to set down that all the world need not know — " now my amours to Deb. are past, and my eyes hindering me in almost all other pleasures ".

So Deb. fades into the crowd by the Temple Gate, smiling across her shoulder as she goes.

There still remained for Samuel Pepys many years of honour-able and laborious life, and not a few pleasures of a more credit-able kind than his trysts with poor Deb. For more than thirty of these years he was a widower, his house being in the care of a succession of housekeepers, among whom even the least com-petent was probably a better manager than his pretty, feckless Elizabeth had been. Mrs. Edwards, *née* Jane Birch, looking after Will Hewer's establishment, lived hard by ; and old friends — and their wives — never ceased to take an active interest in his domestic affairs. Faithful to one of the oldest of his friends, his former chief at the Admiralty, King James, he resigned all his official appointments when Dutch William came. It was shortly before his final retirement that he received from Dutch William's own capital of The Hague a letter which must surely — even after twenty years — have " made his heart and head to work ", if the writer were indeed the original Deb., the only Deborah who figures in the long roll of the Pepys's Abigails. It began, " Honoured Sir, having had formerly the honour to serve you ", and continued with a humble request that Mr. Pepys should be kind to the bearer, the writer's husband. It ended with friendly messages to " Mr. Yures " — *i.e.* Will Hewer — his mother and aunt and all the family ; and it was signed " Deborah Egmont ".

CHAPTER V

Enter " Those Golden Augustans " — and their Abigails

WHEN Mary II came over from Holland with her husband, William III, it is perhaps hardly surprising — in view of the excess of wifely over filial sentiment in her nature — that she should have arrived wearing an orange-coloured petticoat and mantle, and sporting ' cornettes ' of orange ribbon in her hair : but it still seems as strange as it did to certain shocked observers at the time, that she should have scampered about the deserted apartments at Whitehall, " laughing and jolly ", peeping into the closets and turning back the bed-quilts " as people do at an inn ", and playing with uncommon gusto the rôle of Regan — or, if preferred, Goneril.

Among the most perturbed and disapproving of those who watched her then, the bedchamber-women and chamber-maids of Queen Mary Beatrice must undoubtedly have been numbered. Indeed, anxiety grew, and spread through all the palaces, when it became clear that Her Majesty could — or would — do nothing to soften the hardships imposed by William's relentless parsimony. Next to the art of war, economy was one of his best-loved pursuits, more especially when practised at the expense of the English and for the benefit of the Dutch. It soon became apparent that this dour thriftiness of his was something quite different from the dull but honourable scrupulosity of his father-in-law, James II, in such matters : and little surprise was felt when, eleven years later, he stopped the wages of all the servants in the household of his nephew, the young Duke of Gloucester, on the very day of the child's death.

None the less it was thought fitting by him as well as by his English followers that his wife's establishment should be of a size and stateliness corresponding to her rank as a Queen demi-regnant. In addition to a sufficiently imposing array of ladies-in-waiting and maids of honour, Mary had her full tale of chamber-maids, her Necessary Woman and her Starcher. Each of the last-named functionaries was allowed a regular daily quantity of " faggots, billetts, pit-cole, charcole and fewell " : and for " wages, board-wages and necessaries " the Necessary Woman received £91 : 5s. a year. An annual sum of £36 : 10s. was paid " for sweeping the house at St. James's below-stairs, cleaning above-stairs, and necessarys of the same " — which sounds cheap, yet exceeds by £6 : 10s. the sum set aside for the " reliefs " to be given in cases of sickness or poverty among " the under-sort of servants ". Many of the pensions granted by Charles II and granted or continued by James II were discontinued by William III ; but one at least he forbore to cancel — the £6 a year bestowed in the reign of King Charles upon " Cath. Mason, a painfull old servant in the scullery ".

In 1702 the reign of Anne opened, and the curtain rose upon the stage where " those incomparable, those golden Augustans " were to play their several parts. Somewhere upon that stage, though nowhere near the centre of it, stood the meek, incon-spicuous figure of Abigail Hill, recently appointed — by favour of her powerful kinswoman, Sarah Churchill — dresser to the new Queen. There could have been no more striking contrast than that presented by the two cousins, one so arrogant, so impetuous, so well-favoured, the other so low-voiced, so soft-footed, and so far from being a beauty that the constant faint redness of her nose was almost the only thing that anyone noticed about her.

Her mother had been one of the twenty-two children born to that truly patriarchal Hertfordshire knight, Sir John Jennings, Member of Parliament for St. Albans. Her uncle, Richard Jennings, had the privilege of fathering those two dazzling creatures, Sarah and Frances Jennings, both of whom were early attached to the household of the Duke and Duchess of York and both of whom were to die holding the rank of Duchess. It was hardly to be expected that these much-admired yuong beauties should take the trouble to make and keep themselves acquainted with the fortunes of all their surviving aunts, uncles and cousins : and we have Sarah's own word for it that at the time of the Princess Anne's marriage to Prince George of Denmark, and her

own appointment as Lady of the Bedchamber to the bride, she
" never knew there were such people in the world " as her aunt,
Mrs. Hill, and her four Hill cousins, two girls and two boys.
Hill *père*, a Levant merchant, had fallen on evil times and sunk
low in the world ; but he, as well as his wife, was connected in
blood with a future maker of history, for he had an ambitious
young nephew, a barrister by profession, whose name was Robert
Harley. The misfortunes of his uncle's family appear to have left
Mr. Harley's bowels of compassion quite unmoved ; and as far
as is known he did nothing to mitigate their hard lot. Not for
another twenty years was he to become conscious of the remarkable, though long-occluded, gifts and capacities of his cousin
Abigail.

Very different was the conduct of Lady Churchill. Having
been informed of the existence and of the present plight of her
unknown kinsfolk, her first step was to send them ten guineas by
the hand of her informant. Another gift of money soon followed;
and she then bestirred herself with characteristic vigour to provide
for younger members of the group. One son she placed in the
Custom House, the other in the household of the little Duke of
Gloucester ; the younger of the two daughters she installed as
laundress in the same service, " which ", she observes, " was a
good provision for her " : and the elder, Abigail, she took with
her to that unassuming and agreeable home at St. Albans, Hartwell
House, always more dear than any other to herself and her
illustrious lord. Exactly what this poor relation's status was in
the Churchill *ménage* it is difficult to tell. Duchess Sarah said
years afterwards that she treated her " like a sister ", but this
assertion does little to remove our uncertainty. The girl's calling
— whatever her status may have been — was that of a humble
and useful confidante, and she filled the part to admiration.

Sarah's character was as frank as Abigail's was disingenuous,
and the amazed dependent must have been made amply aware of
the extraordinary degree of friendship and familiarity prevailing
between her cousin and the Queen. The Shakespearean image of

> a double cherry seeming parted
> But yet a union in partition,
> Two lovely berries moulded on one stem,

HOGARTH'S SERVANTS, AS DEPICTED BY THEIR MASTER

would have served well enough to describe " Mrs. Morley " and " Mrs. Freeman " if it were possible that one should be a bitter berry and one a sweet. That friendship, foolishly fond on the Queen's side, despotic and possessive on Sarah's, begun in their childhood and seeming likely to end only with their lives, was at its height when Anne ascended the throne. The rise and fall of its strong tides were to leave deep ripple-marks upon the shore of history, and its violent disruption was to alter the whole course of Europe's destiny.

Even if Abigail Hill did not read — either clandestinely or at her cousin's invitation — the letters passing between the two friends, she must soon have realized how completely the Queen's wish was realized that there should be no form or ceremony in her relations with her beloved " Mrs. Freeman ". As Princess, and for a time as Queen, the simple, stupid, affectionate woman could not bear to hear from Sarah's lips, or to read written by her hand, " words which implied in them distance and superiority ". Before long she was to hear, and also to read, many words implying, it is true, no distance in station, but a large measure of superiority — on Sarah's side. It is strange that John Churchill, who, with his wife, had staked all their joint fortunes upon Anne's continued favour, should not have seen that everything might be lost if " Mrs. Freeman's " arrogance soared too high.

That royal favour would ever be withdrawn from her or transferred to another Sarah's pride did not permit her to imagine, much less to fear. Her habitual candour being what it was, it seems rather more than probable that she expounded to her cousin-confidante the rule of conduct she had formulated for her own guidance in her relations with the Queen. Desiring to deserve and maintain her advancement, she resolved to serve her mistress " with an absolute fidelity and a constant zeal ", to keep her secrets, be true to her trust, and to avoid everything that looked like dissimulation and flattery — even though she saw that this might displease her. Such was the system imposed upon herself — without much effort — by Sarah Churchill : and for many years nothing could have worked better. But a shrewd, attentive observer like Abigail Hill could hardly fail to reflect that though this sometimes brutal frankness might answer very well in a person like her cousin, different methods, diametrically opposite methods, might prove even more rewarding if employed by a totally dissimilar person — in fact by someone more like herself.

Slow though she was in speech and action, she was not slow in perceiving that if the Queen valued frankness there was something else that she might be brought to value even more — and that was sympathy. As Anne's health deteriorated, as the cares and duties of state weighed ever more heavily upon her, and most especially when death took from her side her uninteresting but loyal Danish consort, her weary spirit needed an anodyne rather than an astringent — and that anodyne Abigail Hill was at hand to provide.

In her life of the Queen Miss Strickland gives a startling but no doubt substantially faithful account — derived from " a venerable Countess " — of an episode which may well have marked the turning point in the " Morley-Freeman " friendship. As Abigail was not appointed dresser till 1702 her ladyship's memory must have tricked her when she gave the date as " not many weeks after the death of the Duke of Gloucester " in July 1700. According to this story, Anne — whether as Princess or Queen is immaterial — happened to observe one afternoon that she had omitted to put on her gloves. Abigail Hill was in attendance, and she was bidden to fetch them from the adjoining room where her mistress remembered having left them on the table. She obeyed, but failed to find the gloves in the place indicated, for Lady Marlborough had picked them up, and, not knowing whose they were, had put them on. Abigail meekly pointed out what she had done : whereupon the lady, stripping off the gloves in violent haste, exclaimed aloud, " Ah, have I on anything that has touched the odious hands of that disagreeable woman ? Take them away ! " The dresser gathered up the royal gloves from the floor, and retired, " carefully closing the door after her, which she had previously left ajar " ; directly she entered the room where Anne was sitting, she plainly perceived that " every word of the dialogue " had been overheard.

" All unconscious of her doom ", Sarah Marlborough swept on, chiding, railing, patronizing, rewarding. To her humble and obliged kinswoman, the Queen's dresser, she continued gracious, even taking her with her to the opera and thereby — ironically enough — bringing upon herself a mild rebuke from " Mrs. Morley " : but with every day that passed, whether the sky were stormy or merely changeable in the Marlborough quarter, the Queen must have become more conscious of the contrast between her Mistress of the Robes [1] and her recently-appointed dresser, Abigail Hill.

" At first," as Mr. Churchill remarks, " and for some time, their relations were those of mistress and servant, or patient and nurse." " Mrs. Freeman's " rough handling of " Mrs. Morley " had made the poor woman grateful for a gentler touch, and Abigail was nothing if not gentle. In 1704, the year of Marl-borough's great victory at Blenheim, the name of Abigail Hill appeared on the list of Her Majesty's bedchamber-women, and her unobtrusive figure was moved one stage further away from the semi-menial status of her earlier years.

For the information of Mrs. Howard, afterwards Countess of Suffolk, and at one time bedchamber-woman to Caroline of Anspach, Abigail Hill some years later dictated to Dr. Arbuthnot a full account of the duties of such a functionary. The day's duties began " before the Queen's prayers and before Her Majesty rose " ; if any lady of the bedchamber were present, the bedchamber-woman handed her the Queen's linen and the lady put it on Her Majesty. Every change of royal raiment, whether into state robes, hunting-habit, or négligée, was carried out in the same manner, the ' woman ' serving her kneeling, the ' lady ', standing. When the Queen washed her hands, " her page of the backstairs brought and set down upon a side-table a basin and ewer. Then the bedchamber-woman placed it before the Queen, and knelt on the other side of the table over against the Queen, the lady of the bedchamber only looking on. The bedchamber-woman poured the water out of the ewer on the Queen's hands. The bedchamber-woman pulled on the Queen's gloves when Her Majesty could not do if herself " ; but it was the page of the backstairs who had the task of putting the shoes

[1] Sarah Marlborough also held the posts of Groom of the Stole and Keeper of the Privy Purse.

on the gouty feet of royalty. Then, when the long, arduous day closed, when the spur of conscience might prick but the whip of duty was laid aside, when Lady Marlborough's tantrums were past for that time, and ceremony itself was bated, Abigail Hill brought a cup of hot frothed chocolate to the Queen's bed-chamber and gave it to her " without kneeling ".

There we must leave her, for the rest of her story is not that of a bedchamber-woman but of a royal favourite powerful enough at the height of her power to mould the destinies of Europe. Not till 1707 did Sarah Marlborough scent danger in that quarter, and already the proud, passionate creature was doomed, doomed to pass into the outer darkness and ultimately to drag her husband after her. It was in that year that Abigail was married to one of Prince George of Denmark's pages, Samuel Masham, scornfully described by Sarah as " always making low bows to everybody " : the wedding took place under conditions of anxious secrecy in the apartments of Dr. Arbuthnot, and it was with the cautious stealth of a conspirator that the Queen came to grace it with her presence.

Before the year ended there took place the famous final interview between the two cousins, when Sarah told Abigail that she could not attribute the Queen's altered attitude to " anything but her secret management ", and received the grave reply that Abigail was sure the Queen, who loved her extremely, would always be kind to her. " It was some minutes ", relates Sarah, " before I could recover from the surprise with which so extraordinary an answer struck me. To see a woman whom I had raised out of the dust put on such a superior air, and to hear her assure me, by way of consolation, that the Queen would always be very kind to me ! " We can well believe that words failed the dispossessed favourite, but Lady Touchwood in Congreve's *Double Dealer* could have furnished her with some : " What shall I do ? Whither shall I turn ? Hold in, my passion, and fall, fall a little, thou swelling heart ! Let me have some intermission of this rage, and one minute's coolness to dissemble."

Whatever we may think of " Mrs. Freeman's " conduct to " Mrs. Morley " it is impossible to acquit Abigail Masham of ingratitude and duplicity. Her kinsman, Robert Harley, after-wards Earl of Oxford, in whose interest she was now intriguing, had left her and her sisters in the dust from which Sarah Churchill had raised them ; for all he did, for all he cared, they might have continued to eke out a meagre existence as waiting-women, or even chamber-maids ; and he might never have shown himself aware of Abigail's existence, much less of any kinship between them, had she not filled with such unforeseen results that post about the Queen's person procured for her by the soon-to-be-superseded Sarah.

The Duchess had an attached maid, Grace Ridley by name. It was to her that she confided the task of destroying unread the long-hoarded packet of faded love-letters, Marlborough's and her own, which she herself had twice — once in 1736 and once in 1743 — lacked the strength of mind to destroy. That these letters still exist may be due to no failure of fidelity on Grace's part ; it is possible that she never got access to the precious packet. Under her mistress's Will she received an annuity of £300 ; a lump sum of £15,000 ; half of the Duchess's wearing apparel ; a painting of Her Grace by Kneller ; an enamel picture of the Duke ; another of him " in a locket " ; and the striking watch " which was the Duke of Marlborough's ". Another striking watch was bequeathed to Jane Pattison ; it had formerly belonged to her mistress, Lady Sutherland, *née* Lady Anne Churchill, the dearly-loved and long-lamented Lady Anne.

Hearing in 1733 that Lady Bab. Herbert wanted a servant " to wait upon her in her chamber ", Duchess Sarah wrote to her granddaughter, the Duchess of Bedford, asking her to put in a word for a sister of Grace's who had been dismissed from her situation with a Mrs. Hanbury at Scarborough because the lady's third son had fallen in love with her, he being " very amorous " and the waiting-woman " extremely modest and honest ". This, says the old Duchess, " Mrs. Hanbury herself wrote to me, and that she would recommend her to anybody. I don't wonder ", adds Her Grace, " that Mrs. Hanbury was frighted, for nobody would be pleased to marry their son to their woman." It is perhaps not unworthy of remark that " Mr. B." in *Pamela* — published only eight years after this letter was written — had no surviving parent to lament or condemn his marriage with his deceased mamma's maid.

By the end of the seventeenth century the practice of inserting advertisements in order to find places for servants or servants for places was well established. A great step forward was made in July 1693 when John Houghton, Fellow of the Royal Society, and dealer in tea, coffee and chocolate, of Bartholomew Lane, Smithfield, began to append to his weekly pamphlet, *A Collection for the Improvement of Husbandry and Trade*, a half-sheet of miscellaneous advertisements. The feature proved so popular that he continued and developed it, finding room to recommend such diverse merchandise as coffins, spectacles, onions, brandy, whale fins and "joynted babies", *i.e.* dolls, and such a variety of would-be-employed persons as school-ushers, curates, housekeepers, footmen, gardeners and cook-maids.

The eager form of the aspirant to the post of housekeeper or maidservant to a single gentleman soon detaches itself from the throng. For example :

> If any wants a Housekeeper I can help to a Gentlewoman who through misfortune of a bad Husband is reduced . . . she is sober, diligent, and careful, and has been used to all manner of business fit for a housekeeper, as also to rise early and sit up late.

We shall meet her again and yet again, this anxious, hopeful advertiser, and though the wording of her announcement varies from century to century, its temper and purport vary hardly at all. She usually has, or has had, a husband, and is careful to mention the circumstance, presumably to reassure the single gentleman — though why he should have felt reassured it is not easy to imagine, especially if the husband were — as above — both alive and unsatisfactory. Elsewhere Houghton states that he knows of " several curious women that would wait on ladies to be housekeepers " ; also " one that has waited on a lady divers years, and understands all affairs in housekeeping and the needle . . . she seems ", he adds, " a discreet, staid body ". Of a lady's-maid seeking a situation with his aid he remarks, " and truly she looks and discourses passing well ".

We are indebted to Mr. Houghton for some interesting information about the materials used by the chamber-maids and waiting-women when washing tiffanies and sarsenets for their ladies, and also on the subject of household clothes-washing

in general. " Formerly " he wrote in 1700, " bucking with lees
made of our English ashes and hogs' dung were very much used
for the washing of clothes " — such would be the methods
employed in the Windsor of the Merry Wives — " but ", he
adds, " for aught I can learn, wherever soap comes it gets ground
of these, as being more neat, sweet, and less troublesome ". He
noted that it was " extraordinary dear ", but confidently hoped
that its continued use would soon reduce the price ; and its
cheapness, " with a fashion of a great deal of clean linnen and
clean houses ", would be " some of the best ways to encourage
its consumption ".

Some years previously he had given his readers a full account
of the process of soap-making and a scientific explanation of its
cleansing properties. The ingredients were alkali salt, obtained
from potash, tallow and olive oil, " intimately mixed by boiling :
in help whereof the unctuous parts of the tallow and oil do in-
corporate with the grease that is on foul linen, etc., and the alkali
salts do so far divide the greasy particles that they are capable of
being diluted (mixed with water) which by themselves they
would not be ". Houghton's efforts to calculate the amount of
soap then (1694) made in London were complicated by the fact
that the London soap-boilers served the greater part of the
kingdom. " I find upon enquiry " he writes, " that in good
citizens' houses they wash once a month, and they use, if they
wash all the clothes at home, about as many pounds of soap as
there be heads in the family, and the higher the people be, the
oftener they change, the less pains the washers are willing to take,
and the more soap is used : but on the other side the poorer the
people are (and the poor are the most numerous) the seldomer
they shift, and so use the less : and 'tis probable we may allow
a pound a head once a month for every soul in the bills of
mortality." The price was 3d. a pound or 16s. the firkin. In
large households washerwomen were employed to help the servants, but in a more modest establishment, such as that of Mr. and
Mrs. Pepys, the mistress and the maid tackled the task together.

Usually under the pleasant generic name of 'Betty', the
English Abigail flutters in the background of much light verse of
the earlier and later Augustan periods. The maid whom the

dying Narcissa exhorted to " give this cheek a little red " was
called Betty ; and Betty was the name of " the inferior priestess "
officiating at the toilet of Belinda in *The Rape of the Lock*.
Familiar though the passage may be, it is too enchanting not to
be quoted in full :

> And now, unveiled, the toilet stands display'd,
> Each silver vase in mystic order laid.
> First, rob'd in white, the nymph intent adores,
> With head uncover'd, the cosmetic powers.
> A heavenly image in the glass appears,
> To that she bends, to that her eyes she rears ;
> Th' inferior priestess, at her altar's side,
> Trembling, begins the sacred rites of Pride.
> Unnumber'd treasures ope at once, and here
> The various offerings of the world appear ;
> From each she nicely culls with curious toil,
> And decks the goddess with the glittering spoil.
> This casket India's glowing gems unlocks
> And all Arabia breathes from yonder box :
> The tortoise here and elephant unite,
> Transform'd to combs, the speckled and the white.
> Here files of pins extend their shining rows,
> Puffs, powders, patches, Bibles, billets-doux.

The canto ends with the delicious whimsy of the sylphs assisting
the maid in her task :

> These set the head, and those divide the hair ;
> Some fold the sleeve, while others plait the gown ;
> And Betty's prais'd for labours not her own.

A companion picture of less charm but of extraordinary vividness
is painted by Gay in one of his *Town Eclogues*. Lydia, a peevish
belle, is consumed with jealousy of Chloe, who has supplanted
her not only in Damon's heart but in her hitherto acknowledged
supremacy as a ' toast ' ; the circumstance that she has another
admirer — with the less Arcadian name of ' Harry ' — in reserve
does little to abate her spleen. How, she asks herself on rising in
the morning, how shall she spend the " hateful day " ? Shall she
while away its first half " at Chappel " ? But then,

> Who there frequent at these unmodish hours
> But ancient matrons with their frizled *tours*,
> And grey religious maids ? My presence there
> Amid that sober train would own despair.

Shall she then dress, go forth, and take her usual walk

> Through every Indian shop, through all the 'Change ?

But memories of the perfidious Damon would walk with her, and the superseded fair one gives way to sobs and tears — " Thus love-sick Lydia raved " ; and then, hey, presto ! the scene changes as

> . . . her maid appears ;
> A bandbox in her steady hand she bears.
> " How well this ribband's gloss becomes your face ",
> She cries in raptures, " Then, so sweet a lace !
> How charmingly you look, so bright, so fair !
> 'Tis to your eyes the head-dress owes its air."
> Strait Lydia smiled : the comb adjusts her locks,
> And at the Playhouse Harry keeps her box.

Gay returns to the scene in *The Fan*, where he lingers with even greater and more obvious pleasure upon " the mysteries of *Bona Dea* " :

> What force of thought, what numbers can express
> Th' inconstant equipage of human dress !
> How the strait stays the slender waist constrain,
> How to adjust the manteau's sweeping train ?
> What fancy can the petticoat surround,
> With the capacious hoop of whalebone bound ?
>
> .   .   .   .   .
>
> Let a just distance be to beauty paid ;
> None here must enter but the trusty maid.

In all these episodes it is the personal handmaid who figures, deft, tactful or ecstatic as the course of events may demand ; but Gay vouchsafes us a more active glimpse of the lower ranks of the Abigail's calling in that section of his *Trivia* entitled " How to Know the Days of the Week " :

> When dirty waters from balcónies drop
> And dextrous damsels twirl the sprinkling mop,
> And cleanse the spattered sash and scrub the stairs,
> Know Saturday's conclusive morn appears.

The name of ' Betty ' is also found in Young's fifth satire in the sequence entitled *Love of Fame the Universal Passion*, where there

is a lively sketch of a hypochondriacal lady, Rosalinda, a languid
and languishing lady, too feeble to enunciate a complete phrase.

> My fan ! let others say who laugh at toil ;
> Fan ! Hood ! Glove ! Scarf ! is her laconic style ;
> And that is spoke with such a dying fall,
> That Betty rather sees than hears the call :

Of very different stuff is Lemira fashioned in the same satire. Sir
Hans Sloane is summoned in haste :

> He comes ; But where's his patient ? At the ball.
> The doctor stares ; her woman curtsies low,
> And cries, " My lady, Sir, is always so :
> Diversions put her maladies to flight ;
> True, she can't stand, but she can dance all night :
> I've known my lady (for she loves a tune)
> For fevers take an opera in June :
> And, though perhaps you'll think the practice bold,
> A midnight park is sovereign for a cold.
> With colics, breakfasts of green fruits agree ;
> With indigestions, suppers just at three."
> " A strange alternative," replies Sir Hans,
> " Must women have a doctor or a dance ? "

These are all scenes of town life ; in the country, domestic
comedies were played against a background that had changed
little since Stuart times. The local fair was still the great event
of the year ; the gypsy sybil was still consulted with eager faith ;
the vendor of chapbooks, with crude woodcut illustrations in
which the same block was made to do duty for Bevis of Hampton,
Guy of Warwick and St. George, always found ready patronage
among the maids clustering round the kitchen door.

It was dangerous, however, for these simple sentimentalists
to give expression to any sympathy for the exiled Stuarts : as Sir
Charles Petrie reminds us, one unhappy servant girl who had
dared to do so was " publicly whipped till her back was in
ribbons ".

Any idea that rural housekeeping was invariably well-ordered
is dispelled in Soame Jenyns's *Epistle* written from the country to
Lord Lovelace in the year 1735. He describes how a person was
likely to fare who, " with ceremony cloyed " on a pre-announced
visit, decided to pay an impromptu call at the house of a country
knight.

" John, John, a coach !   I can't think who 'tis,"
My lady cries, who spies your coach
Ere you the avenue approach.
" Lord, how unlucky !   Washing day !
And all the men are in the hay ! "
Entrance to gain is something hard,
The dogs all bark, the gates are barred ;
The yard's with lines of linen crossed,
The hall-door's locked, the key is lost.

.   .   .   .   .

The servants run, the pewter clatters,
My lady dresses, calls and chatters,
The cook-maid raves for want of butter,
Pigs squeak, fowls scream, and green geese flutter.

The humbler ranks of the domestic calling were sometimes —
though not invariably — recruited from the workhouse ; but
even in that dolorous place there might be more humanity than
Oliver Twist found under the eye and the rod of Mr. Bumble
nearly a hundred years later.   A realist like Defoe would hardly
soften the harsh outlines of the picture, or seek to spare the
sensitive reader the extreme rigour of the truth : yet in *Moll
Flanders* we meet a small, friendless child whose mother had been
transported for stealing three ells of holland from a draper's shop
and whose maintenance devolves upon the Poor Law authorities
at Colchester.   It is reassuring to learn that the woman with
whom the magistrates ' put her out to nurse ' was both sensible
and kind, and that the children in her care were taught to be
pious, cleanly, housewifely and well-mannered ; but it is a little
startling to read that their Worships proposed to send Moll into
domestic service at the tender age of eight.   The unfortunate
child was terrified, fearing that the older maids would beat her,
and " make her do great work ".   The good old foster-mother
interceded for her, however, and before long she was able to earn
threepence a day by spinning and fourpence by needlework.

At the age of fourteen Moll Flanders was chosen by a lady
to be a sort of companion-attendant to her young daughters.   In
that capacity the girl learnt dancing, music and French ; and when
she was eighteen that happened to her which must have happened
to only too many pretty girls, especially if they were, as the disapproving phrase sent, " educated above their station " ;   she

was seduced by the son of the house. Her later career of crime is as little relevant to our present subject as her subsequent conversion and edifying end ; but it is worth remarking that, after the improvement in Moll's fortunes which occurred when she was transported to Maryland, she bought an English woman-servant who had just arrived from Liverpool in a convict ship.

In *Everybody's Business, Nobody's Business* Defoe gives a more detailed and definite picture of the Augustan Abigail. It is strange to hear rising from the world of the South Sea Bubble, the *Tatler*, the *Spectator*, the aged Dryden and the youthful Pope, the same cry that John Gower sent up to heaven from Plantagenet England — no more distinctions between the upper classes and the lower ; and the lower ape their betters ; and this is abomination. In short, " red ruin and the breaking up of laws ".

It was hard, according to Defoe, to tell the mistress from the maid — and the maid was very often the finer of the two. Her neat's-leather shoes were transformed into laced ones, with high heels ; her yarn stockings had turned into fine woollen ones with silk clocks ; and her high wooden pattens were " kicked away for leathern clogs ". She had to have a hoop, too, as well as her mistress, and her " poor, scanty, linsey-woolsey petticoat " was changed into a good silk one, four or five yards wide at the least. In short, plain country Joan had been transformed into a fine London Madam, who could drink tea, take snuff and carry herself as high as the rest. In order to maintain all these fashionable habits the Abigail needed more money than she was able to come by honestly, even though the wages might be " as much as £8 a year " : so the sessions were crowded with maids who had robbed their employers. The evil was not new, but it was growing : and mistresses became (and remained for many generations) gloomily convinced that no girl who dressed in gay colours, set her hat at a coy angle, or made the best of such personal advantages as God had given her, could possibly be a young person of good principles and virtuous behaviour.

Voltaire, visiting England in 1726, was amazed to see servant-maids at Greenwich Fair so elegantly dressed, and managing their hired horses with so much ease, that he took them for " people of fashion ". He was also greatly impressed by the beauty of

their complexions and the " graceful vivacity of their move-
ments ".

Swift's *Directions to Servants* carries us one stage further on
the steeply sloping descent of domestic morality under Queen
Anne and the first George. Where Gay gives a more or less
cheerful glimpse of the tactful personal maid, the active, mop-
twirling housemaid, and Defoe, though not indifferent to the
darker shadows in his picture, lays on some vivid and not unpleasing colour, Swift supplies a series of savage etchings, drawn
with fierce but telling strokes, and unredeemed by a single lighter
touch.

The question of pay soon crops up and servants are aided with
advice as to how they may coerce their employers into adding
five or ten shillings a quarter to their wages. Having won the
master's favour, give warning "on the grounds that, though you
would rather live with him than with anybody else ", poor
servants are not to be blamed for trying to better themselves ;
that the work is great and the wages are small, and so forth.
" You may ", Swift tells the household, " quarrel with each other
as much as you please, only always bear in mind that you have
a common enemy, which is your master and lady, and you have
a common cause to defend." The keen eye that marked all the
dilapidated chattels at Laracor, the " broken, oaken elbow chair ",
the " curtain worn to half a stripe ", is now bent upon the
kitchen-quarters of the Augustan house.

> Let it be a constant rule that no chair, stool, or table in the
> servants' hall or kitchen shall have above three legs, which has been
> the ancient and constant practice in all the families I ever knew and
> is said to be founded upon two reasons : first to show that servants
> are ever in a tottering condition ; secondly, it was thought a point
> of humility that the servants' chairs and tables should have at least
> one leg fewer than those of their masters.

General instructions, applicable both to men-servants and to
women, all emphasize the habitual dishonesty, cunning and carelessness of those to whom they are addressed, and also, it must
be added, the gullibility and complaisance of the average master
and mistress. Take, for example, the remarks intended for the
guidance of the chamber-maid.

If she breaks any china on the " mantel-tree " or in the cabinet with her whisk, she must gather up the fragments, put them together as well as she can, and place them behind the rest, so that when the lady comes to discover them the maid may safely say that they were broken long ago, " before she came to the service ". This, she is told, " will save your lady many an hour's vexation ". If, while she is sweeping a room, the long end of her brush should shatter a looking-glass, she has a choice of three excuses : that she was blinded by a flash of lightning and supposes the mirror to have been struck ; that she observed it to be covered with dust and, " going very gently to wipe it ", supposed the moisture in the air had dissolved the glue or cement and " made it to fall to the ground " ; or, having first cut the cords fastening the glass to the wainscot and laid it flat on the ground, she can rush to the lady, curse the upholsterer and declare what a narrow escape she has had of it falling on her head.

Here are a few more precepts :

> Oil the tongs, poker and fire-shovel up to the top, not only to keep them from rusting but likewise to prevent meddling people from wasting your master's coals by stirring the fire.

> When you are in haste, sweep the dust into the corner of the room, but leave your brush upon it that it may not be seen, for that would disgrace you.

> When you sweep your lady's room never stay to pick up foul smocks, handkerchiefs, pinners, pincushions, tea-spoons, ribbons, slippers, or whatever lies in your way, but sweep all into a corner and then you may take them up in a lump.

> Making beds in hot weather is very laborious and you will be apt to sweat : therefore, when you find the drops running down your forehead, wipe them off with the corner of the sheet that they may not be seen on the bed.

Allowances are ironically made and excuses provided for a young woman's natural curiosity, her instinctive desire to stare, to idle and to dally.

> You are sometimes desirous to see a funeral, a quarrel, a man going to be hanged, a bawd carted, or the like : as they pass by in the street, you lift up the sash suddenly ; there, by misfortune, it sticks ; this was no fault of yours : young women are curious by nature : you have no remedy but to cut the cord and lay the fault

upon the carpenter, unless nobody saw you, and then you are as innocent as any servant in the house.

When you spread bread and butter for tea . . . let the mark of your thumb be seen only upon *one* end of every slice, to show your cleanliness.

The Directions to the Waiting-Maid are rich in picturesque ' period ' detail. Two things, it is observed, much lessen the comforts and profits of the employment : " that excrable custom got among ladies of trucking their old clothes for china, or turning them to cover easy chairs, or making them into patchwork for screens, stools, cushions, and the like ", and the regrettable invention of " small chests and trunks with lock and key wherein they keep the tea and sugar " without which it is impossible for a waiting-maid to live, for " by this means you are forced to buy brown sugar and pour water upon the leaves when they have lost all spirit and taste ".

As for the former, a general confederacy of servants against the china hucksters is recommended ; " and as to the latter there is no method to relieve yourselves but by a false key ". If she is handsome, the Waiting-Maid will have a choice of three lovers, — the chaplain, the steward and my lord's gentleman : she is advised to choose the steward. If she waits upon a young lady of fortune, she must be an ill manager if she cannot get five or six hundred pounds " for disposing of her ".

> Take care to let it be known what lady you live with ; how great a favourite you are ; and that she always takes your advice ; the fine fellows will soon discover you and contrive to slip a letter into your sleeve or your bosom ; pull it out in a fury and throw it on the ground — unless you discover at least two guineas along with it.
>
> It is a great presumption in me to offer you any instructions in the conduct of your lady's amours, wherein your whole sisterhood is already so expert and deeply learned.

The Directions to the Housemaid begin with some Rabelaisian passages about bedroom-ware, and go on to exhort the damsel to this effect :

> Leave a pail of dirty water with a mop in it, a coal-box, a bottle, a broom, a chamber-pot and such unsightly things either in a blind

entry or upon the darkest part of the backstairs, that they may not be seen; and if people break their shins by trampling on them it is their own fault.

Brush down the cobwebs with a broom that is wet and dirty, which will make them stick faster to it and bring them down more effectually.

When you have scoured the brasses and irons in the parlour chimney, lay the foul wet cloth upon the next chair, that the lady may see you have not neglected your work.

When the rooms towards the street are washed overnight, the foul water should be thrown out of the street door. If the lady chides, and gives positive orders that the pail should be carried all the way down and emptied into the sink, the pail should be so carried that the water will dribble on the stairs, by which not only your load will be lighter but you will convince your lady that it is better to throw the water out of the windows or down the street door-steps.

The Dean's cynical views were formed no doubt when he himself, young, ambitious, gifted and obscure, lived in a sort of shifting no-man's-land between the servant's hall and the parlour; and it is worthy of remark that in many of his minor poems maidservants are made to play ignoble parts. For example, in *A Dialogue between a Member of Parliament and his Servant*, where the servant contrasts his own casual and promiscuous pleasures "at Peter Wood's" with his master's adulterous, clandestine love-making:

> . . . you, the grave and sage reformer,
> Must go by stealth to meet your charmer:
>
> .   .   .   .   .
>
> Some Abigail must then receive you,
> Bribed by the husband to deceive you:
> She spies Cornuto on the stairs:
> Wakes you, then melted by your prayers,
> Yields, if with greater bribe you ask it,
> To pack your worship in the basket.

Elsewhere it is the Abigail herself who is the delinquent, as in *A Description of the Morning*:

> Now Betty from her master's bed has flown
> And softly stole to discompose her own.

Augustan drama, tragedy and comedy alike, teems with Abigails, some high-minded and expostulatory in the manner of Lucilla,

Calista's confidante, in Rowe's *Fair Penitent*, others sly or sycophantic, in the manner of Congreve's Foible.

Lucilla has a great deal to say in the earlier scenes of the tragedy, and is dubbed by Rossano, the gay Lothario's friend, the keeper of her mistress's secrets. When she describes Calista's anguish and roundly rails at the graceless cause of it, Lothario retorts, entirely in character,

> Oh, no more !
> I swear thou spoilst thy pretty face with crying
> And thou hast beauty that may make thy fortune ;
> Some keeping Cardinal shall doat upon thee,
> And barter his church treasure for thy freshness ;

a speech which provides Lucilla with the cue for six lines of admirable sentiments. Later in the play she expostulates eloquently with Calista about her infatuation for Lothario, and commends to her favour that very different person, Altamont,

> Kind as the softest virgin of our sex
> And faithful as the simple village swain.

Swift would have found it hard to believe that Altamont had not slipped a couple of guineas into her hand on more occasions than one, but as conceived by Rowe Lucilla is of virtue all compact. Her creator forgets about her, none the less, before the play ends, and she does not appear either to exhort or to console her mistress in the final scene — pure Webster-and-water — where Calista is " discovered on a couch, in black, her hair hanging loose and disordered ", on one side, Lothario's body on a bier, on the other a table with " a skull and other bones, a book and a lamp upon it ".

Congreve also, in *The Mourning Bride*, reverts to what one may call the *materia scenica* of the more lurid Elizabethans, giving us, with a lavish hand, " bones and skulls and mouldering earth ", daggers, disguises, distressed ladies, a faithful waiting-woman — everything, indeed, except a tragic ending. It is to her devoted Leonora that Almeria, the heroine, speaks the famous opening lines of the first Act :

> Music hath charms to soothe a savage breast,
> To soften rocks or bend a knotted oak.

She has a good deal to say for herself, this damsel — sometimes she almost plays the part of Chorus — and she describes with some eloquence how it had been her wont compassionately to creep at midnight to the grating of the cell where, until he died, the father of the hero had been held captive by the father of the heroine ; she supports Almeria well in the scene under the " arch'd and pondrous roof" of the antique pile ; but she is unconvincing ; and it is a relief to turn from Augustan blank verse to the prose comedy of manners.

An indirect but vivid sidelight on the daily routine of a woman of fashion and her maid — or maids — may be found in Sir John Vanburgh's comedy *The Provoked Wife*. Sir John Brute, one of the characters, disguises himself in his lady's gown, is involved in a tipsy revel, and is haled before a Justice of the Peace, who, failing to penetrate the disguise, demands :

> Pray, Madam, what may be your ladyship's common method of life ?
> If I may presume so far——
> *Sir John* : Why, that of a woman of quality.
> *Justice* : Pray, how may you generally pass your time, Madam ? Your morning, for example.
> *Sir John* : Sir, like a woman of quality. I wake about two o'clock in the afternoon — I stretch and make a sign for my chocolate. When I have drunk three cups, I slide down again upon my back with my arms over my head, while my two maids put on my stockings. Then, hanging upon their shoulders, I'm trailed to my great chair, where I sit and yawn for my breakfast. If it don't come presently, I lie down upon my couch to say my prayers, while my maid reads me the playbills.

Later on, explains the supposed woman of fashion, when her " idle servants are all presumptuously set down " to their dinner, she calls her coach and pays a round of visits. There is at least this to be said in favour of life in this lazy and frivolous woman's household — the day did not begin early, and there must have been many opportunities for a quick-witted and quick-fingered handmaiden to appropriate pinners, tuckers, sugar and tea.

In Richard Steele's comedy, *The Conscious Lovers*, there is a pert, pretty housemaid, Phillis, who delights in hearing her admirer, Tom the footman, talk of the fashionable world, of plays, operas and ridottos. " Oh, Tom, Tom," she says to him, " is it not a pity that you should be so great a coxcomb and I so great a coquette, and yet be such poor devils as we are ! " He recollects their first meeting :

> *Tom* : I remember I was ordered to get out of the Window, one pair of stairs, to rub the Sashes clean — the person employed on the inner side was your charming self, whom I had never seen before.
> *Phillis* : I think I remember the silly accident. What made ye, you oaf, ready to fall down into the street ?
> *Tom* : You know not, I warrant you. You could not guess what surprised me. You took no delight when you immediately grew wanton in your conquest, and put your lips close, and breathed upon the glass, and, when my lips approached, a dirty cloth you rubbed against my face : and when I again drew near, you spit, and rubbed, and smiled at my undoing.
> *Phillis* : What silly thoughts you men have !
> *Tom :* We were Pyramus and Thisbe, but ten times harder was my fate.

How the servants, male and female, might sometimes amuse themselves is shown in Congreve's *Love for Love*. Valentine, who proposes to ' commence playwright ', is doubtful as to his ability to knock together the rhymed couplets with which each act of a fashionable comedy had to conclude, and he accordingly instructs his man-servant, Jeremy, to " get the maids to Crambo in an evening, and learn the knack of rhyming ". This was the ancient game, now more common in nurseries than in servants' halls, popularly known as Dumb Crambo, and undeniably calculated to cultivate that knack. Five years later, in his greatest comedy, *The Way of the World*, Congreve introduced to the public no fewer than *four* Abigails : Foible, woman to Lady Wishfort ; Peg, her ladyship's maid ; Mincing, woman to Millamant ; and Betty, a maid at a chocolate-house.

Mincing figures in the famous and incomparable scene between Millamant, Witwoud and Mrs. Fainall, famous, yet never hackneyed, and not too familiar to be quoted yet again :

> *Mrs. Fainall* : You were dressed before I came abroad.
> *Millamant* : Aye, that's true. Oh, but then I had — Mincing, what had I ? Why was I so long ?
> *Mincing* : Oh, mem, your la'ship stayed to peruse a packet of letters.
> *Millamant* : Oh, ay, letters. I had letters — I am persecuted with letters. I hate letters. Nobody knows how to write letters, and yet one has 'em, one doesn't know why. They serve one to pin up one's hair.

Witwoud : Is that the way ? Pray, Madam, do you pin up your hair with all your letters ? I find I must keep copies.

Millamant : Only with those in verse, Mr. Witwoud. I never pin up my hair with prose. I think I tried once, Mincing ?

Mincing : Oh, mem, I shall never forget it.

Millamant : Ay, poor Mincing tift and tift all the morning.

Mincing : Till I had cramp in my fingers, I'll vow, mem, and all to no purpose. But when your la'ship pins it up with poetry, it sits so pleasant the next day as anything, and is so pure and so crips.

It will be remembered that a plot is concocted by which the low-born Waitwell shall woo lady Wishfort in the character of a rich uncle of the hero, Mirabel : but in case she should agree to marry him he is first hastily united to her maid, Foible. The audience is soon gratified with a sight of the deluded dame seated at her toilet-table, clamouring for the said Foible, and awkwardly waited upon by an understudy called Peg.

" Bring me the red ! " she cries. " The red ratafia does your ladyship mean ? " asks Peg, " or the cherry brandy ? "

Lady Wishfort : Ratafia, fool ! No, fool ! Not the ratafia — grant me patience ! I mean the Spanish paper, idiot — complexion, darling. Paint, paint, paint ! dost thou understand, changeling, dangling thy hands like bobbins before thee ? Why dost thou not stir, puppet— thou wooden thing upon wires ?

Peg : Lord, Madam, your ladyship is so impatient. I cannot come at the paint, Madam. Mrs. Foible has locked it up and carried the key with her.

Lady Wishfort : A pox take you both ! Fetch me the cherry brandy then.

Peg departs, but soon returns bearing a bottle and a diminutive china cup, and immediately finds herself again under fire.

Lady Wishfort : Wench, come, come, wench, what art thou doing ? Sipping ? Tasting ? Save thee, dost thou not know the bottle ?

Peg : Madam, I was looking for a cup.

Lady Wishfort : A cup, save thee ! And what a cup hast thou brought ! Dost thou take me for a fairy, to drink out of an acorn ? Why didst thou not bring thy thimble ? Hast thou ne'er a brass thimble clinking in thy pocket with a bit of nutmeg ? I warrant thee. Come, fill, fill. So — again.

A knock at the door interrupts this edifying colloquy, and Lady Wishfort issues hasty instructions to Peg. She must set down the bottle first — here, here — under the table. What, would she go with a bottle in her hand, like a tapster ?

" As I am a person," exclaims her Ladyship, " this wench has lived in an inn upon the road before she came to me, like Maritornes the Asturian in *Don Quixote* ! "

The contrast between Lady Wishfort's treatment of the uncouth Peg and of the highly sophisticated Foible is amusing : to the underling she is by turns irascible and half-playfully indulgent, to the confidante she is without gloss or subterfuge her vain and foolish self. When waiting for the supposed Sir Rowland — Waitwell in disguise — she eyes with anxiety her own image in the glass.

> *Lady Wishfort* : This wretch has fretted me that I am absolutely decayed. Look, Foible.
> *Foible* : Your ladyship has frowned a little too rashly indeed, Madam. There are some cracks discernible in the white varnish.
> *Lady Wishfort* : Let me see the glass — cracks, sayest thou ? Why, I am errantly flayed. I look like an old peeled wall. Thou must repair me, Foible, before Sir Rowland comes.

The arrangements for the reception of ' Sir Rowland ' are superintended by Foible ; she sees to the wax lights in the sconces, plants the footmen along the hall in their best liveries, and has " pulvilled " the coachman and the postillion " that they may not stink of the stable when Sir Rowland comes by ".

When the plot is exposed, Lady Wishfort hurls upon her treacherous waiting-woman those amazing bursts of invective than which nothing of the kind is more effective in all English drama :

> *Lady Wishfort* : Out of my house . . . thou bosom traitress that I raised from nothing ! Begone, begone, begone — go ! go ! That I took from washing of old gauze and wearing of dead hair, with a bleak blue nose over a chafing pot of starved embers, and dining behind a traverse rag in a shop no bigger than a bird-cage. Go, go ! Starve again, do.

Apparently not relishing that prospect, the cringing Abigail offers to sue for pardon on her knees ; but in vain.

> *Lady Wishfort* : Away ! Out ! Out ! Go, set up for yourself again ! Do, drive a trade, do, with your three-pennyworth of small ware flaunting upon a packthread under a brandy-seller's bulk or against a

dead wall by a ballad-monger ! Go, hang out an old Frisoneer gorget
with a yard of yellow colberteen [1] again, do : an old, gnawed mask,
two rows of pins and a child's fiddle, a glass necklace with the beads
broken, and a quilted nightcap with one ear. Go, go, drive a trade !
These were your commodities, you treacherous trull ! This was the
merchandise you dealt in when I took you into my house, placed you
next myself, and made you governante of my whole family.[2]

It was imprudent on her ladyship's part to take into her
service this tatterdemalion huckstress, a woman who had had no
special training, and who had not graduated by the recognized
degrees from the servants' hall to the housekeeper's room.

The life of a maid " next her lady's person " was beset with
temptations in the guise of opportunities : for example, she
would be entrusted with the key of the corner cupboard and the
preparation of the tea-tray — not then a pantry business : this
would give her access to other precious commodities besides tea.
What these were we may guess from Mirabel's resolve to banish
" all foreign forces, all auxiliaries ", from Millamant's tea-table,
such as orange-brandy, aniseed, cinnamon, citron and Barbados
waters,[3] " together with ratafia and the most noble spirit of
clary ".[4]

The personal maid would also enjoy a prescriptive right to
all her mistress's discarded tuckers, pinners, ruffles, buckles and
fans, as well as such petticoats and gowns as were no longer in
favour. The truth of Defoe's picture of Country Joan turned
Fine Madam may be judged from the circumstance that when
Millamant, the very plume and pearl of elegance, breaks her
fan, she promptly borrows Mincing's : it may well have been a
discarded one of her own.

[1] A kind of open lace with a square mesh named after Louis XIV's minister, Colbert.
[2] ' Family ' in eighteenth-century parlance often meant ' household '. Horace Walpole's at Strawberry Hill included both his servants and his pet animals.
[3] A strong cordial flavoured with orange and lemon peel.
[4] A sweet liquor consisting of a mixture of wine, clarified honey and various spices
such as pepper and ginger.

CHAPTER VI

Pamela, her Brother Joseph, and Some of their Contemporaries

WHEN young Samuel Richardson made a habit of helping maidservants to compose their love-letters and thereby acquired that intimate knowledge which afterwards enabled him to write *Pamela, or Virtue Rewarded*, he incidentally provided for students in later ages a most interesting maid's-eye view of English social life in the middle years of the eighteenth century. Pamela may have been, as Professor Oliver Elton says she was, " to speak metaphorically, the pure idea of a Minx " ; but she was also a perfectly conceived character, in three dimensions, and to follow the course of her adventures up to the morrow of her marriage to " Mr. B." is an instructive experience.

She was the child of very poor but very, very virtuous parents, the family facility in the art of penmanship — not then widely diffused among the masses — being explained by the circumstance that her father had at one time kept a small, un-assuming writing-school. When the story begins she is fifteen, and has lived between three and four years in the service of the benevolent Lady B. So far she has received no wages, but she has been supplied with " cloaths and linen that a gentlewoman need not be ashamed to appear in " ; she has also been " put to write and cast up accounts ", and has become " a little expert with her needle ". At this juncture, when she is at the height of her youthful beauty, her benefactress dies, commending her servants to her son, " Mr. B.", on her death-bed.

The young man, a hardened rake, orders mourning for them all, a very usual manner of expressing regard for the deceased ; he also, " with encouraging and condescending words ", slips four golden guineas into Pamela's hand — an action only too liable to be misconstrued in a cynical world. Pamela's parents, though the reverse of cynical, are greatly alarmed at the intelli-gence, and hastily conclude that " Mr. B." is planning thei

child's ruin, and that what they (and she) usually describe as
" the worst " must inevitably happen before long.

In their distress they take counsel with a neighbour, "good
old Widow Mumford ", who had formerly lived " with the best
families " ; and she reminds them that such rewards are not uncommon, after a death, when the waiting-maid and " such as sit
up " with the sick person often receive tokens of the survivor's
satisfaction. The parents remain a prey to anxiety ; and it soon
becomes evident that " Mr. B." 's married sister, Lady Davers,
has observed with a derisive eye his graciousness to " the pretty
wench, Pamela ". In the presence of Mrs. Jervis, the housekeeper ("a gentlewoman born, who had had misfortunes "), he
bestows upon her a suit of his late mother's " cloathes ", half a
dozen of her shifts, six fine cambric handkerchiefs, three of her
cambric aprons, and four holland ones : but his next bounties are
showered upon her when they are *tête-à-tête* — " two suits of
fine Flanders laced head-clothes, three pairs of fine silk shoes,
several ribands and top-knots of all colours, four pair of fine white
cotton stockings, two pair of silk ones, and two pair of rich
stays " : this last gift she receives with equanimity, but the
stockings seem to her to savour of indelicacy, and bring blushes
to her cheeks. Well may she turn back with wonder to the time
when, not yet twelve years old, she was " fitted out for my good
lady's service with a grey russet ". But her virtue, ever on the
alert, rings a prompt alarum : " though ", she remarks in her
next letter to her parents, " I have lived above myself for some
years past, I would be content with rags and poverty, and bread
and water, and would embrace them, rather than forfeit my good
name ".

Is she already contemplating " Mr. B." with hope as well as
with terror ? Has his profligate charm already made a dint upon
her chaste and fluttering heart ? It would appear so : for she
evinces no regret when he stamps firmly upon the suggestion of
Lady Davers that she should enter her service and go home with
her. It is true that the pretext he gives is that the husband's
nephew, young Davers, might " draw Pamela in " : but the net
result was the same — she remained attached to the household of
that scapegrace young bachelor, " Mr. B." Small wonder that

Mrs. Jervis shook her head : small wonder that the fears of the parents mounted ever higher.

It must be admitted that poor " Mr. B." had a good deal to put up with. His ultimate intentions were the reverse of honourable, but it must have been very trying to find every word and gesture interpreted as a prologue to " the worst ". The wench's " scribbling ", as he calls it, of constant lengthy letters to her father and mother also exasperated him ; even though, as she observed in one of these letters, she is busy at all hours with her needle upon his linen and the fine linen of the family, and was " about flowering him a waistcoat ". She also had to ' get up the linen '.

When Mr. B. carries Pamela off to his other country house in Lincolnshire the plot thickens, for Mrs. Jewkes, the houskeeeper there, is of very different stuff from the conscientious and apprehensive Mrs. Jervis. It is indeed surprising that Richardson was able to lay aside the pastels with which he was wont to work, and paint this coarse, flaunting creature with a force of line and a depth of colour worthy of Hogarth. Her cynical counsels, her depraved outlook, her fidelity to her master and her readiness to further all his designs, however deplorable, add greatly to Pamela's afflictions, and not a little to her dangers, both the imaginary and the real.

Here it may be noted that in these large country houses, large enough to be classed as mansions, or even as ' seats ', a comparatively small staff of servants seems to have been thought sufficient. In Bedfordshire " Mr. B." employed, in addition to Mrs. Jervis and Pamela, Rachel the housemaid, " four maidens " unnamed, a cook and a silver-haired butler ; in Lincolnshire we hear only of Mrs. Jewkes, a cook and " Nan ". How light Pamela's duties had always been is shown by her experience when, intending to escape from " Mr. B." and seek refuge with her parents, she tries to finish scouring a pewter plate which Rachel had begun to clean. " I see," she reflects, " I could do it by degrees : it only blistered my hand in two places."

Though she is full of fluttering eagerness to flee from " Mr. B." and all the perils inseparable from his alarming yet delightful company, she does not propose to hide herself in some place where he could not possibly find her : quite obviously he would look for her in her own home, and it is difficult to resist the conclusion that that is what she hoped he might do. Richardson lingers over the scene describing her preparations for her flight. Fearing to be misunderstood if she should reappear in her lowly (but virtuous) abode with a silk night-gown, silken petticoats, cambric head-cloths, etc., she carefully assembles an outfit more suited to her station : a homespun gown, two petticoats, a quilted camlet coat, some " facings " of a " pretty bit of printed calico ", two flannel undercoats, two round-eared caps, a little straw hat, a pair of knit mittens turned up with white calico, two pairs of blue worsted hose with white clocks, two yards of black ribbon for shirt sleeves, " and to serve as a necklace ".

When she gets down to the task of packing her bundle several other items appear : " a remnant of Scots cloth which will make two shirts and two shifts, the same I have on, for my poor father and mother. And here are four other shifts, one the fellow to that I have on, another pretty good one, and other two old fine ones that will serve me to turn and wind with at home, for they are not worth leaving behind me ; and here are two pair of shoes ; I have taken the lace off, which I will burn, and may be will fetch me some little matter at a pinch, with an old silver buckle or two." She also put in several pieces of printed calico, remnants of silk and such-like, " that," she says, " if good luck should happen and I should get work, would serve for robins [1] and facings and such-like uses ".

Her creator still cannot bear to relinquish the task, so congenial to his trivial, rather feminine mind, of enumerating Pamela's various garments, and suggesting, with no small skill, how well they became her. Here is her description of herself when she was — as she fondly imagined — on the very brink of flight :

> I tricked myself up as well as I could in my new garb, and put on my round-eared, ordinary cap, but with a green knot, however, and my homespun gown and petticoat and plain leathern shoes — but they are what they call Spanish leather ; and my ordinary hose, ordinary I mean to what I have lately been used to, though I shall think good yarn may do very well for every day. A plain muslin

[1] A trimming in the form of bands or stripes.

tucker I put on, and my black silk necklace, instead of the French
necklace my lady gave me, and put the earrings out of my ears.
And when I was quite equipped I took my straw hat in my hand,
with its two blue strings, and looked about me in the glass as proud
as anything. To say truth, I never liked myself so well in my life.

It is not necessary to follow here the course of the story, or to
trace the rising curve of " Mr. B." 's ardour as Pamela continues
to resist him : but her troubles were not over until some time
after virtue was rewarded with a wedding-ring : for " Mr. B."
insists that the marriage shall be kept secret for a time, and it is
hardly surprising that when Lady Davers pays him a visit she
should conclude that " the worst " has happened, and that Pamela
is her brother's mistress. This opinion is shared by her personal
maid, whom she takes into her confidence, and whom she commands to accompany her when, in quest of confirmation of her
suspicions, she bursts into the bedchamber where " Mr. B." and
Pamela are installed, and which she believes to be a temple of
illicit love. There is an admirable illustration (reproduced
opposite page 112) in the 1802 edition of the novel, showing the
ex-Abigail cowering in bed, the Abigail *in esse* looking on in
respectful dismay, and " Mr. B.", in nightcap, dressing-gown and
slippers, forcibly removing his sister from the room.

The story of Pamela, her Virtue and its Reward swept over
England and then over Europe in a resistless torrent, to the
annoyance of supercilious persons like Horace Walpole, who
could perceive all its weaknesses and none of its merits. That the
plot was not inherently improbable is shown by the circumstance
that Lady Mary Wortley-Montagu (no sentimentalist) at once
perceived a striking resemblance between the heroine and her own
sixteen-year-old chamber-maid, Fanny. This girl had had a
rather better education than was common in her class, and she
was exceedingly pretty. Lady Mary took her into her service on
learning that she had conceived a violent desire to wait upon her.
" I do not yet repent it ", wrote her ladyship, " from any part of
her behaviour — the young creature never stirring from my
apartment, always at her needle, and never complaining of anything."

Amid the almost universal chorus of praise one or two slightly apprehensive voices made themselves heard — the voices of mothers who feared that their sons might, in the fashion of " Mr. B.", find a wife in the ranks of their maidservants. One such utterance, worded with some degree of obscurity, was to this effect : " the moral meaning of Pamela's good fortune, far from tempting young gentlemen to marry such maids as are found in their families is, by teaching maids to deserve to be mistresses, to stir up mistresses to support their distinction " : this consideration, it is argued, should " reassure the mothers and grandmothers in all families of affluent fortune who, though they may have none of Lady Davers' insolence, may be apt to feel one of her fears — that the example of a gentleman so amiable as Mr. B. may be followed by the Jackies, their sons, with too blind and unreflecting a readiness ". One can only hope that they *were* reassured.

When in 1759 General Hawley drew up his Will with his own hand the shadow of Pamela certainly fell upon the paper. He left £100 to his servant, Elizabeth Buskett, because she had " proved herself a useful and agreeable handmaid ", and the residue of his estate to his adopted son, with the proviso that if the young man should be foolish enough to marry " the said Elizabeth " neither he nor she should inherit a farthing.

The satisfaction kindled in the mild breast of Samuel Richardson by the success of his first novel must have been all but obliterated by the mortification caused by Henry Fielding's *Joseph Andrews*, in which the whole idea of *Pamela* is made ridiculous by the simple, fatal expedient of changing the sex of the principal character. The first intention of this book was merely to satirize and so to stultify ; and then several of Fielding's puppets sprang to life, and proceeded to do with him what they would.

Joseph, the chaste young footman and eponymous hero, is not among those subtly self-animated figures. He is a dummy, personable, pious and smug, the congenital virtue of the Andrews family having been fortified in him by the perusal of his sister Pamela's letters. The foolish woman of quality in whose service we meet him is a connection of Pamela's " Mr. B." — whose mother's name was, it appears, Lady John Booby. This amplification of the discreet and enigmatic single initial must have

PAMELA.
N.B. — parrying Lady Davers out of her
Chamber, where she had rudely obtruded.
Vide Volume II. Page 296.
Printed for C. Cooke May 30 1801.

VIRTUE REWARDED

Illustration from Cooke's edition of *Pamela, or Virtue Rewarded*

infuriated poor Richardson ; but he might have consoled himself with the reflection that whatever his hero-villain may have been, a booby he could not justly have been called. Lady Booby has a maid, Slipslop, whose resemblance to Mrs. Jewkes is so remarkable that they might well have been sisters, though " Mr. B." 's housekeeper was probably less repellant in appearance. She is described sometimes as her ladyship's ' waiting gentlewoman ', sometimes as her ' chamber-maid '.

The daughter of a poor curate, Slipslop has pretensions to a sort of shabby gentility, and is " a mighty affecter of hard words ". She is " an antient maiden Gentlewoman of about forty-five years of age, who, having made a small Slip in her Youth, had continued a good Maid ever since ". Short, corpulent, with a red, pimply face, a nose too large, eyes too small and one leg shorter than the other, affected, bad-tempered and unscrupulous, she is one of the most famous and certainly the least likable of all the Abigails in English literature. In addition to her other faults, she is a tippler, and we see her exploiting to the full her command of Lady Booby's keys, not only to refresh herself but to conciliate the adamantine Joseph of whom, like her mistress, she is enamoured. She gives him tea, sweetmeats, wine and other delicacies ; and on one occasion she presses a glass of ratafia upon him as a prelude to an assault upon his heart. On her own showing, unsupported by any outside evidence, she gave the Poor many a Cordial that they would have lacked if Lady Booby had been her own Keeper of the Keys : and the sum of her accomplishments is completed by her " excellent knack of delivering cuffs with a good grace ". This knack she had acquired " by frequent practice on the inferior servants ". Small wonder that when Joseph falls in love with one of them, an exceedingly pretty girl called Fanny, who had been " bred up in Lady Booby's family ", *i.e.* in her household, the egregious Slipslop dismisses her.

Absurd as Lady Booby is, it is difficult not to sympathize with her annoyance when Joseph, repelling her advances, declared that, " as Pamela's brother ", he would be ashamed " that the Chastity of his Family ", which is preserved in her, should be stained by him. Her Ladyship thereupon flies into a rage, dubs Pamela " a little vixen ", and vows that she always wondered the late Lady John Booby ever kept her in her house. Unluckily for her, Slipslop's ear has been at the keyhole during this edifying colloquy, and the pert behaviour of the waiting-woman soon betrays her knowledge of her mistress's folly. "Do as I bid you," cries Lady Booby, "and don't shock my Ears with your beastly Language." "Marry come up," retorts Slipslop, "People's Ears are sometimes the nicest Part about them." After an acrimonious dialogue the lady says, "I desire you would provide yourself" — meaning 'look for another situation'. "With all my heart," snaps Slipslop. They are soon reconciled, none the less, for on reflection neither finds that she could do very well without the other ; and Lady Booby weakly makes the woman " a Present of a Gown and Petticoat " as an instance of her future favour : after which we are told that Slipslop " with great tranquillity paid a Visit to a Stone Bottle which is of Sovereign Use to a Philosophical Temper ".

Standing in the direct line of succession between Mrs. Quickly and Mrs. Gamp through Mrs. Malaprop, the creature lards her conversation with garbled words and phrases. For example, during one of her altercations with Lady Booby she informs her that " she talks of servants as if they were not born of human *specious* ". Her accent was presumably not unlike that of Millamant's Mincing, for she apostrophizes her mistress as " O Meam ".

Of Slipslop's ultimate fate we are left in ignorance, but we may hope that Parson Adam's eldest daughter got her place — for what it was worth — and comported herself more creditably in it than she had done. The last episode in which she figures is broadly farcical : it is when in one night two gentlemen successively invade her bedchamber, the first, Beau Didapper, under the impression that it is the lovely Fanny's room, the second, Parson Adams, mistaking it for his own.

Pamela makes a brief appearance, carrying her oats very badly and disdainful of Fanny as her sister-in-law until, by an incredible twist of the plot, it comes to light that Fanny is her sister, and that Joseph's virtue is not hereditary but innate, he being a foundling and no Andrews at all.

Before the young man reaches journey's end and is united to his Fanny he has various adventures, including an encounter with footpads, who wound him and strip him of his clothes. Incidentally, we meet two Abigails, one tactful, the other good-hearted. The first is in attendance upon an affected lady travelling by coach, who protests that she has never in her life tasted such a thing as a dram. When a highwayman attacks the vehicle, the maid " in her Fright " delivers up a little silver bottle of about a half-pint size, " which the Rogue, clapping it to his Mouth and drinking her Health ", declares to contain some of the best Nantes brandy he has ever tasted. This, the lady afterwards assures the company, is the mistake of her maid, whom she had ordered to fill the bottle not with brandy but with Hungary water.[1]

The name of this maid does not transpire, but the maid at the inn whither the travellers repair is yet another Betty, sitting up late " to attend the Coachman and serve him with Cold Meat and a Dram ". She is justly described as " a good-natured Wench ", and before making up a bed for the languishing Joseph and warming it with a warming-pan, she claps " a large Faggot on the Fire " ; then she runs off to fetch a surgeon. The landlord is going to give her one of his own shirts for the wounded man, but the less merciful landlady threatens to throw the chamber-pot at her head if she carries out this order. Ultimately she borrows for Joseph's benefit the shirt of one of the ostlers " who was her sweetheart ", and crowns her acts of charity by bringing him some tea, " for which he was pining in his Fever ".

Fielding comments on the dangerous situation of a chamber-maid at an inn, " daily liable to the Solicitations of Lovers of all Complexions, to the dangerous Addresses of fine Gentlemen of the Army . . . and above all exposed to the Caresses of Footmen, Stage-coachmen and Drawers ".

It is one of the agreeable little ironies of literary history that Henry Fielding should have married his own housemaid *en secondes noces* : she was an excellent creature, made him a good wife, bore him a son, and went with him on that sad journey to Lisbon from which he never returned. That such alliances were not subjects of amazement at the time is shown by Northcote's anecdote of Lawrence Sterne's comment on the marriage of " old Dr. ——" with *his* housemaid, " Ay, I always thought him a

[1] Spirits of wine mixed with " the more essential part of rosemary flowers ".

genius and now I'm sure of it ". What Sterne meant, explains the narrator, was " that Dr. —— saw a thousand virtues in this woman which nobody else did, and could give a thousand reasons for his choice that no one about him had the wit to answer : but nature took its usual course, and the event turned out as he had been forewarned, according to the former experience of the world in such matters ".

In 1759 appeared a comedy, *High Life Below Stairs*, long attributed to David Garrick and included in his collected works as late as 1798, but actually the work of a parson-schoolmaster called James Townley who, in the very year of its anonymous production, became headmaster of the Merchant Taylors' School. The principal characters are members of the London household of a certain Mr. Lovel, a wealthy West Indian merchant, who has complete confidence in his butler, Philip, but is inclined to under-rate Tom, the solitary honest servant among them all. The cast includes five women-servants, four white and one black, the part of Kitty having been created with great success by the incomparable Kitty Clive. " The Duke's Man " and " Sir Harry's Man " are seen meeting in the Park, addressing each other respectively as " Duke " and " Baronet ", and aping their betters with the inevitable grotesque results. To them enter " Lady Bab's Maid " and " Lady Charlotte's Maid ", disputing as to the superior gentility of Vauxhall or " Runelow ". " Lady Char " — usurping her mistress's name as does also her friend, " Lady Bab " — cries, " O, my stars ! Why, there's nobody there but filthy citizens ! " " Lady Bab " replies, " We were in hopes that raising the price would have kept them out, ha, ha, ha ! "

Lovel, incited by his friend, Mr. Freeman, pretends to go on a journey to Devonshire, but actually disguises himself as a lumpish lad supposed to come from that gentleman's estate and " wanting to be made a good servant of ". Believing that their master is far away in the country, Lovel's servants decide to have " a roaring night ", and to " make his cellar bleed ". The young ' yokel ' is of the party, and wanders about gaping at the splendour of everything. When Kitty enters, he ejaculates, " La, la, what a fine lady is there ! This is Madam, I suppose ! " Asked by Philip, the butler, where she has been, Kitty replies, " I have been disposing of some of his Honour's shirts and other linen, which it is a shame his Honour should wear any longer " : and this is followed by the polite assurance that the evening's entertainment is intended as a compliment to her. " But," adds Philip sternly, " I beg I may see none of your airs or hear any of your French gibberish with the Duke." This precious pair, Philip and Kitty, intend ultimately to marry and set up a chocolate-house upon the proceeds of their dishonesty : and it is to this scheme that she refers in the course of the ensuing dialogue :

> *Kitty* : You know my education was a very genteel one. I was a half-boarder at Chelsea, and I speak French like a native. (*Awkwardly*) *Comment vous portez-vous, Monsieur ?*
> *Philip* : Psha, psha !
> *Kitty* : One is nothing without French. I shall shine at the bar.

To prepare " Jemmy " to wait upon the " gentlefolks ", *i.e.* his fellow-servants, she ties and powders his hair and reads aloud to him from a rhymed manual, *The Servants' Guide to Wealth* by Timothy Shoulderknot, formerly servant to several noblemen — a cynical work full of bad advice such as,

> Let it for ever be your plan
> To be the master, not the man,
> And do as little as you can.

Later, the honest Tom says to her, " Egad, madam, the gentry may well complain when they get such servants as you in their houses. There's your good friend, Mother Barter, the old clothes woman, the greatest thief in town, just now gone out with her apron full of His Honour's linen." Kitty calls him " a mealy-mouthed cur " for his pains.

When " the Duke " arrives there is some bandying of elementary French phrases between them, and then a would-be-modish colloquy in the course of which she asks, " Your Grace loves a play ? " and he answers scornfully, " No, it is a dull, old-fashioned entertainment ; I hate it." As he offers to kiss her, " Sir Harry " comes in and does likewise, whereupon " the Duke " roars, " Stand off ! You are a commoner. Nothing under nobility approaches Kitty." " O lud ! " cries the damsel, after some further bickering, " This is charming — to see two noblemen quarrel ! "

" Lady Bab " is carried in sitting in a sedan-chair; she apologizes for being late, but explains that she " got into " her favourite author.

The Duke : Yes, I found her ladyship at her studies this morning. Some wicked poem——
Lady Bab : O, you wretch, I never read but one book.
Kitty : What is your ladyship so fond off ?
Lady Bab : Shikspur. Did you never read Shikspur ?
Kitty : Shikspur ! Shikspur ! Who wrote it ? No, I never read Shikspur.
Lady Bab : Then you have an immense pleasure to come.
Kitty : Well, then, I'll read it one afternoon or another.

" Lady Char " now arrives, also in a chair, and, when " Sir Harry " begins to make gallant speeches, spurns him as a " trumpery baronet ". Presently the general gaiety is heightened by the entry of a one-legged fiddler who " can play anything from a jig to a sonata ", and Philip proceeds to arrange the guests for the dance. " I'll couple you," says he. " My lord Duke will take Kitty, Lady Bab will do me the honour of her hand : Sir Harry and Charlotte — Coachman and Cook — and the two devils dance together " — these last being the negroes, no doubt brought from the West Indies by their master, though black servants of either sex had been common in England since Stuart times.

" Lady Char ", with graceful persuasiveness, begs that " the Duke " and Mistress Kitty will give them a minuet ; but that nobleman pleads his " poor gout ", so Sir Harry and Kitty tread a clumsy measure to the tune called for by the rather vague name of " Marshal Thingumbob's Minuet ".

Then Mr. Lovel's wine begins to flow, his claret, burgundy, champagne and " Tokay for the ladies " : the company becomes boisterous ; " the Duke " and the " Baronet " challenge each other to a duel with pistols — and seconds — " behind Montague House ", only to be rebuked by Philip for brawling in the presence of " the ladies ". Meanwhile " Jemmy " has slipped away unperceived, and at this juncture, in his own character and costume as Mr. Lovel, accompanied by Mr. Freeman, he presents himself at the front door and knocks loudly. A scene of the maddest confusion follows, and the guests are hustled and pushed into the pantry. As Lovel's voice is heard ' off ', calling for Philip, the butler says in a hasty aside to Kitty, " Kitty, have you never a good book to be reading of ? " " Yes, here is one," she answers promptly : and when the two gentlemen enter and Lovel asks, " What the Devil makes you up so early this morning ? " the man replies unblushingly, " Mistress Kitty and I had got into a good book, your Honour."

" The Duke " most imprudently peeps out of the pantry and Lovel, hearing a movement, asks Kitty what she has got there. " In the pantry ? " she retorts. " Lord, your honour, we are at board-wages." During the action which follows Kitty makes a sign to Mr. Freeman that Lovel is tipsy, and suggests officiously that he had better go to bed : but " Sir Harry " calls softly, " Mistress Kitty, Mistress Kitty," and then someone in the pantry sneezes.

> *Kitty* (*aside*) : We are undone, we are undone !
> *Philip* (*aside*) : Oh, that is the Duke's damned rappee.
> *Lovel* : Damn it, there are thieves in the house !
> *Kitty* : Lackaday, Sir, it was only the cat. They sometimes sneeze for all the world like a Christian. Here, Jack, Jack — he's got a cold, Sir. Puss, puss !

Lovel wagers Freeman two to one that with his pistol he could shoot the animal right through the pantry door, but when he cocks and aims the weapon, a loud shriek is heard from within, and all the servants troop out. " The Duke " and " Sir Harry " are ejected with derision, and have little to say for themselves ; but the two maids are by no means abashed. " This," remarks " Lady Char ", " comes of visiting commoners," and " Lady Bab " replies with conviction that they are " downright *Hottentops* ". Philip is discharged on the spot, but Kitty is allowed till the following morning to prepare for her departure. Her exit-line is a cry of " I am ruin't and undone ! "

Seven years after *High Life Below Stairs* had diverted play-goers, lovers of sparkling, not over-decorous, light verse were equally diverted by Christopher Anstey's *New Bath Guide*, show-ing how Sim and Prue, the fat and bean-fed son and daughter of Lady Blunderhead, their cousin Jenny, and their maid, Tabitha Runt, are sent to Bath so that the two young Blunderheads may recover from the effects of the excessively rich and abundant diet chosen for them by their indulgent mamma. The narrative is assigned to various persons, now Sim, now Jenny, now Prue, taking up the tale. It is Jenny who describes the arrival of the party at Bath :

> And here they are, all bile and spleen,
> The strangest fish that e'er were seen,
> With Tabby Runt, their maid, poor creature,
> The queerest animal in nature.

They put up at The Bear, and it soon becomes evident that Tabitha as well as ' Quality ' is to enjoy the full benefit of medical attention, for when the doctor has been summoned, and has prescribed for Sim, we immediately hear his diagnosis of " Tabby's " case, and his prompt treatment of her symptoms : Sim is the narrator here :

> He gives little Tabby a great many doses,
> He says the poor creature has got a Chlorosis,
> Or a ravenous Pica, so brought on the Vapours
> By swallowing Stuff she had read in the Papers !
> And often I've marvel'd she spent so much Money
> In Water-Dock Essence and Balsam of Honey,
> Such Tinctures, Elixirs, such Pills have I seen,
> I never could wonder her face was so green.
> Yet He thinks He can very soon set Her to right,
> With *Testic. Equin.* that she takes every night ;
> And when to her spirits and strength He has brought Her
> He thinks she may venture to bathe in the Water.

When that day arrives Sim describes the scene in a letter to Lady Blunderhead :

> This morning, dear Mother, as soon as 'twas light,
> I was wak'd by a noise that astonished me quite,
> For in Tabitha's Chamber I heard such a Clatter
> I could not conceive what the deuce was the Matter.
> And, would you believe it, I went up and found her
> In a Blanket, with two lusty Fellows around her,
> Who both seem'd a-going to carry her off in
> A little black box just the size of a Coffin.
> " Pray tell me," says I, " What you're doing of here ? "
> " Why, master, 'tis hard to be bilk'd of our Fare,
> And so we were thrusting her into a Chair :

> We don't see no Reason for using us so,
> For she bad us come hither and now she won't go.
> We've earn'd all the Fare, for we both came and knock'd her
> Up, as soon as 'twas light, by Advice of the Doctor ;
> And this is a Job that we often go a'ter
> For Ladies that choose to go into the Water."

Tabitha's terrors are easy to understand : but ultimately she is persuaded to brave the perils of the transit, and is borne downstairs,

> just as safe and well
> And as snug as a Hodmandod rides in his Shell.

A brief interpolation may here be permitted upon that deeprooted and long-persisting habit among young women of Tabby Runt's class and calling — the habit of " swallowing Stuff they had read in the Papers ". Some of the concoctions they trustfully gulped down may have been harmless enough, though on the drastic side — was not Horace Walpole made ill by drinking some medicine intended for his housemaid ? — but others were harmless neither in their composition nor in their purpose. The following advertisement of this period illustrates this point — it refers to a compound sold at five shillings a bottle " at the Golden Ball in Stonecutter's Street, Fleet Market " :

> This liquour is the study of a Jesuit, one Mr. Delore, and is sold by his nephew, Mr. John Delore, and I promise very fair if it don't perform all I say, I'll have nothing for my pains : and if any young Master has debauched a Servant and won't have her, let her give him a bottle of this liquour, and if he don't marry her I'll have nothing for it : therefore I promise very fair : no performance, no pay.

Spas and watering-places seem from the first to have exercised a sort of gravitational pull upon religious quacks of all kinds : bethels and tabernacles tended to spring up, and to lure visitors and invalids away from what used to be called " the Establishment " — the Church of England as by law established. John Wesley — not to be numbered among the quacks, but, like them, a powerful counter-attraction to conformity — was preaching at Bath in the same year that the Blunderheads were there : but

I

unfortunately the evangelist to whom Tabitha Runt inclined her ear was not a Methodist but a Moravian :

> Tabby from Scruples of Mind was releas'd
> When she met with a learned Moravian Priest
> Who says there is neither Transgression nor Sin ;
> A doctrine that brings many Customers in.

Miss Prudence, more genteel, is converted to Methodism by a dream ; and in relating her conversion in a letter to her friend, Lady Betty, she gives an uncharitable account of her fellow-travellers :

> Brother Simkin's grown a Rakehell,
> Cards and Dances every day,
> Jenny laughs at Tabernacle,
> Tabby Runt is gone astray.

That the Moravian missionary is responsible for Tabitha's downfall is made only too clear in four lines of Simkin's *Farewell to Bath* :

> The Man without Sin, the Moravian Rabbi,
> Has perfectly cur'd the Chlorosis of Tabby,
> And if right I can judge by her Shape and her Face
> She soon may produce him an Infant of Grace.

Poor Tabby was not the only Abigail in eighteenth-century literature to accompany her employers to Bath, but the experiences of Smollett's Winifred Jenkins (in *Humphrey Clinker*), though occasionally disconcerting, were far less disastrous. She was in attendance on Miss Bramble, the cross-grained spinster sister of the good-humoured bachelor, Matthew Bramble, and their young niece, Lydia Melford. The story is told, *à la Pamela*, in a series of letters, among them quite a number from Winifred to her fellow-servant, Mary Jones, left at home at Brambleton Hall. Miss Melford, writing to her friend, Miss Willis, describes the King's Bath, crowded with all sorts and conditions of people, all jostling each other without ceremony, the ladies wearing jackets and petticoats of brown linen and chip hats " in which they fix handkerchiefs to wipe their flushed faces ". Miss Bramble insists that Winifred shall " attend her in the water " : and, writes Miss Melford,

. . . as for poor Win, who wore a hat trimmed with blue, what betwixt her wan complexion and her fear, she looked like the ghost of some pale maiden that had drowned herself for love. . . . When she came out of the bath she took asafoetida drops and was fluttered all day. . . . Her mistress says it will do her good, and poor Win curtseys, with tears in her eyes.

Win gives her own version of the episode in a long letter to Mary Jones. At first she was mortally afraid and flustered all day, and made believe she had " got the heddick " : but Miss Bramble said that if she did not go in again she would have to take a dose of " bumstaffy ", and Win, remembering the effects of a mere pennyworth of that concoction upon the housekeeper at Brambleton Hall, " chose rather to go again with her into the bath ".

Winifred is shocked at the dishonesty of the Bath servants, and calls them " devils in garnet ". Three-quarters of a yard of blond lace, a remnant of muslin, and a silver thimble " which was a gift of true love ", disappeared from her work-basket when she left it for a short time on the table in the servants' hall : " and they say as how the very teeth ain't safe in your head if you sleep with your mouth open ". Yet life in this perilous city has its compensations. Attendance upon Miss Bramble and Miss Melford was not so continuous or so laborious that it did not leave their Abigail ample leisure to see the sights — " the prades, the squires, and the circlis, the Craskit, the Noctogon ". She confidently expected to make a havoc among the " mail sex " with the aid of a " killing collar " given to her by the younger lady and " a full suit of gauze as good as new " purchased from Madame Friponneau, the French " mulliner ". No doubt to the extreme admiration of Mary Jones, Winifred relates how she has formed creditable connections in Bath, where, to be sure, they have " the very squintasence of sasiety ". Mrs. Patcher, my lady Kilmaculloch's woman, has taught her how to " refash rusty silks and bumbeseens by boiling them in winegar, chamberlaye and stale beer " — an interesting receipt of which at least one item goes straight back to the more insensitive methods of an earlier age.

Meanwhile Miss Bramble has been writing elaborate instructions to her housekeeper at home, urging that fires shall be kept constantly burning in her room and Mr. Bramble's. The wine-cellar being padlocked, the maids " may go very well without beer in hot weather. Water will make them fair and keep them cool and temperate." The hotness of the weather did not, however, make it undesirable that they should be " kept a-spinning ".

It is inevitable that the sentimental Winifred shall lose her heart before she returns to Brambleton Hall ; romance is already in the air in the person of Miss Melford, hopelessly enamoured of an obscure young play-actor. The maid's affections are won by the eponymous hero of the book, Humphrey Clinker, who from poor and humble beginnings is raised by his merits to comparative dignity and prosperity, as well as being discovered (it was common form in the fiction of the period) to be not what he had been supposed, but an irregular offshoot of the Bramble family tree. As the tale draws to its close the characters pair off as if for a minuet — Lydia and her young play-actor, who, of course, was nothing of the sort, Miss Bramble and the eccentric, impecunious but somehow likable Scottish soldier, Captain Lismahago. Clinker consults Lydia's brother as to whether he himself might not with propriety " play the fool in the same fashion " with Winifred Jenkins. Young Melford thinks he might look higher, and advises him to wait a little.

Poor Win, on her part, is much agitated at the discovery of the young ostler's origin and at his patently improved fortunes : he is out of livery, he wears ruffles : though still " umble and compleasant ", he dwells upon the necessity for patience and for trust in Providence in a manner that fills her with misgiving. And why, she asks, should Squire Bramble object to their union ? " My parents ", she writes, " were married according to the rights of holy mother Crutch in the face of men and angels. Mark that, Mary Jones ! . . . but then I have such vapours, Molly — I sit and cry by myself and take ass of etida, and smill burnt feathers and kindal snuffs."

After some demur Squire Bramble's consent is given. " I would have wished ", he confided to his friend, Dr. Lewis, " that Clinker had kept out of this scrape, but as the nymph's happiness is at stake and she has already had some fits in the way of despondence, I, in order to prevent any tragical catastrophe, have given him leave to play the fool in imitation of his betters." As Clinker had some skill in farriery it occurred to his patron that, under the Doctor's instruction, he might in a little while be qualified to act as a village apothecary.

A triple wedding concludes the narrative : Lydia and young Dennison, Miss Bramble and her old Scottish Captain, Winifred Jenkins and Humphrey Clinker. Lismahago gives Winifred " an Indian purse made of silk grass containing twenty crown pieces " ; Miss Bramble and Miss Melford furnished her with their " superfluities of clothes and linen ".

Writing to her old crony at Brambleton Hall Mrs. Humphrey Clinker is suddenly very high and mighty, though she does condescend to give her a full account of the wedding, with a description of her own costume on the occasion. " Your humble servant ", she confides, " had a plain pea-green tabby sack, with my Runnela cap, ruff toupée and side-curls. They said I was the very moral of Lady Rickmanstone, but not so pale. . . . As our appartments ", she continues, " are to be the yellow pipper in the third story, pray carry my things thither. Present my compliments to Mrs. Gwyllim, and I hope she and I will always live upon dissent terms of civility. Being, by God's blessing, removed to a higher spear, you'll excuse my being familiar with the lower sarvants of the family, but as I trust you'll behave respectful and keep a proper distance, you may always depend upon the good will and protection of yours——"

An Abigail of this period in real life who was removed to an even higher " spear " was Elizabeth Cullen, waiting-maid to the beautiful Duchess of Hamilton, *née* Gunning. She married her fellow-servant, the Duke's valet William Almack — probably *né* MacCall — and as he rose in the world she was adaptable and enterprising enough to rise with him. From the proprietorship of the Thatched House Tavern in St. James's Street Almack passed to that of the Assembly Rooms erected by himself in King Street, where for many years there was housed the most modish and exclusive mixed club in London. The inaugural reception was held in February 1765, when the sharply contrasted figures of Butcher Cumberland and Horace Walpole were among the numerous company. Another guest, Gilly Williams, wrote to

George Selwyn on this occasion : " Almack's Scotch face in a bagwig waiting at supper would have diverted you, as would his lady in a sacque, making tea and curtseying to the Duchesses ". Few ex-Abigails would have been less likely to be abashed by the presence of these great ladies ; and none could have had a keener sense of the benefits that could hardly fail to ensue.

From that delightful book, *The Russells in Bloomsbury*, we learn that, in the eighteenth century, " outside the kitchen the proportion of the female staff to the male staff remained very much as it had been for the past hundred years or more " in that noble household ; " that is to say, the female staff were entirely subordinate in number and salaries to the male staff ". Among the women the housekeeper received twelve pounds a year, the housemaids never less than five and never more than six pounds. Though her wages were not fantastically high by the standard of the times, the housekeeper lived with some degree of elegance in a suite of three rooms. Her breakfast-room contained some objects the very names of which cause a modern collector's pulse to accelerate — a round mahogany pillar-and-claw table ; a dressing-glass in a mahogany frame ; an old Persia carpet ; a chamber clock by Tompion. The kitchen-maids' room does not sound attractive : it contained little beyond wooden beds and their complement of bedding, three old chairs, a deal chamber-table with a drawer, a dressing-glass with a beech frame, and a fender.

Mr. H. Clifford Smith printed in *Country Life* (February 11, 1944) extracts from another Russell inventory, that of Houghton House, near Bedford, made in 1767. The room "over my Lady's apartment ", evidently a maid's room, sounds more snug, with its blue check bed-hangings and window curtains, its four ' matted ' chairs, old elbow chair frame (into which a squab could easily be fitted), and its old inlaid table with a green " bays " cover.

CHAPTER VII

The Eighteenth-Century Abigail — In the Witness-Box and Elsewhere

WHEN, in the month of March 1752, Mary Blandy, spinster and gentlewoman, was tried and condemned for the murder of her father, the incriminating evidence came chiefly from two servant-maids, Susan Gunnell and Elizabeth or Betty Binfield, both of whom had been for some time in the service of the Blandy family at Henley-on-Thames. While lodged in Oxford jail awaiting execution, Miss Blandy uttered some highly disparaging remarks regarding the trustworthiness of servants in general, and, alluding to Susan as " my mother's maid ", she observed that she was disagreeable to her, " but yet, on account of money due to her, which I could not pay, it was not in my power to dismiss her ". Vehemently, and for more reasons than one, must she have regretted her folly in diverting her house-keeping allowance into the pockets of her worthless lover, Captain Cranstoun, the instigator of her crime.

The tale may best be told as it unfolded itself before the eyes of Susan, Betty and their fellow-servant, Robert Harman. In that small, middle-class household they must all have been well aware that their master, Francis Blandy, attorney-at-law, together with his wife, was anxious to find a suitable husband for their only child, born in 1720 and still, in 1746, unmarried. Her good points included fine dark eyes, thick dark hair, and a figure of the redundant type then most admired : but her face was pitted with smallpox and, if contemporary prints ever approximate to the truth, her features were too angular and strongly marked for beauty. Her father, who kept house " in such a manner as to substantiate local opinion that he was rather better than well off ", let it be known that he would give his daughter a marriage portion of £10,000. This inspiring intelligence was circulated not only in Henley itself, but at Bath, whither the Blandys repaired with Mary, and whence they returned with a ' catch ' in the person of a certain " Captain D." Unfortunately, he was almost immediately ordered abroad.

On a summer evening in the year 1746 the three Blandys were invited to dine with General Lord Mark Kerr, son of the first Marquess of Lothian, at his riverside house poetically called ' The Paradise'. Thereafter Susan and Betty could not fail to note how very frequently his lordship's nephew, Captain the Honourable William Cranstoun, visited the Blandys' home. In looks he was not a favourable representative of that ' quality ' whom Mr. Blandy naïvely revered : small, ungainly, freckled, pock-marked, his foxy red eyebrows indicated the colour of the cropped hair beneath his fashionable wig — hair inherited, with other amiable characteristics, from his Campbell ancestor, Archibald the Ugly, Marquis of Argyll. Yet he had undeniably a curious charm of manner ; he dressed well ; his snuff-box and his clouded cane would be of the mode of to-morrow rather than of to-day ; and he is said to have been the original of the *petit maître*, Beau Didapper, in *Joseph Andrews*.

After being ' out in the '45 ' on the Jacobite side, Cranstoun had ' ratted ', and while staying with his uncle he was, as Mr. Roughead says,[1] " beating up recruits in Henley to fill the vacancies caused in the Hanoverian ranks by the valour of the ' rebels ' ". All the Blandys, male and female, found him irresistible. " Captain D." on his return from foreign service had failed to renew his suit, and the way was left clear for another and rather different holder of that military rank. The circumstance that Cranstoun had a lawful wife in Scotland did not deter him from making a bid for the mythical £10,000 — for mythical it later proved to be ; and when his uncle tried to frustrate his plans by revealing that circumstance, he contrived to persuade the infatuated attorney that there was no binding contract, only " an unfortunate entanglement ".

Presently, however, something happened which shook Mr. Blandy's faith in his daughter's wooer, though Mary herself and her mother never wavered for a moment. In March 1748 the Commissary Court at Edinburgh declared that William Henry Cranstoun and Anne Murray of Broughton were man and wife,

[1] In *The Trial of Mary Blandy*.

that their child was born in wedlock, and that he must pay her an annuity of £40, £10 for the child, and £100 for costs and expenses. More than ever must the £10,000 have seemed alluring to the little wretch, who protested that the Commissary Court's findings would inevitably be quashed on an appeal to the Court of Session.

Still believing in him, still anxious to see him married to her daughter, Mrs. Blandy died in 1749. Some time after her death, Cranstoun, who had been held captive by bailiffs in London, arrived at Henley, and it must have been as clear to Susan and Betty as it was to him and to Miss Blandy that the worthy attorney's attitude towards him was radically altered. It was at this time, according to Mary herself, that Cranstoun suggested obtaining from a wise woman in Scotland some white powder " warranted to heal differences between lovers or friends " ; and it was at this time that the lady, with a face of great gravity and concern, informed her maids that Captain Cranstoun had had supernatural warnings of Mr. Blandy's approaching end. He had heard music, footsteps, rappings and other inexplicable, unearthly sounds. Miss Blandy, in conversation with Susan and Betty, expressed the fear that, from what Captain Cranstoun had told her of similar happenings in Scotland, her father would be dead within the year.

It is not difficult to imagine in what excited whispers the eerie tale was retold to Ann Emmett, the charwoman, when next she came to give her regular assistance with the work of the house. Mary Blandy had chosen her audience with skill.

Shortly afterwards Cranstoun went north again, and from Scotland he sent to his *fiancée* some ornaments of Scotch pebble, such as were much in vogue that year, and some white powder with which to clean them. Less than four months later Francis Blandy was dead. The events preceding his death were graphically related by Susan at Mary Blandy's trial. Betty Binfield and Robert Harman also appeared in the witness-box, but their depositions unsupported by their fellow-servant's evidence might not have availed to secure a conviction. Susan's story incidentally gives some vivid glimpses of domestic life in a provincial lawyer's family under George II.

Her usual duties seem to have included valeting her master, sewing on his buttons, preparing his water-gruel and lighting him up to bed. A week before his death she made the gruel in the wonted way and left it standing in the pantry. Miss Blandy remarked that she had gone in there to stir the gruel up, and had eaten some of the oatmeal out of the bottom of the pan. The next evening Susan saw her stirring up her father's gruel before it was taken to him. Shortly after he had drunk it, the maid lighted him up to bed, and before she had herself retired for the night Mr. Blandy was calling to her to bring a basin. He was violently sick for several hours.

Two days later Miss Blandy came into the kitchen and said, " Susan, as your master has taken physic he may want some water-gruel, and as there is some in the house you need not make fresh, as you are ironing." Susan replied, perhaps with characteristic obstinacy, that the gruel was stale, and went and made some more. Then she brought out the pan with the stale gruel and, having tasted it to find if it still had the peculiar taste she had noticed the night before, she looked closer and saw with surprise " a whiteness " in the bottom of the pan. She took it out to the kitchen, and after the cook, Betty Binfield, had commented on the peculiar, flour-like paleness of the oatmeal, she carried it to the door to see it more plainly ; she " saw and felt something white and gritty at the bottom ", and at once suspected poison.

At first sight it would seem as if only a hysterical, ill-balanced type could have conceived such a suspicion, especially as Miss Blandy had always seemed to be the most dutiful and devoted of daughters : but several curious incidents had occurred since the white powder had been sent from Scotland " to clean the Scotch pebbles ", and Susan had forgotten none of them. Though illiterate and no longer young, she was a shrewd and resourceful woman, and, putting these incidents together, she drew conclusions that later proved to be only too well founded.

First of all, Miss Blandy had warned her against taking water-gruel, " for ", said she, " I am told water-gruel hurts me, and it may hurt you ". Then, in June, Susan became ill after drinking the remains of her master's tea, which he always drank from a special ' dish ' of his own : at the time she ascribed her discomforts to having " eat plentifully of beans at dinner ", but she thought again when Ann Emmett also became ill from the same cause. The old woman was rather a favourite with Mary Blandy, who sent her white wine, whey and broth while she lay ill in her own home : but when Ann returned to work she imprudently tasted some of Mr. Blandy's gruel, with even more devastating results. And then Miss Blandy told Betty Binfield to warn Susan Gunnell that if she eat any of the master's gruel, " she might do for herself — a person of *her* age ".

With all these recollections fresh in her mind, Susan locked the pan away and on the following morning bore it round to the house of a certain Mrs. Mounteney, a great friend of the family and Miss Blandy's godmother. The lady immediately sent for Mr. Norton, the apothecary, who removed the white deposit, folded it in a paper, and told her to put it away under lock and key.

Meanwhile Mr. Blandy's brother-in-law, a parson called Stevens, had come to visit him, and into his horrified ears Susan poured her story. He advised her to tell her master ; and it was noticed that the poor old man showed more grief than surprise. It is not necessary here to detail the method he employed to test his daughter, but she soon realized that she was under suspicion. Dashing upstairs, she collected all Cranstoun's letters to her, and all that remained of the fatal white powder : then, descending to the kitchen, she pretended to want to dry the superscription of a letter to her Uncle Stevens, and went close to the fire. Susan and Betty saw her drop some papers quickly into the grate and " stir it all with a stick " : and Betty chose that moment to heap on more coal. Perhaps by accident, but more probably from design, she prevented the total destruction of the papers. As soon as Miss Blandy had quitted the kitchen, Susan called Betty's attention to " a small piece of paper with some writing on it, folded about three inches long ", and Betty drew it out with the tongs. On it was inscribed in Cranstoun's writing, " *The powder to clean the pebbles with* ". Both maids could see that a little of the powder remained in the creases of the paper which, later in the same day, they showed to Mr. Norton. He made the somewhat oracular comment, " Let it be what it will, it should not be there."

A harrowing scene took place in the dying father's bedroom, when, in the presence of Susan Gunnell and the apothecary, he declared that he would forgive his daughter, " if she would but endeavour to bring that villain to justice ". Evading that stipulation, Mary Blandy swore upon her kness that she was innocent — not, indeed, of having mixed with the water-gruel the powder sent from Scotland by Cranstoun, but innocent of attempted murder. The powder, she declared, was sent and administered " with another intent " — *i.e.* to soften the old man's heart towards her lover.

Striving to the last to avert suspicion from " the poor love-sick girl " to Cranstoun, Francis Blandy died on August 14, 1751.

Eighteenth-century methods of scientific detection and analysis were crude and clumsy by modern standards, but the celebrated Dr. Addington needed only a red-hot poker to demonstrate that " the powder to clean the pebbles with " was white arsenic. A post-mortem on Mr. Blandy's body showed that he had died from inflammatory poisoning : and in March 1752 Mary Blandy was tried at the Oxford Assizes for the wilful murder of her father.

Writing about the affair in the previous September, Lord Hardwicke remarked that " it is thought that the Maid and the Charwoman (who I presume are the two material witnesses) cannot long survive the Poison they partook of ". Ann Emmett's fate is uncertain, but Susan Gunnell certainly survived long enough to help to send her mistress to the gallows. There is nothing in her evidence which suggests that she had been weakened either in body or mind by the ordeal she had undergone. Mary Blandy's comment upon Susan's account of the scene by Mr. Blandy's death-bed is interesting : " The mutual sorrow, love and grief that then appeared are truly described by Susan Gunnell ; but, poor soul, in other respects she is much mistaken ".

Cranstoun had already fled to the Continent, whence he sent a threatening letter to Betty Binfield — he probably knew that Susan Gunnell could not read, and so spared her an example of his now notorious penmanship. He died in great agony at Furnes eight months later, leaving many debts, a number of embroidered waistcoats, and a *Confession* in which he maintained that " Miss " had been " perfectly well aware of the character and purpose of the powder ".

Twenty-four years after the trial and execution of Mary Blandy all England was thrilled by another *cause célèbre* in which one of the most important witnesses was an Abigail — or, at least, an ex-Abigail. This was at the impeachment of Elizabeth, *née* Chudleigh, commonly known as the Duchess of Kingston. A great part of the story can be fitted together from the evidence then given by Ann Cradock, formerly in the service of the defendant's aunt, Mrs. Hanmer, at Lainston, in the county of Hampshire.

In the summer of 1744 the already notorious Elizabeth, protégée of Mr. William Pulteney, maid of honour (by his favour) to Augusta, Princess of Wales, and all-but-betrothed of the young Duke of Hamilton, paid a long visit to Mrs. Hanmer at Lainston. Attending Winchester races with her aunt, the fair one met and completely captivated Lieutenant Augustus Hervey, R.N., the second son of John, Lord Hervey, of enigmatic memory, and the charming though slightly *précieuse* Molly Lepell. The handsome young sailor proceeded to woo Miss Chudleigh with all the headlong and triumphant impetuosity of his profession as reflected in ballad and legend. He was not much of a match for a girl who had been setting her cap at a Duke, but it appeared that His Grace, then making the Grand Tour, had been abating something of his ardour and it may be that she was slightly swayed by pique ; if she was not, then she must have felt a *coup de foudre* at least as sudden and as violent as that which smote Augustus. They were married by the light of one candle at eleven o'clock on the night of August 4, 1744, in the presence of only four witnesses of whom one was the maid Ann.

Three months later the bridegroom rejoined his ship, H.M.S. *Cornwall*, at Portsmouth and proceeded to the Jamaica station, while the bride returned to her post, of which she would have forfeited the much-needed emoluments — £400 a year — if the marriage had been made public. Ann seems to have accompanied her to London and was certainly several times in her company during the ensuing year or so : she ultimately married Augustus Hervey's man-servant.

More than twenty years later the parties to the ill-assorted and long-unreal union were anxious to break its bonds and form other lawful connections. Augustus had fallen in love with a surgeon's daughter at Bath and Elizabeth's ' protector ', the Duke of Kingston, was anxious to make an honest Duchess of her. So the lady brought " a suit of jactitation of marriage " before the Consistory Court, and, as Horace Walpole put it, " appeared at Doctors' Commons and swore by the Virgin Mary and Diana that she was never married to Mr. Hervey ". It was, of course, a grotesque miscarriage of justice, the result of collusion between all the parties : and the sequel came in 1776, after the Duke's death, when his heirs, disputing the validity of the marriage, obtained a reversal of the findings of the Consistory Court. Then, to the no small delight of an excited public, Elizabeth was impeached before the House of Peers on a charge of bigamy. Their lordships declared her marriage with the late Duke of Kingston illegal — which was equivalent to a verdict of ' Guilty ' ; but she pleaded her privilege as a peeress — and a peeress she had certainly been ever since her only lawful husband, Augustus Hervey, Vice-Admiral of the Blue and a Lord of the Admiralty, had succeeded his elder brother as third Earl of Bristol in the previous year. She got off with no heavier penalty than " paying the fees ".

If she be indeed the original of Thackeray's Beatrix we must picture her at her trial as she appears, not in *Esmond*, but in *The Virginians*, her beauty gone with her youth, but her vivacity, her arrogance and her effrontery dimmed hardly at all. To confront her came a figure from her distant past — the maid Ann, called as a witness to prove her marriage with Hervey and by her evidence unfolding one by one the romantic, the pitiful and the homely chapters in the story.

Ann described how she had been present at the clandestine nocturnal ceremony at Lainston : how she had abetted the lovers by keeping the other servants out of their way ; and how on the morning of the bridegroom's departure to join his ship she called him, as instructed, at five o'clock — " and entering the chamber found them both fast asleep. They were ", she added, " very sorry to take leave." Asked what was her reason for thinking that the wedding took place in August, she replied without hesitation, " My reason is that it was in the time of Maunbill Fair, and also that there were greengages ripe, which the lady and gentleman were both very fond of ".

In November 1747 the only child of the marriage was baptized in Old Chelsea Church. This is what Ann Cradock had to say upon the subject. The " lady herself " — *i.e.* Elizabeth — told her she had had a child, " a boy, and like Mr. Hervey ", and she promised to take her to see it one day, " in one of the Princess of Wales's coaches " : but the promise was never fulfilled. " When ", said Ann, " I expected to go and see it the lady came in great grief and told me it was dead." Asked whether she had ever heard where the child was buried, she answered, " I did hear that it was buried at Chelsea." Asked, " Who told you so ? " she replied, " The lady at the bar told me so herself when I was airing in the coach with her that way ". From all these things it is clear that Mrs. Augustus Hervey had made a sort of humble friend and confidante of this woman upon whose discretion so much must depend and from whom — as events proved — so much was to be feared. Even if Ann never saw the Hervey baby, she had, at least, the satisfaction of ' airing ' in the Princess of Wales's coach, with the royal blazons upon the hammer-cloth and the harness.

Ann Cradock does not seem ever to have been attached to the lovely, wayward, wanton creature's household ; and an anecdote related by Horace Walpole in 1750 showed that, even when the Duke of Kingston was paying the piper, that household was on a comparatively modest scale. In June of that year " the virgin-mistress " gave a gorgeous entertainment in honour of the birthday of the Prince of Wales, so soon to be King George III. She desired, says Walpole, that gambling guests should go up into the garrets, and then added, " Nay, they are not garrets — it is only the roof of the house hollowed for upper servants — but I have no upper servants ".

A leap of twenty-one years through time and space, from the House of Lords in 1776 to the borough of Bury in 1797, will bring us to another Abigail in the witness-box — herself on trial. Margaret Catchpole was the youngest of six children born to a labourer employed by a celebrated breeder of Suffolk Punches. She entered the service of Mr. John Cobbold, an Ipswich brewer, one of whose children she saved from drowning. This action was probably the main though, it seems, not the only reason why she was valued by her employers and befriended by them at a critical point in her career. Unfortunately she fell in love with a young man called Laud, the son of a boatman at Landguard Fort, ostensibly himself a boatman but actually engaged in contraband trade. In vain her parents and her mistress strove to dissuade her : she was completely infatuated ; and in order to keep tryst with him in London she donned a suit of sailor's clothes — doubtless of his providing — and set off on a horse stolen from Mr. Cobbold's stable.

As soon as the theft was discovered, hastily printed handbills (the ink scarcely dry) describing the girl and her mount were dispatched by every coach leaving Ipswich. Two men sent in pursuit along the London road having been falsely directed were about to turn off in the direction of Maldon when they chanced to meet a person who had seen Margaret riding towards London. She was caught and apprehended in the act of selling the horse to a dealer.

Brought to trial at Bury, she was sentenced to death — as she might then have been for a far slighter felony — but Cobbold interceded so vigorously on her behalf that the sentence was commuted to a term of seven years' imprisonment. Three years of that term she served in Ipswich jail, and then, with the aid of Laud, she broke out of prison " in a very bold manner ", and let herself safely down from the spikes along the top of the wall. Her plan was apparently to go to sea on board her lover's boat, for she was captured on the seashore in the very act of embarking. A scuffle followed, in which Laud was killed, and for a second time Margaret Catchpole appeared at Bury Assizes, and the same judge, Chief Baron Macdonald, sentenced her for a second time to death.

To anyone familiar with the savage severity of the penal code of the period it must seem astonishing that the death sentence should have been commuted once again — this time to transportation for life. She set sail for Botany Bay in May 1801, and, after a seven months' voyage which must have given her ample opportunity for meditation, landed in Australia. There by her exemplary conduct she obtained a considerable remission of her sentence, and there she ultimately married a prosperous settler — indeed, it is the story of Moll Flanders in real life. Margaret did not lose touch with her friends at home in Suffolk, and she gratified them with gifts of curiosities and rarities from the Antipodes. The skin of a lyre-bird sent by her is still to be seen in the Ipswich Museum.

By the middle of the eighteenth century there was in existence a class of sharp practitioner whose activities (if disclosed) were liable to bring them within the reach of the law, though not before they had involved many unfortunate maidservants in ruin. At Drury Lane Theatre in 1761 was produced a farce by Joseph Reed entitled *The Registry Office*. It is a crude and not over-decorous production, but it undoubtedly represented through the medium of caricature a great and increasing evil in social life. When the first act opens we find that Mr. Gulwell, the proprietor of the office, has inserted a most alluring advertisement in the press with the result that " a crowd of deluded females " has flocked round to answer it. It is not only in domestic situations that the rogue traffics. He deals in curacies, military commissions, secretaryships, scholastic posts : he acts now as a matrimonial and now as a theatrical agent. At one time he attempts to trepan a needy Irishman into slavery " at the Plantations ", at another he is obviously on the look-out for recruits to fill the ranks of the *filles de joie*. Only one of the persons whom he interviews is a maidservant, Margery Moorpout from Yorkshire, nineteen years of age, who had been engaged at the hiring-market with a " God's penny " when she was not yet nine. She runs over a list of her accomplishments in broadest Yorkshire dialect ; she can milk, churn, bake, brew, knit, spin and sew. Mr. Gulwell thinks she will do very well for a housekeeper's place with " a substantial farmer in Buckinghamshire " and bids her call again next week. " You must give me half-a-crown, my pretty maid," says he. " Our fee is only a shilling for a common place, but for a house-keeper's we always have half-a-crown."

Margery counts out the money in the form of " twea shilling, and yan, tea, three, four, five, saxpennorth o' brass ", and departs well satisfied, leaving the audience convinced that the " substantial farmer " is a myth or legend, and that a grim fate awaits the " pretty maid " unless she can extricate herself in time from the claws of Gulwell.

These unhappy dupes, all of whom paid a shilling or half a crown for situations (or the prospect of situations) that did not even exist, were much to be pitied, but they were at least free. The " God's penny " received by Margery at the hiring-fair confirmed her engagement but did not prevent her from seeking other employment ten years later. Very different was the fate of the coloured girls who were bought and sold in London as regularly, though not perhaps as frequently, as they were in the East and West Indies and in America. Here is an extract from the *Publick Advertiser*, 1769 :

> To be sold, a Black Girl, the property of J. B. — eleven years of age, who is extremely handy, works at her needle tolerably, and speaks French perfectly well : is of excellent temper and willing disposition. Inquire of W. Owen, at the Angel Inn, behind St. Clement Danes Church in the Strand.

All the coloured (or half-coloured) Abigails in eighteenth-century England were not slaves. Roubiliac the sculptor had a negress in his employment, who died of " de smallpoc " : " poor Mary," he then said, " she vos my hos-maid for five-six-year-more ". Another — and less amiable — sculptor, Joseph Nolle-kens, had a maid called Elizabeth Rosina Clements, who, " from her complexion being of a chestnut-brown colour somewhat tinctured with olive ", acquired the nicknames of " Black Bet " and " Bronze ". She possessed, we are told, " a considerable share of drollery ", and when she and her master were both well stricken in years it used to amuse him to see her dancing the cat, " Jenny Dawdle ", round the studio. " Bronze " was probably a half-caste, but the total absence of soap from the Nollekens' kitchen may have contributed to the duskiness of her colouring.

Two years before the announcement in the *Publick Advertiser* appeared there died at Lichfield an Abigail whose name will be remembered and whose memory will be honoured as long as there are people living who read Boswell and love Johnson.

Catherine Chambers, then fifteen years of age, entered the service of Mrs. Michael Johnson "about 1724", when the elder son of the house, the short-sighted and ungainly Samuel, was the same age as herself : she was not, therefore, the same maid who used to conduct him home from Dame Oliver's little school. With the Johnsons Catherine remained, a faithful and valued dependent. Unlike the majority of her class, she was not illiterate : she was able to attest the indenture of mortgage of the Johnsons' house in Market Street, Lichfield, in 1739 : and from the circumstance that she took charge of the bookselling business when Mrs. Johnson died twenty years later it may be conjectured that serving in the shop had been among her duties. Writing to his stepdaughter, Lucy Porter, about that time Johnson declared that he would ever remember " Kitty's " services to his mother, and that he would like to hear from her as well as from Lucy. He suggested that the two should set up house together, as he was loth to put Catherine " out of a house where she had lived so long and with so much virtue ". Her health was already failing, and though his own circumstances were not easy at the time, Johnson was anxious to help her " to pass the remaining part of her life in quietness and competence ". Eight years of invalidism remained for her ; and then, in August 1767, he noted in his *Prayers and Meditations* : " I am now about to receive with my old friend, Kitty Chambers, the Sacrament preparatory to her death " : and later, " I have communicated with Kitty, and kissed her. I was for some time distracted, but at last more composed, I commended my friends and Kitty. Lucy and I were much affected. Kitty is, I think, going to Heaven." Two months later occurred that touching farewell scene related in a letter to Boswell :

Yesterday, October 17, at about ten in the morning, I took my leave for ever of my dear old friend, Catherine Chambers, who came to live with my mother in 1724, and has been but little parted from us since. She buried my father, my brother and my mother. She is now fifty-eight years old.

I desired all to withdraw, then told her we were to part for ever : that as Christians we should part with prayer ; and that I would, if she was willing, say a short prayer beside her. She expressed great desire to hear me ; and held up her poor hands as she lay in bed, with great fervour, while I prayed, kneeling by her —

The words of the prayer follow, and then, with a simplicity that was one of his most endearing though not his most frequently manifested characteristics, Johnson relates the sequel, using the briefest terms, almost all monosyllables, and eschewing the surge and thunder of his wonted style altogether :

> I then kissed her. She told me that to part was the greatest pain she had ever felt, and that she hoped we should meet again in a better place. I expressed, with swelled eyes and great emotion of tenderness, the same hopes. We kissed and parted. I humbly hope to meet again and to part no more.

The various segments of the Johnson circle were not infrequently united at Sir Joshua Reynolds' high, bleak house in Leicester Square, and the Doctor may thus serve as a point of contact with a certain other Abigail of that precise period — 1771, to be exact — who, though her name has not been preserved, fills a modest niche in the history of painting in England. The story may be told in the words of James Northcote, R.A., at that time living as a pupil with Sir Joshua.

> I had, for the sake of practice, painted the portrait of one of the female servants ; but my performance had no other merit than that of being a strong likeness. Sir Joshua had a large macaw, which he often introduced into his pictures, and was always kept in the dining-parlour, where he became a nuisance to this same housemaid, whose department it was to clean the room after him : of course they were not upon very good terms with each other.
>
> The portrait, when finished, was brought into the parlour one day after dinner, to be shown to the family, that they might judge of the progress I had made. It was placed against a chair while the macaw was in a distant part of the room, so that he did not immediately perceive the picture as he walked about on the floor : but when he turned round and perceived the features of his enemy, he quickly spread his wings, and in a great fury ran to it, and stretched himself up to bite at the face. Finding, however, that it did not move, he then bit at the hand, but perceiving it to remain inanimate, he proceeded to examine the picture behind, and then, as if he had satisfied his curiosity, left it and walked again to a distant part of the room ; but whenever he turned about and again saw the picture, he would, with the same action of rage, repeatedly attack it.
>
> The experiment was afterwards repeated on various occasions in the presence of Edmund Burke, Dr. Johnson, Dr. Goldsmith, and

most of Sir Joshua's friends, and never failed of success : and what made it still more remarkable was that when the bird was tried with any other portrait, he took no notice of it whatever.

Some years earlier Hogarth had painted the heads of his whole household, men and women, on a single canvas. The women wear becoming caps, with frills and ribbons, but their faces are so closely similar, so slightly differentiated, that at first sight it seems as if they must all have belonged to one family. They share, of course, the typical Hogarth face, with the close-set eyes and the wide, full mouth — the face that appears under the turban of Lord George Graham and upon the artist's own shoulders in his self-portrait. Just *how* decorative an eighteenth-century Abigail could be, with her becoming high-poised headgear, her dainty apron and her long-handled " whisk ", may be imagined with the aid of Gainsborough's unfinished painting of " Mrs. Graham as a Housemaid ".

In the same year that Sir Joshua's macaw was diverting his distinguished friends by its domestic feud, a young woman entered the service of Lady Mary Greathead at Guy's Cliffe, Warwick, whose arrival must have caused intense astonishment and some raising of eyebrows both in the housekeeper's room and the servants' hall. " What ", one imagines the butler saying, " what can her ladyship be about, to take into the house the child of a strolling player — a chit that had sold packets of tooth-powder to the public in the playhouse where her family were performing ! Heard you ever the like ? "

But Lady Mary was a great enough lady to be a law unto herself. *Née* Lady Mary Bertie, daughter of Peregrine, second Duke of Ancaster, she had been a widow for five years, and had an eleven-year-old son who, apparently, shared her love for poetry and play-acting, and who, in course of time, himself wrote a blank-verse tragedy — but of that more anon. The strolling player's daughter whom she engaged as a sort of personal maid or maid-companion in 1771, was a dark-eyed, handsome girl of sixteen, Sarah Kemble by name. Though she was useful in a variety of ways to her parents, had played Ariel in *The Tempest*, Princess Elizabeth in Havard's *Charles I* and Rosetta in *Love in a Village* and could be trusted to make ' noises off ' at the right moment, they dispensed with her assistance and hustled her into domestic service in the hope that she might thus be induced to forget Henry Siddons, an impecunious and not particularly promising member of the Kemble troupe, who had dared to win the heart of Sarah.

Many years later Bertie Greathead told Miss Williams Wynn that he " had been in the habit of hearing Mrs. Siddons read *Macbeth* even from the period of her being his mother's maid " ; and Lady Mary observed to " Conversation " Sharp that she used always to feel an irresistible inclination to rise from her chair when her queenly-looking dependent entered the room.

Sarah's salary was £10 a year — a very high rate of pay for an untrained girl of sixteen whose previous experience had not been such as to prepare her to wait upon a lady of quality. None the less, she remained for two years at Guy's Cliffe, with occasional absences in attendance upon Lady Mary. On one occasion she attended her ladyship to the Duke of Ancaster's seat in Lincolnshire and is said to have been " fond of spouting in the servants' hall ". Indeed, it seems highly probable that she ingratiated herself with her colleagues by treating them to recitations from her extensive repertoire. If " Shikspur " was too much for them, she could always oblige with selections from *The Mourning Bride*, *Venice Preserved*, *The Distrest Mother* or *Love in a Village*.

From time to time a visitor for Miss Kemble would appear at the servants' door and be received in the servants' quarters, no doubt regarded there with that mixture of wonder and disparagement reserved by that class for the play-actor. It was Henry Siddons, as impecunious, as unremarkable, as faithful as ever. In November 1773 Sarah took leave of her noble patroness and of the storeyed bowers of Guy's Cliffe, and went to Coventry to be married to her Henry. Many years later the Kemble and Siddons families revisited as honoured guests what Mrs. Siddons called " that truly charming and to me uncommonly interesting place ", where the Greatheads received them with a warmth most refreshingly undiminished by any class-conscious qualms.

In 1788 came the opportunity to make some practical return for all this gracious hospitality. Bertie Greathead, as befitted one whose youthful ears had been filled with the sonorous accents of Sarah Kemble, wrote a blank-verse drama and aspired to see it ' put on '. Thanks to the good-will of the Kemble family he had his wish. *The Regent*, with John Philip Kemble in the title rôle and Mrs. Siddons as the heroine, was produced — and ran for eight nights. On the second night the " buzz of inattention " from boxes, pit and galleries so upset the actress that she threw up her part — but she spared the author's feelings by pleading indisposition. The Kembles had done their best ; and there is no record of any resentment on the part of the Greatheads that they could not do more.

About five years after Lady Mary Greathead's " queenly dependent " had married Henry Siddons, a young girl of extra-ordinary beauty was employed as a nursemaid in the family of a certain Mrs. Thomas at Hawarden. Whether she ' gave satis-faction ' is not known : but there is little in the later life of this auburn-haired dazzler to suggest that she had any strong natural affection for young children. Her own, unless they were of some use to pin down a lover, seem to have won only a small and shallow patch of her capacious heart. Presently she gravitated to London, and entered the service of Dr. Budd, one of the physicians at St. Bartholomew's Hospital and a medico of some note. The medical gentlemen of that period felt it to be in accordance with their dignity that they should live in a handsome style. There was not likely to be any bleakness at Dr. Budd's, or any dearth of comforts above stairs and below. He occupied one of a row of large, somewhat pretentious houses at the northern end of Blackfriars Bridge. The bridge had at first been known as the Pitt Bridge, in honour of the Great Commoner, and the houses continued to be known as Chatham Place when he was a commoner no longer. It was not a healthy situation, for the rise and fall of the pollution-laden river filled and emptied the cellars ; but Emma Hart (or Lyon) opposed to this miasma a far more robust constitution than did another auburn-haired " stunner ", Lizzie Siddal Rossetti by name, in the same environment about ninety years later. Emma continued to bloom during the eighteen months that she spent on Thames-side ; and there must have been some lively interludes in Dr. Budd's kitchen when the day's work was done, for the beautiful wench had already in her the histrionic streak that was later to inspire her " attitudes " and her fellow-servant was a stage-struck young woman, Jane Powell, who in after years won a measure of success as an actress. It is recorded of Emma that when, in her palmy days (as Sir William Hamilton's wife and Nelson's mistress), she visited the theatre, she always made a point of advancing to the front of the box and applauding with vigour if her former fellow-servant was in the caste.

The Abigails of eighteenth-century literature, prose and verse, early and late, were very apt to find themselves in Bath. One of the best known of those who *did* is Lucy, Lydia Languish's maid, in *The Rivals*. She is a pert young woman, with a great deal to say for herself : she indulges in objurgations such as " Burn it ! " and " O Gemini ! " Lydia addresses her as ' child ', or as ' my dear Lucy ', and in the famous first scene between them, when Lucy returns from the circulating library with a dozen novels, it is clear that they understand each other perfectly. One fragment of the dialogue sounds like a far-off echo of the exchange between Lady Wishfort and Peg in *The Way of the World* :

Lydia : Heigh ho ! What are those books by the glass ?
Lucy : The great one is only *The Whole Duty of Man*, where I press a few blonds, ma'am.
Lydia : Very well. Give me the *sal volatile*.
Lucy : Is it in a blue cover, ma'am ?
Lydia : My smelling-bottle, you simpleton.
Lucy : Oh, the drops ! — here, ma'am.

In another scene, Mrs. Malaprop, who addresses her as ' girl ', exhorts her (quite unnecessarily) not to let her simplicity be imposed upon, and entrusts her with a *billet-doux* for Sir Lucius O'Trigger. After the lady has withdrawn, the damsel's manner alters, and she expounds her own philosophy with candour. " Let girls in my station," says she, " be as fond as they please of appearing expert and knowing in their trusts : commend me to a mask of silliness and a pair of sharp eyes for my own interest under it ! " She counts up the gifts and the guineas that she has acquired in the most nefarious manner — " for Mrs. Malaprop — for betraying the young people to her — when I found matters were likely to be discovered — two guineas and a black paduasoy ", or " from Mr. Acres for carrying divers letters — which I never delivered — two guineas and a pair of buckles ". No doubt it was these emoluments, ill-gotten as they were, together with the " hats, ruffles, caps, etc., etc., numberless " bestowed on her by Miss Languish, which enabled " that little traitress Lucy " to deck herself out so smartly that Sir Anthony Absolute's coachman, seeing her afar off in conversation with his master's son, asks Fag, the man-servant, whether she is " the lady " — *i.e.* the lady with whom young Absolute was in love.

How human and approachable great — and even royal — ladies might be towards their maids is well illustrated by two examples : one traditional in the family of Lady Sarah Napier (*née* Lennox) and one recorded by Lady Louisa Stuart.

In her extreme old age the still kind and charming Lady Sarah lived alone, with a household sternly ruled by a certain Mrs. Jones, in the corner house of Cadogan Place. One day her lady-ship went up to her bedroom and found a young housemaid in front of her looking-glass using her hairbrushes. Not surprisingly the girl was transfixed with horror — but it soon became apparent that what she dreaded was the wrath of Mrs. Jones, and that for her there were no terrors in the probable annoyance of her more tolerant mistress. Lady Sarah's descendants cherish this anecdote as evidence of her kindness of heart ; but that it should have been related — obviously by herself — may also be taken as evidence of her sense of the ridiculous.

When Charlotte Augusta Matilda, Princess Royal of Great Britain, was married in 1797 to the Hereditary Prince of Württem-berg, one of the clauses in the marriage treaty stipulated that she must be allowed to take three English female servants " from hence ". In her last years " it was her custom on Sundays to make her English maid read her an English sermon " : and on the day before her death, in October 1828, she said, at the con-clusion of the pious exercise, " There, my dear, you have done, and I thank you — you will never read me another."

All " the dear Sisterhood ", as their brother, George IV, called them, were well served by trusty Abigails. Living mewed up in almost cloistral seclusion, under the dragon-glare of Queen Charlotte's eye, they were happy to have the assistance of humble adroitness and discretion. Letters not intended for mamma to see could be sent " under cover " — Princess Elizabeth's to her maid Brawn, Princess Amelia's to one or other of the two Gaskoins, aunt and niece.

Brawn accompanied her particular Princess to Germany when the middle-aged but still blooming " Eliza " was married to the Landgrave of Hesse-Homburg, and she remained with her till her death twenty-two years later. By the Landgravine's Will all her gowns and shawls and an annuity of £100 went to her " excellent and valued Brawn ".

Peculiar pathos attaches to the memory of one of the two Gaskoins — the one who survived Princess Amelia by only three months. When Mary Anne Gaskoin died in February 1811, the old King was hopelessly mad and the Regency had begun. But somehow the news of her death broke through the shadows that encompassed him, and in a brief interval of lucidity he gave orders that she was to be buried in St. George's Chapel, " as near as might be to her royal mistress ", and himself dictated the inscription for the mural tablet in the cloisters " placed there by King George III in Testimony of his grateful Sense of the faithful Service and Attachment of an amiable Young Woman to his beloved Daughter ".

CHAPTER VIII

Regency Spectacle

TO many people interested in English social history the
Regency always seems to fill a wider span than its exact
nine years. George III's mind, steadily darkening as the age of
trousers and top-hats dawned, was in eclipse at least eight years
before his eldest son became Regent in 1811 ; and the personality
of that son was already so clearly projected upon the general
vision that it may almost be said that the new reign began
eighteen years before the old reign ended. The very name of
' George IV ' sounds like a pseudonym for the Prince Regent,
and the King himself remained a sort of ageing *avatar* of the
Prince. These things being so, the first Regency Abigail makes
her curtsy in 1801 and the last in 1823.

In October of the former year the following letter appeared in
The Lady's Monthly Museum or Polite Repository :

To the Editor

SIR,

Can any of your correspondents inform me what is become of
the race of plain-dressing, docile and obedient beings who formerly
served as cooks, or housemaids, or maids of all work, in a family ?
I have lately lost an old servant who lived with me nearly twenty-
five years ; and, though I never expected to meet with such another, I at least thought I might meet with something like her.
During a late excursion to Brighton I enquired, as I passed through
the Weald of Sussex ; when to my astonishment, I found nothing
but *young ladies, delicately arrayed in white*, with their heads *à la
Brutus*, who declared they were all anxious for places, and wished to
go out to service.

One of them informed me that she had lately left her place, and
could have an excellent character, her only reason for quitting being
that her mistress did not suffer her to drink tea twice a day, and
could not abide her wearing feathers in her hat on Sunday.

Mr. Sheridan informs us in *The Critic* that when Queens or

heroines go mad they usually do so in white satin ; I suppose therefore that village maidens when they go mad content themselves with
white calico.

Yours,

" PREVENTER "

With tea costing ten shillings a pound — or more — the
lady's reluctance is comprehensible ; but it was surely short-
sighted on the part of " Preventer " to object to the white gowns
which, if consistently white, were evidence of cleanliness and of
a perfectly proper pride in the damsel's own appearance. The
remark about the feathers in the Sunday hat recalls Rebecca, the
Prices' little maid in *Mansfield Park*, who " discomposed " Mrs.
Price by walking forth on the Sabbath " with a flower in her hat ".

It is a chaotic but not entirely cheerless picture which Miss
Austen gives us of the household of the retired officer of Marines
at Portsmouth, in a small, untidy, shabby house crowded with
boisterous children — " the home of noise, disorder and im-
propriety ", where the mistress spent her days " in a sort of slow
bustle ". Whether " helping, or reprimanding, or indulging "
her maids she was " without any power of gaining their respect ".
She lamented the " shocking character of the Portsmouth
servants " ; " it is quite a miracle ", she said, " if one keeps them
more than half-a-year : I have no hope of ever getting settled ".
Yet Rebecca's life was not wholly bleak. She enjoyed the
assistance and the company of an underling called Sally, younger
and even more feckless than herself ; and she participated un-
disguisedly in the excitement and interest aroused in every
member of the Price family by the coming and going of the
ships in the harbour.

Maidservants usually move decorously and indistinctly in the
background of Miss Austen's novels, but in *Persuasion* young
Mrs. Musgrove utters to this effect concerning the maids of her
mother-in-law :

> " Mrs. Musgrove thinks all her servants so steady that it would
> be high treason to call it in question : but I am sure without
> exaggeration that her upper-housemaid and laundry-maid, instead
> of being in their business, are gadding about the village all day
> long. I meet them wherever I go."

REBECCA WITH A FLOWER IN HER SUNDAY HAT

Illustration by Hugh Thomson to Jane Austen's *Mansfield Park*

Worse still, they were always tempting her nursemaid, Jemima, " the trustiest and steadiest creature in the world ", to take a walk with them. On the side of Mrs. Musgrove the elder there were grave doubts as to the steadiness of Jemima. " She is always on the gad," remarked that lady disapprovingly. " And from my knowledge I can declare she is such a fine-dressing lady that she is enough to ruin any servants she comes near."

At Longbourn the household seems to have consisted of a butler, a housekeeper, two housemaids and a cook. Mrs. Bennet did not attempt to make any of her five daughters domesticated : let Charlotte Lucas occupy herself with mince-pies, but, " for my part, Mr. Bingley," quoth she, " *I* always keep servants that can do their own work ". Mrs. Hill the housekeeper took an obvious interest in the fortunes of the family, and was quick to draw favourable conclusions from the arrival of an express letter to Mr. Bennet from Mr. Gardiner at the beginning of chapter xlix : she was prompt, too, with her congratulations when her mistress exclaimed, " Oh ! here comes Hill ! My dear Hill, have you heard the good news ? Miss Lydia is going to be married ; and you shall all have a bowl of punch to make merry at her wedding." And how exquisitely characteristic it was that Lydia should go after dinner " to show her ring and boast of being married to Mrs. Hill and the two housemaids ", all of whom must have been well aware of the antecedent scandal.

To the cynical observer it might seem that a pretty girl of the lower classes was entering a zone of some peril when she entered domestic service, particularly in a household where the masculine element was of the rakish sort : not so Miss Austen's admired Mr. Crabbe, whose village belle, Phoebe, " correct in thought ",

> judged a servant's place
> Preserved a rustic beauty from disgrace.

In *The Maid's Story* (*Tales of the Hall*) we make the acquaint-ance of Biddy, one of the most lifelike of Regency Abigails. The narratrix has been sent

> With Grandmamma to keep perpetual Lent.

She describes how

> We had a little maid some four feet high
> Who was employed our household stores to buy ;
> For she would weary every man in trade,
> And tease t'assent where she could not persuade.
> Methinks I see her with her pigmy light
> Precede her mistress on a moonless night,
> From the small lantern throwing through the street
> The dimmed effulgence at her lady's feet.

Grandmamma departed this life with some abruptness, and the sale of her effects barely paid " the bills, the burial and the rent " : after which the kind-hearted Biddy took the forsaken young lady to her own " hovel ", assuring her that she would " find the poor had some enjoyments " : and the story proceeds :

> When dinner came, upon the table bare
> Were placed the humblest forms of earthenware,
> With one blue dish on which our food was placed,
> For appetite provided, not for taste.
> I looked disgusted, having lately seen
> All so minutely delicate and clean ;
> Yet as I sate I found, to my surprise,
> A vulgar kind of inclination rise,
> And near my humble friend, and nearer drew,
> Tried the strange food, and was partaker too.

One hazards a guess that the " strange food " was similar to that depicted by Stephen Duck, dumpling with boiled bacon. Good-natured Biddy tries to amuse her guest with conversation, prattling of her plans, and her neighbours, and mingling

> . . . stories, merry jests and warning dreams
> With tales of mirth and murder,

and thereby forging another link in the chain connecting her with the wonder-loving damsels of earlier days.

There could hardly be a sharper contrast between any two contemporary poets than that between Crabbe and Byron, or between any two Abigails than that between the youthful, diminutive Biddy and Mrs. Mule, the " fire-lighter " in Byron's Bennet Street lodgings who followed him when he moved to the Albany and later formed part of the unquiet household in Piccadilly. " I always ", wrote his lordship in February 1814,

" feel in better humour with myself and everything else if there is a woman within ken. Even Mrs. Mule, my fire-lighter, the most ancient and withered of her kind, and (except to myself) not the best-tempered, always makes me laugh — no difficult task when I am i' the vein."

Tom Moore, in a note to this letter, says : " This ancient housemaid, of whose gaunt and witchlike appearance it would be impossible to convey any idea but by the pencil, furnished one among the numerous instances of Lord Byron's proneness to attach himself to anything, however homely, that had once enlisted his good nature on its behalf ". For a whole season she was " the perpetual scarecrow " of his callers in Bennet Street : when, in the ensuing year, he took chambers in the Albany, they fondly thought that they would " get rid of this phantom " : but no ; there she was again ; he had brought her with him. A year later the disastrous marriage had taken place, and Lord and Lady Byron were living " with a regular establishment of servants " in " Old Q's " house, 13 Piccadilly Terrace : it was then concluded that " the witch had vanished ". One of Byron's old friends — apparently the narrator in person,

> happening to call one day when all the male part of the establishment were abroad, saw, to his dismay, the door opened by the same grim personage, improved considerably in point of habiliments since he last saw her and keeping pace with the increased scale of her master's household, as a new peruke and other symptoms of promotion testified. When asked how he came to carry this old woman about with him from place to place Lord Byron's only answer was, " The poor old devil was so kind to me ".

We get a parting glimpse of her in one of those incongruously cheerful letters written by " Pippin " to her husband about that time :

> You would laugh to see, and still more to hear, the effects of your absence in the house. Tearing up carpets, deluging stair-cases, knocking, rubbing, brushing ! By all these I was early awakened, for Mrs. Mew (*sic*) seems convinced that my ears and other seven senses have departed with you. She no longer flies like a sylph on tiptoe but like a troop of dragoons at full gallop.

Evidently Byron's insomnia made a stronger appeal to the

" old devil's " sympathies than did Lady Byron's " interesting condition ".

If a new series of *Dialogues of the Dead* were written, how revealing (and how acrimonious) might an imaginary colloquy be between Mrs. Mule and Mrs. Clermont — Byron's humble friend and Byron's implacable enemy.

In that waspish piece of invective entitled *A Sketch* Byron thus describes the spectacular rise of this erewhile obscure hand-maiden of the Milbankes at Seaham :

> Born in the garret, in the kitchen bred,
> Promoted thence to deck her mistress' head ;
> Next — for some gracious service unexpressed,
> And from its wages only to be guessed —
> Raised from the toilette to the table where
> Her wondering betters wait behind her chair.
> With eye unmoved and forehead unabashed
> She dines from off the plate she lately washed.

There is an element of Byronic exaggeration here ; but it is certain that this woman acquired a strange ascendancy over Lady Milbanke and a less strange but even more disastrous ascendancy over the youthful Annabella at an early stage in their threefold relationship, when she was first the child's nurse, and then —

> Who could, ye gods, her next employment guess ?
> Only an infant's earliest governess !

It may not be true that " she herself, by teaching, learned to spell " ; but it was a peculiar choice even for what would now be called a ' nursery governess '. Her inadequate tuition was soon outgrown, but she remained in attendance upon Miss Milbanke — with whom she had at least one taste in common ; an open and rather unpleasing zest for the delights of the table. It will be remembered that Byron hated to see a woman eating ; and it has been suggested that Annabella's passion for " fleecy mutton chops " was one of the physical traits which he came to find repugnant in her. She was certainly not admonished on this point by her earliest preceptress, whom we find writing eagerly from London to Seaham requesting that portions of goose-pie should be sent south for her enjoyment.

Clermont was fond of admonishing — a fussy, possessive,

officious woman. She was probably the " confidential female attendant " who, according to Moore, pronounced it to be a bad omen that, when the newly-wedded couple were about to depart, the bridegroom should have said, " Miss Milbanke, are you ready ? " She had conducted the bride from her bedroom to the bleak drawing-room where the ceremony was performed ; and, when the hollow toasts and felicitations were over, and the imposing wedding-cake had been cut, it was she who reminded her that she must change hastily into her dove-grey travelling pelisse, for the early dusk of January would deepen into darkness by four o'clock.

In the previous November Annabella's personal maid had to be dismissed, having " erred ". " It is ", wrote Byron to his *fiancée*, " a sad affair in a well-regulated family,[1] but I am glad it did not occur in *ours* — yours and mine that is to be. I would recommend the next to be much in years and frightful as possible." His statement to Medwin that there was a lady's-maid in the carriage with himself and Lady Byron on that nuptial journey was contradicted both by her ladyship and by John Cam Hobhouse, the best man : but it would appear that the maid was sitting outside in the rumble until the coach reached Durham, and at that halt she was invited by her mistress to come inside and occupy the back seat, to shelter herself from the falling snow.

The fine old Cromwellian house at Halnaby where they spent their chequered honeymoon was in the care of a former Milbanke Abigail now married to the resident butler. The moodiness of the fury-ridden bridegroom threw the bride very much upon Mrs. Minns for companionship and sympathy, and the good woman was so much shocked and alarmed by Byron's behaviour that she implored Lady Byron to write to Sir Ralph Milbanke, but this the poor, perplexed, pig-headed young creature would not consent to do. Instead she extorted from Mrs. Minns a solemn promise not to say a word upon the subject.

All this time Clermont was lurking in the background, a swarthy, sinister figure, not to be acquitted — even if Byron's *Sketch* be a wild travesty — of " deepening scandal's tints ".

---

[1] For interesting sidelights on Byron's " housemaid harem " at Newstead in 1811–12 see *To Lord Byron*, by George Paston and Peter Quennell.

Heaven knows that these tints were soon lurid enough to require little deepening.

When the Byrons settled in Piccadilly and the saddest, maddest and worst chapter of his relations with his now-pregnant wife began, Mrs. Clermont was at hand — not in the house, but near enough to take some care of her former charge. Oddly enough, it was at Byron's suggestion that she was installed under his roof before Ada was born on December 10, 1815, " amid the flinging about of furniture and soda-water-bottles " by her father " in the room immediately below ".

Later, when Lady Byron had fled to her parents' protection and was installed at Kirby Mallory, she corresponded confidentially with Clermont regarding Lady Milbanke's probable course of action against Byron. " She will ", wrote Annabella, " break my heart if she takes up the thing in *bitterness* against him." But it is hard to see how the adoring mother could be anything but bitter : and when Clermont went with her to join the fugitives one feels certain that the " hag of hatred " gave full vent to her undoubted talent for making mischief — mingling, in Byron's words, " a thread of candour with a web of wiles ".

His capacity for self-deception was so remarkable that one hesitates to attempt to determine how far *A Sketch* was inspired by honest anger, and by a sincere belief that this " Hecate of domestic hell " had contributed to the break-up of his marriage. No woman could have deserved all — and few women have deserved any — of the loathly epithets he heaped upon Clermont in what Wordsworth austerely summed up as " the Billingsgate of Bedlam " ; and no one who entertains a vestige of half-reluctant affection for him could fail to regret the streak of caddishness which prompted Byron to have a number of copies of *A Sketch* printed by Murray for ' private ' circulation — when well the poet knew that so scandalous a document was unlikely to remain ' private ' long.

Moore's comment was that the poem was " generally, and it must be owned justly condemned as a sort of literary assault on an obscure female whose situation ought to have placed her as much *beneath* his satire as the undignified mode of his attack certainly raised her *above* it ".

Byron's desire that Clermont should suffer (justly or unjustly is of no moment) for the part she played was not unfulfilled. After his death she was dragged into the newspapers again and, according to Lady Byron, " shamefully traduced ". Again, in 1830, when Campbell intervened — not very happily — in *The New Monthly* apropos Moore's *Life* of the poet, the ex-Abigail was hauled out of that retirement at Clifton which she had no doubt desired to enjoy undisturbed, and made once more a bone of contention between two packs of strongly partisan curs.

In the year of Byron's betrothal to Annabella Milbanke — 1814 — Lady Hippisley, wife of Sir John Cox Hippisley, of Ston Easton Park, near Bath, drew up in her *Day-Book* a set of regulations for the management of her household. Selections from these were published by the Rev. J. J. Antrobus in *Country Life*, November 26, 1943, and he, together with Commander Hippisley, the present owner of the book, most kindly permits me to quote from them here. The ' Hall ' means the servants' hall.

> No Maidservant is to go out without applying to the House-keeper.
>
> No strangers or other persons from the village to enter the kitchen, as they may wait in the archway until they obtain the answer required.
>
> A small lanthorn to be given to each Maid, which she is to go about the house with, and use going to bed, and on no account to deviate from this safe rule.
>
> The Maids are to have their allowance of Beer, a pint, served to them after Dinner in the kitchen.
>
> No washing allowed to the Maids excepting a certain proportion of those articles of cook's dress supposed to be dirtied in her kitchen business. A proper proportion of Soap and Starch to be allowed them by the Housekeeper to wash their clothes with themselves.
>
> The two Housemaids or any other Servantmaid who may chance to be in the house are to set *entirely* in the little room by the House-keeper's : in short, no one to set in the kitchen but the Cook and the Kitchenmaid.
>
> Once every month Martha Kingman is allowed to come to clean the Hall pewter and sometimes she is sent for by the Butler to clean bottles (decanters ?) but as helper or charwoman she is never to come in except by express of Lady Hippisley, and it is to be

observed that never but upon extraordinary occasions will this be allowed.

All wages to be paid 1st May and November. No perquisites.

At Ten o'clock the Kitchen Fire and all lights are to be extinguished and all the Maids are to go to bed, except when one of the Housemaids is to set up to warm the Beds : in such case they are to set up alternately.

Life at Ston Easton must have been agreeably (or disagreeably) enlivened by the whims and hobbies of Lady Hippisley, who kept a tame bear, conducted peculiarly odoriferous chemical experiments in her private laboratory, and had her own bathroom with a sunk bath under a ceiling of blue stucco studded with golden stars. Few indeed must the Regency Abigails have been whose duties included cleaning out anything larger than a small bathtub or a foot-bath.

Oddly enough, Caroline, Princess of Wales, so uncouth in her personal habits at the time of her marriage, and on that account so repugnant to her fastidious bridegroom, had a bathroom with elaborate fittings in her house in Connaught Place, though whether she made much or any use of it " is quite another thing ".

To return to Ston Easton and its remarkable *châtelaine*, aptly described by one visitor as a *femme grenadière*. She further lays it down that

The Board Wages at Ston Easton are usually 6/- per week, with vegetables from the Garden, Small Beer, Coal and Candle, but since each has become so very much dearer it has been raised to 7/-, which is to go back to the former sum on the reduction of the price of Bread, Meat etc.

It will be remembered that Kitty, in *High Life Below Stairs*, scouted the idea of there being anything in the larder when the domestic staff were, as she put it, " at board wages ". No butter was ever allowed " in the Hall ", and tea is mentioned only at Christmas-time, when thirty retainers, their wives and their families were entertained, the menu consisting of " Ribs of Beef roasted, Round of Beef boiled, a goose or meat pie, 2 large Mince Pies, 2 Large Plum Puddings, Variety of Vegetables ".

Broth was made for the poor from pot-liquor, when the family partook of boiled beef, but the servants do not appear to

have participated in this *régale*. For them a large Cheshire cheese
was kept in the larder, from which small portions would be cut
by the housekeeper or the butler, that the servants might " take
a little with their beer after dinner ".

" If ", writes Lady Hippisley, " any Servant introduces or
permits the use of Spirits or Tobacco into the Hall, his allowance
of strong beer is to be taken off for a week." The idea that
a female servant might conceivably transgress in this manner
apparently never entered her ladyship's head. All servants, male
and female, were expected to be quiet and regular in their conduct,
and from this rule " either in town, country, or watering-place
they are not to imagine themselves in any degree exempt ".

" It is presumed ", says her ladyship, " that no servant would
attempt to set down to dinner uncombed or with dirty clothes or
hands : if such an indecorum should occur, the Butler should
turn them out."

The men-servants' liveries are described in much picturesque
detail, but no particulars are given as to the women's uniform,
therefore presumably supplied by themselves. There is an interesting picture by Thomas Beech, showing the under-keeper,
bailiff, housekeeper and still-room maid at Ston Easton about this
period or a little earlier. The housekeeper is stately in a light-
coloured linen gown sprigged with blue and a crisp mutch-cap :
the still-room maid wears a dark, steeply-tilted Dolly Varden
type of hat with a hood or snood of linen under it, and an
attractive flowered dress with a long, peaked bodice trimmed with
narrow tucks or frills ; the skirt — or perhaps it is the apron ? —
is gracefully looped up in front.

That remarkable woman, Mrs. Taylor of Ongar, mother of
the more celebrated Ann and Jane, found time among her many
activities, maternal and domestic, to produce several edifying
books. One of these was entitled *A Present to Servants*, and in
the fifth edition she inserted a little compliment to the Rev. John
Trusler, author of *Domestic Management or the Art of Conducting
a Family with Economy, Frugality and Method, the Result of Long
Experience*. There are, says Mrs. Taylor handsomely, servants
of old standing, now living, who acknowledge with gratitude the
great benefit they have received from this work.

John Trusler (1735–1820) was exceedingly active in the matter of manuals, guides and books of instruction, his subjects ranging from longevity to chronology, and embracing by the way philosophy, grammar, midwifery, etiquette and " a satirical novel in the style of *Gil Blas* ". By contrast with the impersonal pomposity of most productions of the sort, his *Domestic Management* is refreshingly coloured by his prejudices and idiosyncrasies. For example, he twice expresses his distrust of young women who come to apply for a situation " dressed in gauze, curls and ribbons " ; and while descanting upon the virtue of willingness, he interjects : " When I hear an insolent footman, if asked to drive a nail, say, ' I'll go for the carpenter ' ; or a pert wench, if desired to shut the stable-door, reply, ' I don't understand horses ', I am ready to brain the fools."

On the question of board-wages, in which he appears to have been of one mind with Lady Hippisley, he cites the impressive example of " a nobleman who was a General Officer and lived in as good a style on an income of £4000 as many did on three times that income ". He kept his thirty servants permanently on board-wages, and assured Mr. Trusler not only that he was a considerable saver by doing so but that the servants were better satisfied, though their standing wages were lower than the ordinary. We are not told what rate was fixed either by this frugal nobleman or by Trusler himself, who had kept *his* servants " for forty years upon the same principle ".

The reverend gentleman's pronouncements are sometimes contradictory, as when he declares that servants should at all times be considered as humble friends, and encouraged by kind words, indulgences and small presents when they do right ; and then that it is idle to expect either method or attachment from them. Zeal is commended, but excess of zeal is rightly deprecated, with the illustrative anecdote of

the ignorant, foolish girl so industrious as to be at the pains of taking pictures out of the frames in order to clean the inside of the glasses, and injure the prints and drawings by so doing ; to injure paintings by attempting to clean them with soap-suds ; and scour off the bronze of a tea-urn quite to the copper in order to brighten it.

" A careful housemaid ", says Mr. Trusler, " will be tender with slight furniture, and not rub it till she breaks it " ; and again he draws upon his personal recollections for a cautionary example :

> I have seen a strong country wench, from a conception that hard rubbing is necessary, raise a cabriole chair on one leg and, in order to rub the opposite leg, lean on it with that force as to make the whole frame crack, and rub a slight table till it has given way under her heavy hand.

" A slight table " — what visions of spindle-shanked elegance, of slim Heppelwhite and gracile Sheraton, does that phrase not evoke !

Vindictiveness, dram-drinking, slovenliness in dress, all come under Mr. Trusler's rod, and he deals with each defect in a characteristic manner. " Don't," he enjoins, " in order to spite him or be revenged, break the butler's glasses in his absence, hide a silver spoon to have the footman thought a rogue, or put anything in the pot to give the meat a bad taste that the cook may be scolded." Women cannot be supposed to need any exhortations to sobriety, but he feels that he may surely caution them without offence against accepting a dram on a cold morning from some tradesman with whom they lay out their master's money. " Dram-drinking ", he warns them, " brings on the dropsy, and will shorten your days and in a very short time will destroy a pretty face."

As regards a woman-servant's dress he delivers himself as follows :

> Dressy servants are women of suspicious character, and however *genteel* they appear in their own eyes, they are less so in the eyes of others. It is not expected that a young woman should dress herself like an old one ; but if she set herself off in her own opinion with fine trumpery or what is called ' fal-lal finery ' she is only a mark of derision. It is necessary that she should have a sufficient change of underclothes, stockings and pocket-handkerchiefs, and outward, useful ones. Indeed, such a wardrobe a prudent mistress will take care to inspect, and take no servant without ; otherwise she [the servant] must be ever at the wash-tub.

It was probably for the benefit of the misguided wearers of " fal-lal finery " that the reverend gentleman adds the warning that a young woman out of a place should not lodge " at a public house or at an improper one ".

Instructions to chamber-maids are in some places borrowed verbatim from Dean Swift, his ironical injunctions being only slightly edited so that they may be read seriously. On the question of chamber-pots a great deal is said. These utensils must never be taken out of the bedroom, much less left upon the landing or the window-seat ; nor should they be emptied out of the window. When the bed has been made, everything in the room must be " put in its proper place, the chamber-pots under the bed, but within the valance, so as not to be exposed to the eye ". An hour or two before bedtime the maid should go round the bedrooms, taking care that the windows are closely shut, that the cat be not locked in any room, and that every " necessary utensil be in its place ". She may, considers Mr. Trusler, " as well not put the chamber-pot in the room as put it under any part of the bed but the place it is expected to be found in ".

If the blankets of the bed are " troubled with fleas " it is the chamber-maid's duty to look for them and kill them ; mopping under the bed with a wettish mop is a preservative against these insects, and bugs can be " effectively destroyed by sweet oil ".

> Should a chambermaid be rung for in the night, she should fly to the room with all speed . . . and take her tinder-box with her. She may not be aware of the consequence of a moment's delay. Many a life has been lost by the nightmare, or a suffocating cough, for want of momentary assistance ; and a person who has just power enough to ring the bell may be suffocated whilst a maid stays to rub her eyes, light her candle, or adjust her cap. Her tinder-box ought, of course, to be in good order, and near her bedside.

Very gravely does Mr. Trusler warn maidservants against combing their hair with their ladies' combs, wearing their shifts or petticoats, making free with their thread, pins, etc., or using their master's razors to cut their corns. But a dutiful servant is not likely to go unrewarded. If she obtains the good opinion of her employer, she will find a friend who will often keep her in sickness, endeavour to make her happy in her situation, frequently give her useful presents, and may either leave her something considerable in the way of a legacy or make some provision for her in the event of her " settling " — *i.e.* marrying.

As the nineteenth century struggled through its first two uneasy decades the number of manuals upon domestic and other arts and sciences steadily grew. Among the most illuminating of these was *The Female Instructor or Young Woman's Companion*, published at Liverpool in 1816. Later it reappeared, considerably augmented but only slightly altered, under the more promising title of *The Female Instructor or Young Woman's Guide to Domestic Happiness*, 1817–18. It is interesting to contrast the definitions of a lady's-maid and chamber-maid's duties in the 1816 volume with Hanah Woolley's remarks in 1677. The first must be capable of doing fine needlework, reading aloud from the best authors, washing lace, muslin, gauze and cambric, and cleaning gold and silver lace. The chamber-maid, we are informed, looks after the lady's clothes. " When your mistress has undressed," she is exhorted, " examine all her clothes with great niceness, and if you discover any spots on them, let them be immediately taken out ; after which fold them up carefully and put them in their proper place." Instructions follow as to the best method of removing spots from a great variety of fabrics, and how to wash black silks, scarlet cloaks and damask curtains.

The housemaid had an arduous life, crammed with small, redundant, niggling tasks. In summer she must begin the day's work by rubbing the stoves and fire-irons with scouring-paper and cleaning the hearths. In winter, after raking out the ashes, she must clean the fire-irons, " which, if the common sort, can be done by rubbing them first with a rag dipped in vinegar and ashes, then with an oily rag, and after that with scouring-paper, rottenstone, or white brick " : how many processes and how many cleaning materials would be needed for fire-irons of an uncommon sort this authority — perhaps mercifully — does not lay down. Our housemaid should then proceed to clean the locks of the doors, having a piece of pasteboard for each " just big enough for slipping over the lock to preserve the door ". Here the media are oily rags, rottenstone, white brick. Next the carpet should be folded back, and damp sand sprinkled on the floor " to lick up the dust and flue ". Carpets, it is reassuring to know, " when they will turn are best cleaned by laying the wrong side upwards for a day or two, and then the dust will fall out on to the floors ". Dust on picture-frames can be blown off with a pair of bellows. Wet sand may be laid on the (evidently uncarpeted) stairs before sweeping.

After these complicated and, by modern standards, deplorably unhygienic activities, the housemaid — providing " the family is up " — should now set about opening the windows of the bed-chamber (closely shut all night) and uncovering the beds " to sweeten and air them, which will be a great help against bugs and fleas. . . . The cleaning of the head of the bed, the valances and the curtains with a brush or whisk is not to be omitted."

The later (London) edition of this instructive work provides more exciting reading. The subjects dealt with include love and marriage, dress, arithmetic, commercial and social correspond-ence, attendance upon the sick, precepts of religion. Short narratives are occasionally introduced to point the moral.

We are told of the tombstone of Ursula Swinburne in Croy-don Churchyard. Having served the same family for thirty-five years and " fulfilling her duty in that station of life which the Creator alloted her ", she died at the age of fifty-five in 1781. A clergyman tells the story of the daughter of a day-labourer, for many years a maid-of-all-work in the house of a tradesman. During the earlier part of her service her wages were forty shillings a year — no advance on the wages of a man-servant in the seventeenth century, as shown by the old folk-song with its refrain :

> He serveth for forty shillings a year,
> How can he be merry and make good cheer ?

Later, upon her undertaking the whole of the washing and ironing without assistance, she received five shillings more annually ; and finally her pay reached the giddy peak of £4. For helping in the shop she received no specific reward.

Then " a bad-tempered old relative who spent much time with the family " was won by the girl's assiduity and gave her a small sum of money, further augmented by her own savings to a sum of £20. Of this she nobly bestowed half on her aged father, who promptly purchased a cow : the other £10, put aside against some future necessity, came in handy to pay the surgeon who operated — successfully — upon Aged P., in spite of the fact that the local apothecary had pronounced the case to be hopeless, " a mortification having in his opinion already taken place ". A few years after she " had made this laudable use of her hard-earned savings ", her master died, leaving her £100 in cash, a quantity of household furniture, and the interest of £300 during her life : and a few months later she was wooed and wedded by " a farmer in comfortable circumstances ".

More pathetic is the story of a young woman from Wiltshire — Sarah — servant in a clergyman's family in Chelsea, related to show at once the kindness of her employers and her attachment to them. In the summer of 1807 she fell sick of a fever, and her mistress tended her devotedly.

> In compliance with medical advice a lodging was hired for her in an airy part of the neighbourhood. A coach was considerately procured to take her thither. Pale as a water-lily, the sick young woman was supported down the stairs. She modestly expressed a wish to see her master once more before she went. Her mistress with kind concern assured her that he stood at the gate in order to see her safely into the carriage.

A touching scene followed. A kindly greeting from the clergy-man (can it have been the Rev. Weedon Butler ? [1]) and the sight of the infant son of the house stretching forth its hands to her, overwhelmed poor Sarah : " She would have spoken, but could not ; she faltered, sobbed, leaned back on her female friend and wept ; then pointed to the coach with a sigh and tottered to it ".

Then the curtain falls : we shall never know whether Sarah survived to requite the kindness of her master and mistress, or died, and so merited (and probably received) a monumental tribute to her worth.

The chapter on " Conduct to Servants " comes next to that on " The Passions ", and in it the writer gives vent to some utterances very rich in time-colour :

> A kind and tender attention is due from the affluent to the deserving part of their fellow-creatures. . . . The Almighty, for wise and good purposes, has thought fit to place His children in very different situations. The good and truly amiable are never

[1] *Regency Roundabout*, p. 105.

severe to their domestics, and they are rewarded with dutiful affection. How pleasant to be received, after any temporary absence from our own house, with the smiling countenance of a worthy domestic — an eye uplifted with humble but grateful delight !

It is, however, highly improper for young people to converse with servants in the same unreserved manner that they would with an equal or a superior — " a proper distinction may be kept up without either pride, reserve, or coldness ". Many of the servants in genteel families have been reduced, perhaps, to their humiliating situations by the imprudence of their parents.

When choosing a situation a maidservant should prefer a sober, regular family, even if the wages be lower. She should beware of giving warning " in a pet ", and should put up with many inconveniences, and even hardships, rather than foolishly " throw herself out of a suitable place " ; but if her health or morals seem to be in danger she must take prompt action. A few pieces of good counsel follow. She must not answer back or mutter to herself if she receives orders that do not suit her fancy. And — shades of Lady Hippisley ! — she must use a lanthorn going to bed, and be careful about fire. By law a servant through whose carelessness a house is set on fire was liable to a penalty of one hundred pounds.

There follows a portrait of the perfect maid. She rises early. She always looks clean and tidy, even when, dressed in a close bed-gown (*sic*) and a plain linen or cotton cap, she is doing dirty work. She is never seen going about the house with holes in her stockings or slipshod shoes. Her cap and bonnets are very neat and becoming but — shades of Mrs. Price ! — without any lace or " fancy work ". Her handkerchief is always tidily put on and pinned close over her neck. Her dress on Sundays and when she goes out is *the same as at other times* (our italics) except that she is then particularly neat and clean.

This paragon never desires to go to races, or feasts, or fairs ; never spends any time and money on silly books of songs, or in running after fortune-tellers, or purchasing lottery tickets. She never plays at cards. A walk in her master's garden or in the fields, either by herself or with sober company, a visit to her friends, or a good book to read, are the amusements she likes best.

All these negatives add up to a positive — the average typical handmaiden of the period, of whom Leigh Hunt traced a delightful picture some two years later — in 1820 to be exact. " Her ordinary dress ", he says,

> is black stockings, a cap, and a neckhandkerchief pinned cornerwise behind. If you want a pin, she just feels about her and has always one to give you. On Sundays and holidays, and perhaps on afternoons, she changes her black stockings for white, puts on a gown of better texture and finer pattern, sets her cap and her curls jauntily, and lays aside the neckhandkerchief for a high body, which, by the way, is not half so pretty.

Leigh Hunt next introduces us into the kitchen where, in a drawer of the dresser or the table, with a duster and a pair of snuffers, may be found some of her property, such as a brass thimble, a pair of scissors, a thread-case, a piece of wax, " much wrinkled with the thread ", an odd volume of *Pamela*, and perhaps a sixpenny play, such as *George Barnwell* or *Oroonoko*. There is a piece of looking-glass in the window.

> The rest of her furniture is in the garret, where you may find a good looking-glass on the table, and in the window a Bible, a comb, and a piece of soap. Here stands also, under stout lock and key, the mighty mystery, the Box — containing among other things, her clothes, two or three song-books of nineteen for the penny ; sundry tragedies at a halfpenny the sheet ; the *Whole Nature of Dreams Laid Open*, together with the *Fortune-teller* and *The Account of the Ghost of Mrs. Veal*, the story of *The Beautiful Zoa*, " who was cast away on a desart island ", etc. Some half-crowns in a purse — a silver penny wrapped up in paper by itself — a crooked sixpence — two little enamel boxes with looking-glass in the lids, one a fairing, the other " A Trifle from Margate " ; and lastly various letters, square and ragged, and directed in all sorts of spellings, chiefly with little letters for the capitals.

Margate was popular with the Regency Abigails. One of them, advertising for a situation in 1811, actually expressed her preference for " a family going to Margate " : others, more adventurous, declared their willingness to go to the East or West Indies.

The advertisement columns of the Regency newspapers open

up a rich and hitherto rather neglected field of social history, and yield a large crop of respectable females eager to " take charge of the domestic concerns " of widowers and single gentlemen. Many of them declare that money is " not so much their object as a comfortable home ", and a few of them mention that they " enjoy a small competence ". Perhaps the following is one of the most unforgettable of their manifestoes — from *The Times*, 1818 :

> A Gentlewoman who has recently become a Widow under the most afflicting circumstances wishes for a situation with a Widower, a Gentleman who may require the presence and exertions of a respectable Female to superintend his family. This advertisement is addressed to the virtuous part of mankind only. The lacerated heart of the writer has but one motive — namely, an asylum for herself and child.

Less harrowing but not entirely dissimilar is the Young Person " whose circumstances have been clouded by misfortunes " and who is desirous of a situation to attend on a young lady or ladies or would " with pleasure dedicate her time to an elderly Lady whose retired disposition or infirmities might render her services available ".

More lively and much more intriguing is another and longer announcement appearing in *The Times* during 1811 :

> A Lady whose obliging disposition and genteel manners gained the esteem of some of the first Families who frequented the house of her friends (well-known in the mercantile world) and under whose roof it became her province to superintend and govern for some years with propriety and elegance, is now reduced to the painful necessity of offering herself to any Gentlewoman who will accept of her services to go out of England or to any gentleman of consequence going to settle in Rio de Janeiro. The loss of friends and the severity of others produces this request to strangers.

This anxiety to " go out of England " suggests active pursuit by creditors, even by Bow Street runners : but why Rio de Janeiro ?

Persons answering advertisements had to direct their letters to a variety of accommodation addresses, among which we find coffee-houses (including Wills's), booksellers, ironmongers and cheesemongers. Many of the aspirants mention their acquirements ; mantua-making, getting up fine linen, and even embroidering court gowns, figure in the list. One young person proclaims herself proficient in " every branch of dressmaking, and child-bed linen if required ".

The two peculiarly English vices of snobbery and hypocrisy are soon to be discerned. Here we have a Young Person who has " no objection to cleaning the *upper* part of the house " ; and there — but she shall speak for herself :

> Wanted, by a Young Person of Respectability a situation as companion to a lady ; she understands dressmaking ; would have no objection to give directions as to sending up dinner or anything in the domestic way that is not menial.

And here is another example of the same sort of thing :

> To wait on a Lady where it is not required to associate with other servants, a young Woman of good connections who has been respectably educated and understands dressmaking.

These particular young women were not seeking — were probably not qualified to fill — situations as lady's-maids where in the ordinary course of things they would not have to associate with other servants except the butler and the housekeeper : they seem to envisage some vague, nondescript sort of post of which only the privileges are plainly defined.

In addition to their acquirements in the way of needlework, mantua-making and so forth, the Abigails lay claim to a variety of merits and virtues : some are cheerful, some are serious-minded ; some are active, some are meek ; some have no followers ; some — it is a pathetic touch — " can bear confinement ". Wages are seldom mentioned, but the " comfortable home " is frequently and hopefully specified ; also the " genteel place where a footman is kept ". It is perhaps a little uncharitable to stigmatize as hypocritical the phrasing of the next specimen, but it is difficult not to hear a faint Pecksniffian twang :

> Wants a Situation, a Young Woman who has been well brought up in a respectable family to attend upon and read to an elderly lady or as attendant upon a young lady. The advertiser is of a religious

turn of mind and meek disposition. Will endeavour to make herself useful to the utmost of her power. She has some knowledge of mantua-making.

Elsewhere we find the parents of a young girl between sixteen and seventeen seeking for her a place " where her morals will be attended to " and asking no salary, and the " serious person of good principles " who would prefer to serve " a religious-minded family " — can she have been reading *The Female Instructor* ?

When we turn to the less numerous announcements of the " Situations Vacant " class we find with some surprise that many of the " genteel families ", living in good style with a considerable domestic staff, reside in districts from which the last shreds of such gentility have long since departed. In the East End of the City, in the City itself, in Hackney, Peckham, Mile End Road, Whitechapel, there were households demanding maids who " thoroughly understood their business ", were used to caring for good furniture, and had *not* lived previously " in a tradesman's family ".

Not only in the closely-printed advertisement columns does the Regency Abigail appear. As a delinquent she sometimes figures in the legal reports, usually for some act of petty theft ; and in small paragraphs tucked away at the foot of the page she may be found in a more tragic guise. In March 1818, for example, the body of a young woman about twenty-six years of age was found floating in the river Medway near East Barming. From the circumstance that her right temple had been " severely crushed as if by a hammer " foul play was suspected, and from her dress and appearance " it was thought that she had been a servant in a respectable family ". No one identified her or came forward to claim the body for burial.

Some such instances as these — of girls losing their characters or their lives — may have been in the mind of the author of a little book, *The Cook's Oracle*, of which a fifth edition appeared in 1823. As its title implies, it deals mainly with culinary affairs, but at one point there is inserted an " Estimate of Expenses of a Female Servant ", with strong comments thereon. As tabulated, these expenses were :

Half pound of tea per month per annum ⎫	
Ditto, sugar, per week ⎭	3. 10. 0
4 pair of shoes, per annum	0. 18. 0
2 pair of black worsted stockings	0. 4. 0
2 pair of white cotton ditto	0. 5. 0
2 gowns	1. 10. 0
6 aprons, 4 check, 2 white	10. 6
6 caps	10. 6
A Bonnet, a Shawl or Cloak, Pattens, etc. Ribands, Handkerchiefs, Pins, Needles, Threads, Thimbles, Scissors, and other working tools, Stays, Stay-tape, Buckram, etc.	2. 0. 0
	9. 8. 0

" Besides these," says *The Cook's Oracle*, " she has to make a Shift and buy Petticoats, Pockets and many other articles. We appeal to the *neatest managing and most economical Housewife* to inform us how this can be done, and how much the poor Girl will have remaining to place to her Account in the Savings Bank for help in sickness, when out of a Place, and for her support in Old Age. Here is the source of the swarms of Distressed Females which we daily meet in our streets."

Many of the items in this list recall Leigh Hunt's maidservant and her belongings ; but it will be observed that nothing is allowed here for amusements, not even a poor penny or two for the purchase of song-books or " tragedies at a halfpenny the sheet ". As £8 was considered a very fair wage for a maid-of-all-work at this time, the figures given form a painful counterpoise to the comments that follow.

Five years before the Regency began, but not before it was realized to be inevitable if not imminent, the Poor Law authorities of Newport, Isle of Wight, fitted out a young girl for service very much as the girl in *The Cook's Oracle* is equipped, though perhaps more meagrely. Her name was Sophy Daw or Dawes, and she was the illegitimate daughter of a man who combined the humble if reputable profession of an oyster-catcher and shellfish-purveyor with the occluded but more profitable activities of a smuggler. Before he abandoned her, her mother, and her numerous brothers and sisters to the mercies of the parish, Sophy, a nimble, well-developed child, had been wont to assist him in his avowed calling by gathering winkles on the rocks. The work of a farmhouse, however rough, must have seemed strange by contrast, and one can only admire the courage of Farmer Cliff's wife when she took into her service this uncouth, disreputable creature. Who tired of the other first is not recorded, but Sophy could not leave lawfully until the time was up for which the Newport authorities had ' bound ' her to Mrs. Cliff, or without their knowledge and consent. Leave she did, before she reached womanhood. She gravitated to London, and to that half-world for which by nature she was predestined. Her later career as mistress and subsequently murderess of the last Prince de Condé does not come into the framework of this book ; but it may be observed that seldom indeed in history has it happened that an ex-winkle-gatherer and farm servant has risen to such a peak of power that the scandal caused by her actions has contributed to the downfall of a dynasty.

CHAPTER IX

Below-Stairs at 5 Cheyne Row

ON a certain cloudy June day in the year 1834, a hackney coach was clattering across the cobbles of Belgrave Square on its way to Chelsea when suddenly there came from its musty depths the gay song of a canary, and a Scottish voice was heard to say, " That is a promising omen, ma'am." The name of the canary was Chico ; the owner of the voice was Bessy Barnet, maid-of-all-work to Mrs. Thomas Carlyle, with whom (and Mr. Carlyle) she was journeying to the house in Cheyne Row [1] destined in after years to be one of the most famous houses in the English-speaking world.

They were not precisely a young couple, these adventurers from the north — he thirty-nine, she thirty-three ; yet there is something engagingly youthful about the blending of courage and apprehension with which they launched themselves upon London. His ruddy, rugged features were as yet unblurred by a beard, but already they were warped by melancholy and dyspepsia : something of the beauty still lingered that had once made Jane Welsh the toast of her native Haddington, but already ill-health and a complexity of cares had given an occasional bitter line to her lips and a stormy expression to her magnificent eyes. They were to be the master and mistress of a long line of Abigails whom her letters and his comments have endowed with certain gleams of immortality.

The line could hardly have begun better than with Bessy Barnet, " of the distinguished qualities and fortunes ", as Carlyle dubbed her. By engaging her " despite strong counsels to the contrary " from their patrician friend, Mrs. Montagu, the Carlyles had deeply offended the lady ; but they seem never to have regretted the decision, and when the optimistic Bessy reappears many years later in circumstances of unexpected gentility, her old devotion to Mrs. Carlyle is seen to be as warm as ever.

[1] Then Number Five, now Number Twenty-Four.

When they reached the house in Cheyne Row, a house " of most antique physiognomy, all wainscotted, carved and queer-looking ", the three of them led for a time a sort of gypsy life, pending the arrival and unpacking of divers boxes and cases from Scotland. They had time to admire its narrow strip of garden, where two vines and a walnut-tree contrived to grow if not to flourish, and to explore its empty rooms from attic to basement. To the front of the basement, then only half-sunk, there was a large kitchen, tolerably well lighted by two windows ; behind this were the back-kitchen or wash-house, the larder and the coal-cellar. A new range was put in when the Carlyles' tenancy began, and another, with a " patent self-supplying boiler " in 1862 — the year in which water was ' laid on ' ; yet the well and its ancillary pump are mentioned as being in use as late as 1864. From Mrs. Carlyle's comparison of an excessively *décolleté* lady to " a servant-girl who has pulled off her gown to scrub her neck at the pump " it seems not unlikely that the ablutions of the maids were sometimes performed in that manner at Chelsea.

In the front-kitchen the monotonous meals preferred by the Carlyles were prepared — the endless mutton chops and legs of mutton, varied by an infrequent fowl or by game supplied by a friend's gun : here was made ready that porridge which a scornful English servant described as " the master's pap " ; and here, in a bed periodically invaded by the *Cimex lectularius*, the maid (or maids) invariably slept until after Mrs. Carlyle's death, when the supposedly sound-proof study up under the skylight became the maids' bedroom.

Jane Welsh Carlyle believed herself to be, on the whole, an indulgent mistress, and she belonged to a race traditionally less aloof and conventional than the English in such matters ; it is therefore with some surprise that we find her in 1860 hotly repudiating the demand of a well-trained maid for " a servants' hall and a bedroom upstairs ". Whatever the austerities and discomforts of life in the Cheyne Row basement may have been — and by modern standards they were neither light nor few — most of her maids were devoted to her, some even to the point of enthusiasm ; and in spite of her occasional hints that Carlyle's exacting and eccentric habits weighed rather heavily on the domestic staff, it is clear that both before and after her death they could find it in their hearts to be attached to " Mr. C."

In her dealings with them, as in her dealings with her husband, her mother and her friends, Jane Welsh was swayed by the fluctuations of her passionate and unpredictable temperament. Avid of affection, not averse from its outward demonstrations, she was a prey to black disillusionment when one of her swans — as so often happened — betrayed the plumage of a goose. Like Burns, " a child of skinless sensibility ", she constantly — with the full concurrence of her medical advisers — sought to soothe her jangled nervous system by taking opium, usually in the form of morphia pills. More unusual at that period but far less reprehensible was the smoking of these " cigarillos " with which she often kept time to Carlyle's churchwarden pipe. Neither her advocates nor her husband's apologists have yet been able — or are likely ever to be able — to prove whether a maladjusted marriage was or was not a contributory cause of this distressing nervous instability ; but in spite of all Froude's misplaced chivalry, in spite of all Carlyle's exaggerated remorse, it is clear that the sometimes brittle-seeming fabric of their married life was built upon an immense deposit of reciprocal love and understanding.

The roll of Mrs. Carlyle's Abigails is too long to be rehearsed in full, but imagination lingers over the Irish specimen who took up her duties in the summer of 1835. At first she was described hopefully as an " active, tidy-looking Irish Roman Catholic ", but a month later Mrs. Carlyle wrote of herself as being " at the mercy of another distracted Irishwoman, or such successors as Heaven in its mercy or wrath may provide, for this one also is on the move ". Carlyle, whose function it usually was to pronounce sentence of dismissal, called her a "mutinous Irish savage ", and recorded with something like glee how he had sent her away for " jingling down her plates as if they were quoits ". " To your room at once ! " thundered the Sage. " Wages tomorrow morning : disappear ! " On another occasion, when discharging the damsel nicknamed " Pessima ", he notes : " My brief request to her was to disappear straightway and in no region of God's universe, if she could avoid it, to let me behold her again ".

In the interregnum between this stormy interlude and the coming of Anne Cook from Scotland, the Carlyles enjoyed the services of the small waif whom Carlyle described, with his habitual gruff tenderness, as " this poor little Chelsea specimen, picked out as a stop-gap from some of the neighbouring huts here — a very feeble but willing little girl, introduced by the too romantic-looking name of Seraether — which, questioning her little self, I discovered to be Sarah Heather — Sar' Eather ". Jane Carlyle called her, but not unkindly, a " peesweep ", with which " swift but ineffectual bird Sereetha seemed ", observes her master, " to have a similarity ".

During a visit from her mother, Mrs. Welsh, Mrs. Carlyle wrote to her husband in Scotland, " Sereetha has attained the unhoped-for perfection of getting up at half after six of her own accord, lighting the parlour fire and actually placing the breakfast things — (*nil desperandum me duce*) — After breakfast mother descends to the inferno, where she jingles and scours, and from time to time scolds Sereetha till all is right and tight there." Meanwhile the lady of the house had swept the parlour and blackened the grate — with the fire lit ? — and in due course the visitor from Scotland ' sorted ' her own bedroom.

Cooking presented few problems in a household where so little was demanded in the way of ' made dishes ' — indeed, one of Mrs. Carlyle's American biographers is deeply shocked by the neglect of fruits and vegetables (and all their vitamins) in the kitchen at Cheyne Row. " A bit of meat ", writes Mrs. Carlyle, " roasted in the oven suffices two days cold and does not plague us with cookery. Sereetha can fetch up tea-things and the porridge is easily made on the parlour fire : the kitchen one being allowed to go out (for economy) when the Peesweep retires to bed at eight o'clock." About a fortnight later the lady records proudly as evidence of her own exemplary patience and good-humour that Sereetha is still there and that she — Mrs. Carlyle — has not yet fallen out with her mamma.

Then Anne Cook arrived from Scotland, convoyed by the homeward-wending Thomas, and the small figure of Sareetha vanishes without leaving any trace. Anne's reign was comparatively brief, but two distinct pictures of her remain. Carlyle had a trick — sometimes alarming to the uninitiated — of rising in the night or early in the morning, smoking pipes, taking cold baths, consulting books, or otherwise beguiling the sleepless hours, so Anne suggests that " if he went staveren aboot the hoose " in this manner he might " give her a cry " at 3 A.M. The second glimpse shows her cheered by Mrs. Carlyle with two penny heather-brooms, bought from a boy at the door " to keep Anne in heart ".

Next in the procession of capped and aproned ghosts comes that " strangest mixture of philosopher and perfect idiot " that Mrs. Carlyle professed ever to have met, Helen Mitchell, commonly known — from her place of origin — as Kirkcaldy Helen. (It is perhaps a little unorthodox to include her and some of the Carlyles' other Scottish handmaidens in a book entitled The English — and not The British — Abigail, but I hope that the circumstance that they play their parts upon the Chelsea stage may justify this stretching of the terms of reference.)

" That poor bit dottle Helen ", as Carlyle called her, arrived by cab on a wet, blustering night, having disembarked at St. Katharine's Docks. She seemed, he remembered, " to have cared no more about the roar and tumult of London on her way hither than a clucking hen would have done, sitting safely in its hand-basket and looking unconcerned to right and left ".

She contributed many quaint sayings to the family store, and he was to write in kindly retrospect of her " gentle, genial lambency of grave humour and intelligence " ; and, he added, " wittiest of wit that ever I heard was poor by comparison ". Escorted to the National Gallery and confronted by a picture of the Madonna and Child, probably by an Italian primitive very free with gold leaf and bright colours, her only comment was, " Ah, how expensive ! " " I would rather ", she remarked on one occasion, " live single all my life than be married to a saft taty." When Cavaignac came to dinner uninvited, she said reassuringly, " It's nae matter what ye gie him, for he can aye mak' the bread flee."

Her characteristic monologue when clearing away the break-fast-things one morning in 1843 has been thus recorded by her delighted mistress. " Indeed, I don't for my part think there is any *love* in the world nowadays, like what used to long ago. There was No. 6 — how soon *she* got over the death of her lover — and Mr. Brimlicombe the milkman was married seven months after *his* wife's death. But I *do* think," she resumed, after some interruption of dusting, " that Mr. Carlyle will be ('admire the tense !' interjects Mrs. Carlyle) a *very desultory widow* ! He is so easily put about and seems to take no pleasure in *new females* ! "

A manual of domestic management about this period lays it down that maids " should not be debarred from out-of-door exercise and the possibility of attending divine worship every Sunday ", adding kindly, " Neither is it wise to deny them entirely the relaxation of reading ". In a formal letter of engagement cited later nothing is said about " time off ", but Helen was certainly able to pay a round of calls on the other domestics in Cheyne Row — " visiting numbers " was her mistress's term ; and we hear of her being bidden to " take herself for a long walk after dinner ". As regards reading, she was not only permitted but encouraged to enjoy that relaxation. She formed a low opinion of Harriet Martineau's *Guides to Service* published anonymously in 1838, and seemed to think that " Miss Martno " had gone rather astray in the section entitled *The Maid of All Work* ; but she unreservedly admired the writings of Carlyle. " Take care," she interjected, when handing some books to her mistress, " that ane's the Maister's *Sartor Resart*, and a capital thing it is — just *noble* in *my* opinion."

One March morning in the year 1843 Helen was heard re-lighting the parlour fire " with a perfectly unexampled venge-ance ". " What ails the creature now ? " Mrs. Carlyle said to herself. " Who has incurred her sudden displeasure, or is it the red herring she had for dinner which has disagreed with her stomach ? " She had specially petitioned that she might have this particular delicacy — having grown a little weary, perhaps, of unending mutton. Descending to the depths, she kept up the same wild hubbub ; and when she brought the tea-tray she " clanked it on the lobby-table as if she were minded to demolish the whole concern at one fell stroke ". The temperamental and officious Geraldine Jewsbury was on a visit to Cheyne Row, and, intrigued by the rumblings below-stairs, she went down to investigate. " Where ", she asked, " is the cat ? " " The cat ! " said Helen grimly, " I have all but killed her." " How ? " enquired the startled Geraldine. " With the besom." " Why, for goodness' sake ? " " Why ? " repeated Helen, bursting out into a new rage, " *Why* indeed ? Because she ate my red herring. I set it all ready on the end of the dresser, and she ran away with it and ate it, every morsel, to the tail. — Oh, if I had got hold of her she would not have got off with her life." " And have you had no dinner ? " asked Miss Jewsbury. " Oh, yes — I had mutton enough ; but I had just set my heart on a red herring."

" A singular humble loyalty and genuine attachment to her mistress never failed in poor Helen as the chief redeeming virtue ", wrote her master many years later. In October 1840, when Mrs. Carlyle was laid up and miserably ill, the poor soul " bent over on her bed as if she were a child and rubbed her cheek on hers " — her own cheeks being wet with tears : On New Year's Day, four years later, she came early to her lady's room, saluted her with a hearty smack on either cheek, " while ", records Mrs. Carlyle, " an immense gingerbread cake — which she had baked more gingery than usual to suit my taste — was thrust into the breast of my night-shift ". The redeeming virtues of humility, fidelity and (unconscious) humour were certainly needed in a young woman who was already at the end of 1844 " getting more and more into the habit of tippling ". Tearful promises of amendment were followed by harrowing occasions when, having stupefied herself with the contents of a hidden bottle of whisky from ten in the morning till the end of the day ", she was found lying on the kitchen floor, " in the midst of a perfect chaos of dirty dishes and fragments of broken crockery ".

From time to time Mrs. Carlyle's friends set about finding her another Abigail, and once Helen's passage was actually booked by sea to Kirkcaldy, for she obstinately refused to look for a situation in London or to take any steps towards quitting Cheyne Row. " Fancy you ill and me not there to take proper care of you," she said to her mistress ; " I think *that* would be a farce ! " Yet it was only at the last moment that her tears, her pale face and her despair procured her one more chance. In September 1846 she had not relapsed, and had grown " like wine

and a few other things, the better by keeping ", when Fate intervened in the person of a brother in Dublin who had been " rising
into great prosperity as a maker of coach-fringes, thanks to the
immense consumption of that article on the railways ". This
worthy, whose attentions to his sister had hitherto been confined
to a quarter of an hour's call when business brought him to
London, now suddenly decided to make " a sort of lady " of her.
" He looks ", noted Mrs. Carlyle, " a foolish, flustering sort of
incredible creature " ; " a silly snob ", said Mr. Carlyle ; and it
was further remarked to his detriment that his eyes were too close
together and his expression was shifty. Helen, however, " felt
no doubt as to the solidity of his basis", and accepted his invitation
to join him in Dublin.

Not the least of her merits had been the cheerful imperturb-
ability with which she had endured various domestic crises and
afflictions — such as the presence of carpenters and workmen
trying to make the upper part of the house sound-proof against
the " accursed pianoforte " of the young lady next door, and —
worse still — the recurrent presence of what Mazzini called
" small beings " and she herself called " bogues ".

At this point perhaps a brief digression may be permitted
upon this subject — one which, however unpleasing in itself, is
not without interest to the student of English social history in the
first half of the nineteenth century. In 1835, the year following
their installation at Cheyne Row, Mrs. Carlyle recorded proudly,
" We have no bugs yet to the best of my knowledge ; and I do
not know of one other house among all my acquaintance that so
much can be said for ". By the late summer of 1842 the kitchen
bed was " impregnated with these small beings ", beyond Mrs.
Carlyle's cleansing powers : it was sold (with all its awful
potentialities) to a broker, and the lady " went the same day and
bought a little iron bedstead for the kitchen for one pound two
and sixpence ". Eleven months later Kirkcaldy Helen espied
" two bogues ", and a carpenter was hurriedly summoned to take
her couch to pieces. He remarked that " they " were " pretty
strong ". The horrified Mrs. Carlyle flung " some twenty pailfuls
of water on the kitchen floor, in the first place to drown any that
might attempt to save themselves. Then ", she adds, " we killed

all that were discoverable, and flung the pieces of the bed . . .
into a tub full of water, carried them up into the garden and let
them steep there for two days." " Ach Gott ! " she exclaims,
" what disgusting work to have to do — but destroying bugs is
a thing that cannot be neglected." In the course of the bug
investigation it was discovered that the woollen mattress was
being " eaten from under " Helen with moths — all of which
reflects rather badly on the housewifery of Jane Welsh.

Four years later the small beings were discovered in the stuff-
ing of a chair presented by Sir Henry Taylor ; and in 1849 all
curtains were frantically torn down and sent to the dyers, " not
so much to have the colour renewed as to have the bugs boiled
to death ". Early in 1856 Mrs. Carlyle put it on record that she
had kept her house for many years free and clean " from all such
abominations " ; but later in that same year the then Abigail,
" Cockney Anne ", being left in charge, permitted Carlyle's own
bed, his sacred green-curtained bed, bought in Dumfries " with
part of the payment for an article on Jean Paul ", to become
infested. Taken severely to task, she expressed astonishment
that " such a fuss should be made about bugs ", and gave a
month's notice — but this she afterwards retracted.

Let us return now to Helen Mitchell, dwelling in brief,
precarious gentility with her fringe-making brother in Dublin.
As might have been foreseen, the plan did not work well, or for
long. Back in Kirkcaldy, she directed wistful glances and appealing letters to Cheyne Row, and asked nothing better than to
return there. " She did return, poor wench," Carlyle records,
" but was at once discerned (not by me) to be internally in a state
of chaos ; and within three months for open and incurable
drunkenness had to be dismissed." The last stages of her down-
ward journey were lamentable. One evening she opened the
door to her master and mistress looking like " a stage ghost very
ill got up — blood spurting from her lips, her face whitened with
chalk from the kitchen floor, her gown ditto, and wearing a smile
of idiotic self-complacency ". Thereafter she sank lower and
lower, the " poor bit dottle ", and was finally sent home to
Kirkcaldy to die.

In her fierce loyalty to Mrs. Carlyle, Helen hotly resented all attempts by outsiders to exploit that lady's romantic kindness of heart, and the vials of her wrath had been poured forth upon the two Mudie girls, Elizabeth and Juliet, unwearying efforts to ' place ' whom as lady's-maids had no enduring results. It was they, according to Helen, who had brought in the " bogues " — on their shawls. " Flary, staring and conceited stolid-looking girls," says Carlyle, " thinking themselves handsome." Their father, a Dundee schoolmaster, had abandoned a scholastic career to seek his fortune in London, died, and left a widow and these two incompetent daughters. " The wretched, stalking block-heads " — it is again Carlyle who sums up — " stalked steadily, fatefully, downwards towards perdition." They performed, however, one useful function, albeit unwittingly : they reconciled Mrs. Carlyle and her adoring but incalculable friend Geraldine Jewsbury, who by associating herself with the quest of situations for the Misses Mudie bridged the temporary gulf yawning between the two friends.

Miss Jewsbury herself was a notable housewife, and had acted most successfully as *châtelaine* first to a widowed father and then to a bachelor brother. In the intervals of writing emotional and incoherent but exciting novels she found time to contribute articles on subjects of general interest to Douglas Jerrold's *Shilling Magazine*, and one of these — she being a member of the Carlyle circle and a frequent visitor to Cheyne Row — may be touched upon here. It was entitled " Hiring a Servant ", and it betrayed a very low opinion both of employers and employed, the former being inclined to regard their maidservants as cattle and to complain of them as if they were " malign Brownies ", while among the latter neither chastity nor honesty could be expected. It must have been in Manchester rather than in Cheyne Row that these views were formed, for Jane Welsh never treated her servants unsympathetically and even the least satisfactory among them do not seem to have been either dishonest or un-chaste. On the other hand, both she and her husband were occasionally goaded into ejaculations which it would be unfair to regard as typical of their attitude to their domestic staff.

Servants, observed Mrs. Carlyle in a letter to her cousin Jeannie Welsh (March 1843), are " a most important, a most fearful item in our female existence . . . what a mercy it is for us that we never discover all the misconduct of the 'vile creatures' till they are gone or going ". " Domesticities ", according to Carlyle in morose mood, were " anarchic exceedingly ; the funnel-neck of all our anarchies." Yet of individual servants — all but the very worst specimens — they could both write with humorous tolerance, infinite kindness and real compassion.

When Helen Mitchell departed for Dublin in December 1846, she left the household at Cheyne Row " in a fearful puddle ", but worse remained behind, for the next Abigail to take up her abode in the basement was the Scottish damsel soon to be nick-named " Pessima ", and almost as soon — *i.e.* after only six days — to be discharged by Carlyle in the vigorous terms quoted above. She had been selected in Edinburgh by an old servant of the Carlyles " more on account of her pretensions to *Free Grace* than on account of any *works* she was capable of ". Finding single service too lonely and becoming suddenly conscious that being a maid-of-all-work would spoil her hands, she threatened to " take fits " if she were not allowed to go, and, very far from being abashed by the wording of her dismissal, she walked off on a Sunday morning " as happy as a pig ".

An advertisement in *The Times* produced only one applicant, and that one " not to be thought of " : but a second attempt was more fortunate, for, after Mrs. Carlyle had interviewed " all sorts of horrid-looking females ", a " cheery little button of a creature " presented herself, who had been for three years in a neighbouring family and left in consequence of the mistress having died and the master gone into lodgings. The bereaved gentleman gave her a promising character : " only one lover who came to see her, and only one female friend, both highly respectable and not too troublesome ". The lover's name was James, and he was a butcher's lad ; once a week he would visit his beloved, and sit for two hours with a taciturnity worthy of Mr. Barkis in a similar situation. It pleased Mrs. Carlyle to know that " a little decent love-making was going on in the house ". Two years later the butcher married her and bore her off to Jersey, where the Carlyles heard of them " doing well in the butcher's business ; but alas, before long, of poor Anne's falling ill and dying ".

A good, willing, handy creature Anne had been ; she learned to poise herself precariously upon a pair of steps in order to dust every book on her master's shelves ; through her acquaintance with " Old John ", the man-servant next door, she put a stop for five long, peaceful days to the incessant piano-practice of the ladies in that house ; and she once delighted her mistress by expressing a doubt as to where there was *another* lady that could stuff chair-cushions and do anything that was needed, " and be a lady, too ! " " So now ", added Mrs. Carlyle, " I think that I am strong enough in Anne's respect to even smoke in her presence."

" Cockney Anne " enjoyed the occasional assistance of a certain Mrs. Piper, of whom she was inclined to be a little jealous. On one occasion, when Mrs. Carlyle had been absent from home, this good dame had slept three nights in her bed " to air it " ; therefore when Carlyle was due to return from a visit to Scotsbrig in October 1847, Anne volunteered to go and sleep in his bed for a few nights, " to take the damp out of it " — so little had English habits gained in fastidiousness since the seventeenth century.

The seven years immediately following — 1849–56 — were chequered and rather uncomfortable years in the Cheyne Row kitchen. Elizabeth Sprague from Exeter, " a high-going, shining kind of damsel ", murdered her mistress's sleep and caused her to become so weak and excited that she had to have recourse to morphia pills ; then came Eliza, who, being only a ' temporary ', was " set to cleaning out the kitchen closets and presses, where many abominations came to light ". She was in the act of swabbing the kitchen floor to make the place "seductively clean for the stranger " when her successor, twenty-year-old Emma, arrived — only to be shut up in the spare room with some sewing till she could " find a place below for the sole of her foot ". Self-possessed, soft-voiced, slow-witted and incompetent, incapable of making mutton-broth and in roasting " far from strong ", she soon faded out, and the procession of flitting phantoms goes on. There was the one who went suddenly stone deaf on New Year's Day, 1851, and thereafter decided to become a kitchen-maid rather than be driven mad by " listening to bells and never hearing them " ; and there was Irish Fanny, " willing

Reproduced by permission of the Proprietors of Punch

"PROTECTOR AND PROTECTEE"

1866

to fly to the moon for her mistress ", who, after having her trunk, her " nice, large new trunk ", rifled by burglars who broke in through the larder window, ultimately " ran away into matrimony of a kind ", probably with one of her compatriots, the Irish labourers who had been at work upon the (alleged) sound-proof room.

Then there was the " great beauty " engaged in July 1852, because she had been six years in her last place and also because Carlyle " distinctly liked her physiognomy ". In addition to being a perfect fool she proved to be a listener at keyholes and a fumbler among papers, and Mrs. Carlyle was grateful to fall back upon another little Chelsea girl, "Little Martha ", who had come to help when Cockney Anne was ill. "I could have told you, ma'am," said Little Martha sagely, apropos of the "great beauty", "the very first day that girl was here that she wasn't fit for a *genteel* place."

Yet another Ann (this time with no terminal ' e ') now fills the scene — a very genteel young person, as the following anecdote proves. Lady Alicia Hill, calling one day, noticed that the maid had a bandaged finger, and asked what ailed it. " I have cut it, my Lady." " How did you do it ? " " Well, I did it — cutting up a fowl." When relating this dialogue to her mistress Ann explained, " You know, ma'am, I couldn't go and say to a *real* young lady that I did it cutting a *bath-brick* ! That sounded so *common* ! I thought a *fowl* was more the thing."

It is hardly surprising that, after five years, she should have decided to accept the invitation of a niece who was going into business as a milliner and wanted her to spend three months with her " to teach her housekeeping ". At the end of that period she announced that it was her intention to take a situation with " a single gentleman who kept an under-servant to do all the rough work ". To her succeeded Miss Cameron, a person of even greater pretensions to gentility, for she claimed to be the daughter of a half-pay Captain and to have filled for eight years the post of maid-companion to " the daughters of General Osborne ". The " Irish impostor ", as Carlyle labelled her, was soon discovered to be a liar and a thief, and after tarrying in Cheyne Row for a fortnight and three days she decamped by stealth between ten and eleven at night.

In June 1858 enter " Little Charlotte ", one of the most engaging of all the Cheyne Row Abigails. " A fine little Chelsea creature ", Carlyle called her ; " clever little Charlotte," wrote Mrs. Carlyle, " far more like an adopted child than a maid of all work " — and a great deal is heard for a time of her virtues and accomplishments. She baked excellent bread ; she crocheted " out of her own head " a large cover for the drawing-room sofa. Finding that there were mice — as well there might be — in the house, she brought home a black kitten which at once made friends with Mrs. Carlyle's beloved dog, Nero ; she also — though from no utilitarian motive — adopted a sparrow, and fed it on scrapings of meat. A faint shadow of mystery hangs about Little Charlotte ; her nearest kin were an aunt and an uncle, whom she called ' Father ' and ' Mother '. When she had been in Cheyne Row for a year she had what must have been the greatest adventure of her life — a trip to Scotland. That country she had conjectured to be " a fresh and airy place ", having noticed that her mistress " did smell so beautiful " on arriving home from the north. She travelled by steamer, with Nero, Carlyle, and Carlyle's riding horse. Once installed with the family in a farm near Aberdour in Fife, she was " filled with wonder and delight " by the kindness of the people. Young men who did not so much as know her name said " Bonnie Lassie " to her, as they passed her on the road ; and the farmer with whom they were lodging gave her a little sugar rabbit and told her that she was " getting quite pretty ". But, alas, this was another of Mrs. Carlyle's cygnets whose plumage betrayed that they were not pure swan. In 1860 Little Charlotte is no longer sleeping in the iron bedstead in the kitchen or hanging her caps and aprons out to dry in the shade of the walnut-tree, and the Carlyles are at the mercy of " Old Jane ", gloomily described as a " complete failure and humbug ".

In the matter of loyalty and affection she had not fallen short of Mrs. Carlyle's rather romantic requirements — there is a delightful story of her pride when Carlyle was made a Knight of the White Falcon in 1859, and of her reply when the charwoman remarked, " Then the mistress is a Lady now ! " — " Yes, but she says she won't go in for it ; such a shame ! " She was gay, she was devoted, but it presently became apparent that she was unmethodical, not over-conscientious, and had " a born tendency to muddle ".

During the brief reign of " Old Jane ", Little Charlotte never ceased to hover round Cheyne Row, and when Mrs. Carlyle fell ill she insisted on helping to look after her. " She really ", wrote her ex-mistress, " loves us both passionately " — and there she still was, " poor foolish thing ", hanging on at her aunt's, " just as untidy in her person with nothing to do as she used to be in her press of work ".

In the meantime the adventure so hazardously begun in 1834 had prospered beyond all expectation. The uncouth, angular philosopher from Dumfries was now a figure of note not only in the literary world of London but in the world at large. The critics who had dismissed *Sartor Resartus* as " clotted nonsense " had undergone a change of heart : and the Carlyle legend was in process of formation. Grand Dukes from Germany and eminent writers from America sought his society ; he was a member of the Athenaeum and a frequent (if incongruous) guest in what Disraeli might have described as the gilded saloons of the great. Contrary to the legend fostered by Froude, he did not for one moment dissociate his Jeanie from his social triumphs, which she shared as fully as she cared to share them. *She* was shining, too, and not with reflected radiance only. Her wit and her charm were becoming known, and in her Chelsea house — growing every year less meagre and ascetic — she held her court as often as her variable health allowed her to hold it. All this augmenting prosperity was expressed by degrees in the external accompaniments of their existence. Already in 1845 Carlyle had bought himself a riding horse, and in 1860 the time was not far distant when his wife would take carriage exercise in her own brougham, instead of hiring one from the livery stable : but perhaps the most memorable turn in the road was reached in the August of that year, when it was decided that the Cheyne Row household should consist of two Abigails instead of one only. The innovation was Carlyle's idea, and does not seem to have been welcomed with unmixed pleasure by Jane.

A " really promising woman " of thirty-four, Charlotte

second of that name, and Sarah, "a remarkably nice-looking girl of sixteen", formed the first pair to be driven in double harness by the inexpert hands of their lady. "I think", she wrote, perhaps a trifle dubiously, "the house will really be more comfortable and orderly"; but disillusionment was round the corner. Charlotte Secunda proved to be a "conceited fool", and also the sort of person who regarded loyalty in a dismissed servant as a proof of foolishness. The following dialogue took place between her and Little Charlotte. "You seem", remarked the older woman, "to like being here." "Of course I do ; I look upon this as my home," rejoined the younger. "But you are a nice-looking, healthy girl, you will easily get another place if you try." "Oh, I know that, I may get plenty of places, but I shall never get another home."

"What a poor spirit that girl has, ma'am," commented Charlotte Secunda to the affronted Mrs. Carlyle. "If anybody had been dissatisfied with *me* it's little that I should care about leaving them."

It was about this time that this *cri de cœur* came from the parlour at Cheyne Row : "So now I am mistress of two servants — and ready to hang myself!"

When contemplating this change Mrs. Carlyle had toyed with the idea of having Little Charlotte back as a stable-companion to the other young maid, but was deterred by the reflection that "she, who couldn't rule herself, would have made a sad mess of ruling a girl nearly her own age". Before the year ended the feckless but warm-hearted child was duly reinstalled, "bursting with ecstasy", and congratulated by the Carlyles' friends upon her triumphant return. Luckily she and young Sarah soon made friends, and Sarah delighted her by the confession that if "Tall Charlotte" had not been dismissed, she herself would have given notice, she disliked her so much.

Always optimistic, Mrs. Carlyle wrote, in one of the gayest and most gentle of all her domestic commentaries, that Sarah's tidiness and method were just what was needed to correct Little Charlotte's born tendency to muddle, while Little Charlotte's willingness and affectionate disposition "warmed up" Sarah's drier, more selfish nature. "It is a curious establishment," noted its head, " with something of the sound and character of a nursery." The two young things, both under nineteen, kept up " an incessant chirping and chattering and laughing ", and, as both had " remarkably sweet voices ", it was pleasant to hear. They slept so soundly, " those fortunate girls ", in their basement bed that the alarum clock at their heads was never heard by either of them, and it was necessary that an old man who lodged with Charlotte's relations should rap on the kitchen window on his way to work at six in the morning. Small wonder that in this cheerful state of affairs Mrs. Carlyle should report " The two-ness is no nuisance to me now ".

It did not — it could not — last. Less than a year later Little Charlotte vanished from the scene — vanished finally except for a fleeting reappearance in May 1863, when she was third housemaid at the Marquess Camden's and " much more sedate and proper " than when her mistress " had to put her away ".

There followed a procession of always transient and often unsatisfactory creatures whose outlines need be traced in a few strokes. There was a new housemaid — what we should now call a ' house-parlour-maid ' — in the summer of 1861, " a little black, busy creature ", who had a mysterious love-affair, and " went to New Zealand out of sight " ; to her succeeded an " affected fool " called Maria who was clever in the care of her master's books and presumed upon it. Then came a Scot, Elizabeth, " that horse ", Carlyle unkindly called her, " that cow, that mooncalf ", and Little Flo, at first ranked as an " incomparable small housemaid " and at last as an " incomparable small demon ". The two maids who welcomed Mrs. Carlyle with flushed faces and tearful eyes when she returned from Scotland in October 1864, were apparently the same whom Carlyle had described as " two idiot servants " during her absence earlier in the same year. " A large, gooseish housemaid ", " a big beautiful blockhead ", these were the flowers of language with which he adorned one of them : she was wasteful, too ; " three pounds of fresh butter at twenty-pence a pound regularly consumed in the kitchen, and half a pound of tea at four shillings made away with in four days ".

It may be interesting at this point to ' put in ' a list of the " usual observances ", *i.e.* rations, for one person for one week, drawn from a manual of domestic management belonging to this period. " Tea, two ounces ; coffee, a quarter of a pound (if for breakfast only) ; cocoa paste, a quarter of a pound, for breakfasts ; sugar, half a pound ; butter, half a pound ; cheese, half a pound ; milk, one quart — varying with the taste of the family ; bread, eight pounds for a woman, sixteen pounds for a man or boy ; meat, six pounds ; beer, one gallon for a woman, seven quarts for a man ; potatoes, three and a half pounds." Except in the articles of milk and potatoes the list is one to cause war-time mouths to water.

And now we come to that halcyon season at Cheyne Row, the last eighteen months of the once unquiet life of Jane Welsh Carlyle : " a second youth," wrote her widowed husband, " almost a second childhood with the wisdom and graces of old age, which by heaven's great mercy were conceded to her and me ". The clouds had already begun to disperse in the summer of 1863 when Mrs. Carlyle paid a few days' visit to her old maid Bessy Barnet, " redeviva, 1862 " as Mrs. Blakiston, the wife of a rather pompous but very amiable and unsnobbish physician in Warrior Square, St. Leonards-on-Sea. This was the same Bessy who had come with them to Cheyne Row nearly thirty years before, and who now hovered over her guest with sweet jellies, champagne and calves'-foot jelly, in the intervals of gliding about her house " looking very natural " as mistress of it, and maintaining " the completest silken dominion " over her husband. She " would not be hindered " from bringing up hot water and waiting on Mrs. Carlyle " as a lady's maid ", and was never so pleased as when talking of the things that had happened when she was her servant in very sooth.

Towards the close of 1864 there enters with majestic, Siddons-like tread the " admirable cook " of the " courteous manners and equable temper ", Mrs. Warren by name. She was a " respectable widow of fifty " whose perfection seems at first slightly to have daunted her employers. Her first coadjutor had been unsatisfactory, but in 1865 Mrs. Carlyle brought back with her from Scotland Jessie Hiddlestone, the daughter of Mrs. Welsh's last Haddington servant, and once in the employment of Mrs. Russell at Thornhill. Mrs. Carlyle had marked her there, " a bonnie young woman who dashed about with great activity, but who made a noise with fire-irons and skuttle and doors " that kept the lady " constantly jumping ".

By extraordinary good fortune Mrs. Carlyle's part of the correspondence preceding the formal engagement has survived. At the beginning it is clear that she felt certain doubts. Would Jessie be happy so far from her own country ? " I dislike ", she wrote, " a gloomy, discontented-looking servant quite as much as an inefficient one " ; and the girl's last situation, wherein she had been very well contented, was in a houseful of servants at Edinburgh, where her chief work had been waiting at table. Still, she felt sufficiently confident to define the duties of a housemaid " where there are only two servants kept ". She had to do the house-work, answer the door, wait at table ; she must be " the least bit of a lady's maid " to her mistress, and " the least bit of a valet to Mr. Carlyle ". The washing, she adds reassuringly, " is all given out ; the servants wash their own clothes — there is a little garden to dry them in ".

Coming to the important question of wages, Mrs. Carlyle writes, " I give my Housemaid twelve pounds a year and one pound ten for *beer money*, which she may drink or save as she likes. Tea and sugar is of course given." Finally, on May 24, 1865, the formal letter of engagement was written. It began with a promise to send Jessie a shilling in postage stamps, " after the good old Scottish fashion of engagement, unknown in London " — and apparently misunderstood there, for Mrs. Carlyle had observed surprise and even terror on the part of the person receiving it, who " supposed it might bind her to Heaven knew what — like the shilling given to enlist a soldier ".

The English habit of engaging servants only by the month is then condemned as " a very bad plan ", giving opportunity to people " to fly asunder in any moment of ill humour on either side ". Jessie had previously been engaged by the half-year, and it was proposed that the present engagement should be upon the same terms. She came south with Mrs. Carlyle in July 1865.

At first all went well. From Folkestone a month later the lady wrote a friendly letter to her Abigail which shows that she had liked being ' maided ' by her. " I need excessively to have my hair combed," she confessed, " and then the Housemaid is so ugly ! I can't bear Her to come within a yard of me." Jessie, it seems, was the possessor of " a face that captivated everyone by its brightness and sweetness " ; and for a time she walked in an air of glory — a fellow-Scot, the daughter of old Margaret of Haddington, the erewhile maid of dear Mrs. Russell of Thornhill. Then, for the last time in her tale of troubled days, Jane Welsh Carlyle suffered the dull pang of disillusionment. She found that " snubbing and riding with the curb-bridle " were what Jessie required. " I make a point ", she wrote, " of being just to her, as *mistress* to a *servant*. So she got the ' nice dress ' at Christmas, along with Mrs. Warren's, but I put no affection into anything I do for her, and let her see that I don't." Whether Jessie saw this or not, she stuck to her post, receiving at Christmas in addition to the ' nice dress ' the sovereign always given to each of the Cheyne Row servants at that season by a certain sparely-built, red-faced, russet-whiskered gentleman whose blue eyes clashed with his neck-tie of another yet not a more vivid blue — John Ruskin.

During the winter of 1865–6 Mrs. Carlyle was — in her own words — " speculating " as to whether she should accompany her husband to Edinburgh, where he was to deliver his address as Lord Rector of the University in the course of the ensuing spring. Finally she decided that the mental strain would be too great even if the physical were not so — for she was haunted by nervous fears that the address would prove a fiasco. Accordingly she remained in Chelsea with Cousin Maggie Aitken, Mrs. Warren and Jessie Hiddlestone.

Perhaps because too much was not demanded or expected of her, Mrs. Warren seems never to have disappointed her mistress. It was to her, an Englishwoman, cool and polite, that was confided the story of the two candles, laid away for a certain solemn purpose twenty-four years before — a purpose even then fast ripening to fulfilment.

When the Carlyles were giving their first party in London, Mrs. Welsh had decorated the table — unknown to her daughter — with candles and confectionery. Mrs. Carlyle had taken umbrage ; had declared that people would say she was extravagant and would ruin her husband ; and had borne off two of the candles and some of the cakes. Poor Mrs. Welsh, bitterly hurt, had begun to weep : and it was then that Mrs. Carlyle had taken that resolution — " bright ", says her husband, " as with heavenly tears and lightning ", that those two candles should stand lighted by her coffin " when the time should come ".

All her three attendants were helping Mrs. Carlyle to dress for John Forster's birthday party when a telegram arrived from the faithful John Tyndall in Edinburgh : " *A perfect triumph* ", it said. Having read it herself, she read it aloud to " the gaping chorus ", which began to dance and clap its hands. " Eh, to hear that ! " cried Jessie : " I told you, ma'am," added the more temperate Mrs. Warren, " how it would be." And then the household proceeded to administer brandy to the agitated and overjoyed lady. *Punch* marked the occasion by a cartoon in which Thomas Carlyle, with cape and wideawake, " made a really creditable appearance ". Terry the greengrocer asked Mrs. Warren whether Mr. Carlyle were the person " they wrote of as Lord Rector " — and Mrs. Warren having answered in her stage voice, " the very same ! " Terry shouted out (" quite shouted, ma'am "), " I never was so glad of anything ! By George, I am glad ! " Forgetting their past differences, which had been neither slight nor few, the cook and the housemaid rushed out to buy copies of *Punch* to send to their families, and then returned to express their joy in a very practical way. " It seems to me ", wrote their amused mistress, " that on every new compliment paid you these women run and fry something, such savoury smells reach me upstairs." If either of the enthusiasts ever had an opportunity of reading the Rectorial Address she would find that in the course of it the Lord Rector remarked that he heard people complaining that maidservants were " getting instructed in the 'ologies ".

Reassured, perhaps, by the cheerful tone of his wife's letters, Carlyle did not hurry back to her side. That she missed him is clear from this passage in the last but one of all the letters she ever wrote : " I have put the women to sleep in your bed to air it. It seems so long since you went away."

On the evening of April 21, a few friends, including Mrs. Oliphant, had been invited to 5 Cheyne Row " to meet the

Froudes " ; but Mrs. Carlyle felt equal to her usual drive round the Park in the afternoon. About five o'clock the Rector of Chelsea met her brougham returning empty, with Old Sylvester, the coachman, sitting in tears on the box : he had come to fetch someone to identify his mistress, lying dead in St. George's Hospital. Jessie undertook the sad errand, and remembered all her life the sight that awaited her in a little dim room at the hospital : Mrs. Carlyle, still dressed in her bonnet and gown, lying on the narrow iron bed, and at her feet the little dog " who had so nearly been run over in the Park and to lift whom tenderly back into the carriage beside her had been her last act on earth ".

Back at Cheyne Row Jessie Hiddlestone showed excellent sense. She looked for and found Mrs. Carlyle's Address Book, and an effort was made to send word to the various friends expected that same evening. Not all of them could be reached in time, so Mrs. Oliphant, an early arrival, undertook to inform any other guests who might appear. Meanwhile Mrs. Warren and Miss Jewsbury were preparing the small panelled first-floor room behind the dining-room, where the long-hoarded candles were burning when the two maids lifted Jane Welsh Carlyle from her temporary coffin and laid her on the bed that they had made ready for her.

Jessie Hiddlestone remained for five months in the service of the widowed Carlyle ; among her duties were these — to rush forth and ' move on ' all street-organs and things of that kind ; to cut up the Sage's pipe tobacco ; and to fill and light the short clay pipe that he was wont to smoke before rising in the morning. Thirty-four years later, as Mrs. Broadfoot, a cheerful, comely widow from Thornhill, she revisited Cheyne Row ; it was after this visit that she sent from Scotland the packet of Mrs. Carlyle's letters still preserved among the treasures of the old house.

CHAPTER X

Victorian Epilogue

IN 1838, a year after the youthful Victoria had grasped her orb and sceptre in such unexpectedly firm hands, Charles Knight and Company, publishers to the Society for the Diffusion of Useful Knowledge, began the issue of a series of small books under the general title of *Guides to Service*. First *The Maid-of-All-Work* and then *The Housemaid* received instruction in both the moral and practical aspects of their respective callings : and in 1839 came the turn of *The Lady's Maid*.

Some readers hastily concluded that the anonymous writer had herself been in domestic service ; others, among whom was the Carlyles' Kirkcaldy Helen, thought poorly of the *Guides*, and considered that they betrayed a degree of inexperience which detracted from their value. The secret of the authorship was soon out — it was Harriet Martineau who, without having been a maid-of-all-work or a housemaid, had set forth to expound their duties, and who, without any intimate personal knowledge of " high life ", was ready to tell a lady's-maid what to do and how to do it.

One prerequisite at least Miss Martineau did possess, and that was an intuitive sympathy with women of the working class. As a child in her father's house in Norwich she had objected to being sent by her mother with " inconsiderate messages " to the servants — for example, when Mrs. Martineau requested that they should not " stamp like elephants over her head " : and we shall see later that this sympathy inspired her dealings with her own maids till the end of her long life. She realized, none the less, that when kindness is ill-requited unpredictable harm may ensue. " If ", she tells the housemaid, " you should have a kind-hearted, gentle-tempered mistress, you really cannot be too thankful . . . if you get into the service of such a mistress, you will not listen to any temptation to leave it, but keep steadily to your duty."

Steadiness in all things is indeed one of the virtues most earnestly inculcated by Miss Martineau. Her ideal maid will not let the summer weather tempt her to stand talking at the door or gossiping out of the window. The baker's man, she remarks admonishingly, " has news and jokes and pretty speeches " for every girl on his round : all the more necessary is it " to keep up the self-respect which everyone respects in another ". No attempt is made to deceive the Abigail into imagining that hers will be a primrose path. " You find you have few pleasures. Your Sunday walk, a holiday now and then, an entertaining book with an hour to read it in, and perhaps a bird, a favourite plant, or a kitten — these are nearly all your indulgences : and they are indeed very few."

It will be noted that Miss Martineau the Unitarian says nothing about a *good* book, or listening to a good sermon : while Miss Martineau the Political Economist naturally does not hint at anything so economically unsound as expenditure on penny ballads, fairs, fairings or personal adornment.

The housemaid, whose wages are stated to average £8 to £9 a year, is particularly warned against being careless with her mistress's glass and china. While examples can be cited to prove that " a careful eye, a steady hand, and a sensible mind " can reduce breakages to a minimum, " I do not see ", declares Miss Martineau, " that ladies are bound to put up with having their sets of china and glass broken into, their lamp-shades cracked, and their wash-basins smashed ". And lamp-shades, she adds, in a feeling parenthesis, " are very expensive ".

When the aspirant comes to the *Guide* dealing with the duties of a lady's-maid, she is at once reminded of the " superior character of the service ", its hardships and advantages being weighed against each other, the importance of discretion and a pleasing deportment being stressed. Strict honesty in all things is commended : some maids who began by taking pins and ends of tape have finally conspired with the men-servants — always the villains of the piece — to steal their ladies' jewels : and so a young person who once felt safe from all temptation finds herself condemned to transportation or the treadmill.

To her own maids at the Knoll, Ambleside, Miss Martineau

was a kind though exceedingly instructive mistress. She would cram their minds with useful knowledge, read aloud to them from her own leading articles, and encourage them to attend her lectures. When Martha, one of her treasures, married the master of the Bristol Ragged Schools, she herself " arranged the flowers, laid the wedding breakfast, shut up the cat, and generally acted as benevolent godmother ".

In 1844 the authoress was persuaded to try mesmerism as a cure for an intractable and elusive malady which had incapacitated her for many years, and the results were so encouraging that her maid, Jane, agreed to reproduce, as well as she was able, the passes she had seen made by the professional mesmerist, while the patient read aloud to her from a pseudo-scientific book on animal magnetism. This Jane was afterwards to become quite celebrated, indeed notorious, as " the Apocalyptic Housemaid ". When she and her future mistress first met, Miss Martineau had been lodging with Jane's aunt at Tynemouth. Characteristically the lady interested herself in the enthusiastic, imaginative girl, hard driven by her elderly relative, whose housemaid (and slave) she was. This interest was immensely heightened when Jane submitted to being put in a trance and, while supposedly " under", gave a vivid description of the wreck of a local ship near Hull, and the escape of the crew. Miss Martineau was convinced of the genuineness of Jane's vision ; so was Elizabeth Barrett ; but doubters like Robert Browning were confirmed in their scepticism by the fact that the news of the wreck and the crew's survival had been commnuicated to the mesmerist's own maid and to Jane herself some hours before the *séance* was held. A heated correspondence raged upon the subject in the columns of *The Athenaeum.*

No argument advanced by the cynical could shake Miss Martineau's faith in her protégée, whom she installed as a member of her modest household at the Knoll. Ultimately the Apocalyptic Housemaid, impressed by one of her mistress's discourses on the subject of Australia, decided to emigrate to that land of promise and vanished from the scene before Harriet Martineau's malady returned and mesmerism failed to repeat its earlier triumph over it.

Calling on her friends the Carlyles any time in the early 1840's, this intellectual though rather cranky lady could hardly have failed to meet one or other of the Italian political refugees who then frequented Cheyne Row. Among them was a portrait-painter, Spiridone Gambardella by name, whose endeavours to find a maid were amusingly described by Mrs. Carlyle in a letter to a relation. He was determined to have a " gu-l " all to himself ; the " gu-ls " in the lodging-house where he was staying were vile creatures who left finger-marks on everything. The Abigail of his artless dreams was to mend his linen, wash his brushes, make fancy-dresses for his models and sit for him her-self, " a beautiful fo'm " being an indispensable qualification. It seems hardly credible, but he inserted an advertisement in *The Times* to this effect : " Wanted a very genteel girl to do very genteel work, not under fifteen, not exceeding eighteen years of age, wages from twenty to thirty pounds per annum ". He was, of course, as Mrs. Carlyle perceived but was too kind to say to him, " exposing himself to the most atrocious imputations ". By nine o'clock on the morning of the day that the advertisement appeared fifty girls were on the door-step and more were arriving every minute. Some of them were escorted by villainous-looking parents, guardians or exploiters ; none of them was under any uncertainty as to the nature of " the very genteel work " ; but whereas some of the bolder, more flaunting types showed every willingness to negotiate, there were others, mostly those who were escorted by avaricious elders, who betrayed a pathetic reluctance.

Not unnaturally the proprietor of the lodging-house raised the strongest possible objections to the scheme and its immediate results. Gambardella engaged none of the deluded applicants, and Mrs. Carlyle assisted him to compose a less ambiguous advertisement — with what sequel, if any, is not known.

Strangely gullible though Miss Barrett tended to be, she can hardly have dreamed when she interested herself in the Apoca-lyptic Housemaid that her own maid, Wilson, most staid, sober and unimaginative of Englishwomen, would in course of time find herself involved in " manifestations ", besides fulfilling a destiny which neither herself nor her friends could conceivably have predicted for her when she took up her post as lady's-maid in Wimpole Street.

During the period immediately preceding Mr. Browning's irruption into the dim, over-heated bedroom of Elizabeth Barrett, Lily Wilson had been in constant attendance upon her mistress, then too feeble to rise from her sofa and cross the room to her bookcase. Her affectionate eye must have noted the improvement in Miss Ba's spirits which began with the opening of her correspondence with Mr. Robert Browning and increased progressively as the exchange of letters proceeded. Hers too would be the hand that confided one-half of those letters to the Wimpole Street posting-box, for nobody understood better than Wilson did that Mr. Edward Moulton Barrett must be allowed to know little or nothing about the new interest that was transforming the half-life of his eldest daughter into a life more full than most women have ever had a chance to live.

How perfect was Wilson's grasp of the whole situation and how warm was her sympathy may be gathered from a letter written by Elizabeth in August 1845, three months after the loud voice (and the even louder trousers) of Mr. Browning had dissipated the gloom of the darkened upper chamber for the first time.

> Wilson tells me that you were followed upstairs yesterday . . . by somebody whom you probably took for my father. Which is Wilson's idea and I hope not yours. No — it was neither father nor other relative of mine, but an old friend in rather an ill temper.

In February 1846 Elizabeth Barrett was anxious about Mr. Browning's headaches and his health generally, and overflowed to Wilson. " When you were gone yesterday," she wrote to him, " and my thoughts tossed about restlessly for ever so long, I was wise enough to ask Wilson how *she* thought you were looking — and ' she did not know ' — she ' had not observed ' — ' only certainly Mr. Browning ran upstairs instead of walking as he did the time before '." Incidentally we learn that by this time there was no question of Wilson preceding him up the stairs and announcing him formally to her mistress.

A month later we get a glimpse of the excellent Wilson which illustrates the essentially prosaic and pedestrian turn of her mind.

Miss Barrett describes how on the morrow of one of Robert Browning's visits Wilson found and held up from her chair a bunch of dead blue violets.

> Quite dead they seemed ! You had dropped them and I had sate on them, and where we murdered them they had lain, poor things, all the night through. And Wilson thought it the vainest of labours when she saw me set about reviving them, cutting the stalks afresh, and dipping them head and ears into water — but then she did not know how you and I and ours live under a miraculous dispensation, and could only simply be astonished when they took to blowing again as if they had never wanted the dew of the garden.

Wilson's duties and activities were divided between Miss Ba and Miss Ba's beloved dog Flush, who, in the summer of the same year, so far forgot himself as to snap at Mr. Browning — in spite of constant amiability on that gentleman's part and occasional propitiations in the way of cake. The delinquent came upstairs " with a good deal of shame in the bearing of his ears ". His mistress would not speak to him : he then went to her sister Arabel, who said, " Naughty Flush, go away ! " And he got no consolation from Wilson, who had already whipped him, because she explained, " it was right ". " Do you imagine that I scolded Wilson when she confessed to having whipped him ? " wrote Elizabeth. " I did not. It was done with her hand, and not very hardly perhaps — though ' he cried ', she averred to me." Later she reassures her lover by telling him, " But nobody heard yesterday of either your visit or of Flush's misdoings — so Wilson was discreet, I suppose, as she usually is, by the instinct of her vocation. Of all the people who are not in our confidence she has the most certain knowledge of the truth."

The next day Elizabeth wrote to her Robert a long letter concerning their joint plans for the future, and confessed, with some hesitation, that she had thought of taking Wilson with her, " for a year, say, if we returned then ". By that time she hoped to be stronger and wiser, and rather less sublimely helpless and impotent. She reminds him that she cannot leave the Wimpole Street house without " the necessary number of shoes and pocket-handkerchiefs " unless she has help from somebody, and she has to contrive " a sheltering ignorance " for her sisters to the last.

There again a confidante was necessary, and to what confidante but Wilson could she have recourse ? " If I left her behind," she says, " she would be turned into the street before sunset. Would it be right and just of me to permit it ? Consider ! "

Further to give Mr. Browning's considerations the bent which she desired, Miss Barrett went on to assure him that she believed Wilson to be attached to her, that she knew her to be ready and willing to follow her to Italy or anywhere else in the world, and that she was " very amiable and easily satisfied ". But — and here obviously is the reason for all this anxious tact and delicacy — she was " an expensive servant " : her wages amounted to £16 a year.

The poet replied with characteristic vehemence that without Wilson, or someone in that capacity, " you — no, I will not undertake to speak of *you* : then *I* should be simply, exactly, INSANE to move a step ". He adds that he would rather propose that they should live on bread and water and sail in the hold of a merchant ship. This letter of his crossed with pages of after-thoughts from his Elizabeth, who was suddenly seized with the conviction that she might have annoyed or frightened him about Wilson.

Wilson's willingness to follow her mistress anywhere led her to a less agreeable spot than Italy. Flush was stolen and held to ransom by a gang of dog thieves, and when Miss Barrett boldly went to seek him in their Whitechapel lair, Wilson went with her in the hackney cab, firmly persuaded that they would both be robbed and murdered, and tugging nervously at her gown when " an immense feminine bandit ", the wife of the gang leader, invited them to enter the house and await his return. They did not accept the invitation, nor were they able to bear Flush home with them in triumph ; but he was ultimately restored, a very thirsty and somewhat chastened dog.

On September 12, 1846, the lovers were married in Maryle-bone Church. Writing to his bride on the very day of their wedding, Browning added a postscript : " Remember to thank Wilson for me " : almost at the same moment she was writing to her bridegroom, describing how she had gone straight from the church to Hugh Stuart Boyd's house, and rested, and drunk

Cyprus wine there, till her sisters, having missed her and Wilson, took fright and, fetched by the maid, hurried to Mr. Boyd's " with such grave faces " that she was fain to go with them in the carriage as far as Hampstead Heath to calm their fears.

" How necessity makes heroes — or heroines, at least ! " she wrote. " For I did not sleep all last night, and when I first went out with Wilson to get to the fly-stand in Marylebone Street I staggered so that we were both afraid for the fear's sake — but we called at a chemist's for *sal volatile* and were thus enabled to go on." Mistress and maid had had a brief, heart-to-heart colloquy the night before, during which Wilson was " very kind, very affectionate ", and her mistress promised enduring gratitude.

Urged by Browning to take " the simplest possible ward-robe ", Mrs. Browning — as she now must be called — answered that she and Wilson had a light box and a carpet-bag, between them — amazingly modest luggage in an age of Noah's-ark-trunks and crinolines. On the eve of their departure from England we hear, however, of " boxes ", safely got away by Wilson, who had been " perfect ". Her mistress, who had formerly been afraid of her timidity, realized her error and remarked, " I begin to think that none are so bold as the timid when they are fairly roused ". The devoted but officious maid, Susan, in *Aurora Leigh* may stand as a sketch of Wilson, especially when Aurora thus apostrophizes her :

> Leave the lamp, Susan, and go up to bed.
> The room does very well.   I have to write
> Beyond the stroke of midnight — get away ;
> Your steps forever buzzing in the room
> Tease me like gnats.

Wilson, says Leonard Huxley in his edition of Mrs. Browning's letters to her sister, " eventually became as Italianate as any dream of her poet-mistress, once she had got over her Puritan shock at the nudes in the picture-galleries ". In 1848 we hear of her " blooming in health and spirits ", talking Italian " with a little licence in the grammar ", and understanding it when spoken. She made little net caps for Mrs. Browning, " washable and very pretty " in various colours, blue, green, lilac and purple, and dressed her long dark hair " in the old Grecian plait behind ", sighing as she did so for the days when " Miss Arabel's looked beautiful plaited that way ". She also " made up beautifully " some dark-coloured material sent by Arabel and Henrietta to Florence, and baked " knead-cakes " to admiration. Italian food and — perhaps to an even greater degree — Italian wine suited Wilson perfectly. " Fancy me and Wilson drinking claret out of tumblers ! " exclaimed Mrs. Browning, whose affection for her deepened as years passed and was made stronger still when the Browning baby, the " Third Incomprehensible ", was born, and Wilson constituted herself his adoring bondwoman.

No such child, Wilson was convinced, had ever existed. She was terrified of his learning anything by heart, even little pieces of poetry, lest the excitement should be too much. But she suffered Ferdinando, the man-servant engaged in 1853, to take the small boy, and Flush — under her superintendence — to swim in the little river at Bagni di Lucca. The child repaid her affection warmly : she was his " Lili ", his own " Lili ", and when Mamma was busy with her poetry, " Lili " was guardian, slave and play-mate all in one.

Even in the more easy and unconventional atmosphere of Italy Wilson retained her British reserve and a strong sense of her own dignity. She went to call on a friend in the household of the Princess of Parma at the Princess's villa, very elegant, with a parasol in her hand, and was equally scandalized and discomfited when the two-year-old daughter of the princely house rushed at her, clasped her round the knees, and seized her parasol.

For a time Wilson was affianced to " Mr. Righi of the Ducal Guard ", a fine-looking man with " a prepossessing counten-ance " ; but the romance fizzled out, and she got over her dis-appointment in a way which did " the greatest credit to her good sense and rectitude of character ". She also had " an offer " from an old admirer in England. Finally, she contracted a happy marriage with Ferdinando, whose devotion to her small charge had done much to commend him to her favour.

It is rather surprising that a woman of such excellent sense should have believed in " candle-omens ", though not at all surprising that Mrs. Browning should have been her eager pupil in the art of interpreting these omens. When the lady became interested in spiritualism, the Abigail followed suit. It was found that Wilson was a medium, "though a weak one" : she also went in for automatic writing, though generally in an indecipherable and incoherent manner. She herself seems to have been an object of sympathetic interest to one of the "controls" with which Mrs. Browning believed herself to have established contact. On one occasion this message "came through" : *Send Wilson to bed — she is ill.* At first Wilson laughed, and said it was a great mistake — she felt so sleepy she couldn't keep her eyes open, but was as well as possible. In the course of undressing her mistress, however, she suddenly plumped down into a chair "in a sort of half-mesmeric, half-fainting affection — the large tears dropping down her cheeks". After "a proper application of hygienic vinegar" she recovered : but it was probably fortunate that marriage with the stalwart Ferdinando delivered Wilson from an influence so enervating.

In the same year — 1847 — that saw Lily Wilson adjusting her stiff Britannic notions to Italian ways, the Brothers Mayhew published an extravaganza, with illustrations by Cruikshank, entitled *The Greatest Plague of Life, or the Adventures of a Lady in Search of a Good Servant* and supposed to have been written by "one who has been almost worried to death". At an early stage it becomes clear that we are not expected either to like or to pity the shrewish, despotic little snob who tells the tale, and begins by announcing that she has had to give up her establishment and take refuge with her husband and children in a boarding-house "all through a pack of ungrateful, good-for-nothing things called servants, who really do not know when they are well off".

Her home had been in Park Village, Regent's Park, and a great source of trouble, scandal and rebellion in her household had been "a set of fellows from those dreadful barracks in Alb–ny Str–t". We meet these too-prepossessing warriors later, but they were not responsible for the downfall of her first maid, whom she engaged at a salary of £10 a year, "finding her own tea and sugar". On their return from their honeymoon at Rottingdean she and her lawyer husband found their treasure, Mary, lying on her back in a state of complete intoxication, while the best linen sheets, airing on a clothes-horse before the fire, were burnt "to perfect rags ". On the day of the first reception given by the bride, Mary drank up all her mistress's eau-de-cologne and then was so ' fuddled ' that she tried to make the guests shake hands with her in the hall and then apostrophized them as " a set of stuck-up things " because they wouldn't. Another time she drank two bottles of choice cherry-brandy and filled them up with cold tea — with devastating results at an At Home. The lady, concluding that she had done the same with the sole remaining bottle, ordered her to drink the contents of that one also : but as it happened to be the only one containing un-diluted cherry-brandy, Mary obeyed with alacrity.

During the domestic crisis which ensued, a charwoman attended, who was rewarded by the sum of 1s. 6d. a day, two pots of beer, and a glass of spirits at night. Then a most suitable-looking, unassuming young person came to apply for the situation. She came wearing " a nice plain cotton gown of only one colour, being a nice white spot on a dark green ground, and a good, strong, serviceable half-crown Dunstable straw bonnet, trimmed very plainly — a nice clean quilled net cap under it, and one of the quietest black-and-white plaid shawls I think I ever saw in all my life ", notes the mistress, who engaged her upon the same terms as the delinquent Mary, with the proviso that " no ringlets, followers or sandals " would be allowed.

When dressed for duty the appearance of this paragon under-went a startling change. She wore " a fly-away, starched-out imitation Balzorine gown of a bright ultramarine picked out with white flowers — on each side of her head a bunch of long ringlets like untwisted bell-ropes, and a blonde lace cap with cherry-coloured streamers flying about nearly a yard long ". Small wonder that during her brief reign the house was besieged by Life Guardsmen from Albany Barracks, creatures " so frightfully handsome that they ought not to be allowed by Government to wander at large in those fascinating red jackets, cracking the hearts of all the poor girls in the neighbourhood as if they were so much crockery ".

This question of " followers " was a burning one with most mistresses : it is easy to understand their apprehensions, but difficult to approve of those prohibitions which, if fully enforced, condemned the vast majority of women-servants to perpetual spinsterhood. In *The Greatest Plague of Life* there is an illustration entitled simply " Followers " which interprets with Cruikshank's habitual savage skill the point of view of the average employer in this regard. We see a trim-waisted maid, broom in hand, leading into the house by the back-door a long, curving procession of men, women and children, each section, and some individuals, carrying a large banner with an appropriate inscription — Father and Mother, Sisters and Brothers, Uncles and Aunts, Cousins in Town, The Young Man as Keeps Company, Acquaintances and Outboard Lovers, Various other Suitors, Friends and Old Fellow-Servants, Country Cousins (wearing smocks), A Strong Body of Police (in tall hats), a Detachment of Military (in shakos and tight-waisted tunics) and so on, till the tail of the procession vanishes out of the top of the picture. In the Friends and Old Fellow-Servants group there is a negro footman with a cockade in his hat who reminds us of Mr. Sedley's Sambo in *Vanity Fair* and also of the curious circumstance that though coloured men-servants were frequently seen well into the nineteenth century, the coloured woman-servant, only a little less usual in earlier periods, had by then almost completely disappeared.

It is clear that the imaginary housewife of the Brothers Mayhew is more concerned with the military section than with any other — very natural, when the headquarters of the Life Guards were so near, providing a boundless contiguity of scarlet-jacketed heroes. " I don't know ", writes the lady plaintively,

> if any of my courteous readers have ever been in Albany Street when the bugle is sounded for these fellows to return to their barracks, but upon my word the scene is really heartbreaking to housekeepers, for there isn't an area down the whole street but from which you will see a Life Guardsman with his mouth full ascending the steps and hurrying off to his quarters for the night.

Like Leigh Hunt's Abigail seventeen years earlier, the maid of 1847 as depicted by the Mayhews has a strong taste for cheap and lurid literature. One girl particularly susceptible to its appeal was wont to march about the house in Park Village with a broom in her hand, fancying herself to be " Ada the Betrayed " or " Amy " in *Love and Madness*. The stories which she loved and re-lived appeared in penny numbers and bore such titillating titles as *The Heads of the Headless*, *Marianne or the Child of Charity*, *The Castle Fiend*, *Mary the Primrose Girl*, *The Maniac Father or the Victim of Seduction*, *Emily FitzOrmond or the Deserted One*. There was also the *Penny Sunday Times*, in which the damsel was found rapt in contemplation of " a large, staring frightful engraving in the middle of the front page ", showing " a great brute of a man in a Spanish hat and a large black cloak all flying about, striking some very grand theatrical attitude and flourishing over his head a big carving knife to which three or four heavy notes of admiration were hanging, while a poor defenceless woman lay at his feet . . . weltering in a pool of ink ". The title would be something in this style : " The Earl in his Rage slaying the Lady Isoline ".

The Greatest Plague in Life is satirical and farcical by turns, but it gives some vivid and authentic glimpses of London life ten years after the accession of Victoria. For example, when we are shown how the romantically-minded Abigail might be tempted to waste her scanty substance upon the *Last Dying Speech and Confession* broadsheets hawked in the streets by " husky vagabonds with cracked post-horn voices ". One particular maid is described as rushing up in all haste to the door, " to have another penn'orth of horrors " : after which she would sit down " and never let the bit of paper go out of her hand until she had got the whole of the affecting copy of verses by heart ". Then for weeks afterwards she would march up and down, chanting some such nonsense as :

> Biddle and Sheriff is our sad names
>   And do confess we were much to blame,
> On the 28th of September last
>   We well remember, alas ! alas !
> The very thoughts causes us to rue
> In eighteen hundred and forty-two.

Two years after the publication of *The Greatest Plague* there appeared an anonymous book entitled *Home Truths for Home Peace or Muddle Defeated*. The writer seems to have been one of those admirable but not invariably amiable people upon whom every token of untidiness, confusion, lack of method and want of care acts like a strong irritant poison. Unfortunately many of her acquaintances seem to have had all Mrs. Jellyby's fecklessness without any of Mrs. Jellyby's excuses, and some of her descriptions of the interiors of their homes, especially when unexpected visitors called, make harrowing reading even now.

This authority is especially severe when dealing with those households where, although the garments of mistress, maids and children are all equally dirty and untouchable, it is explained that " there is no end to the washing in the house ". The " great washes of families in a muddle " were invariably distinguished " for bearing an inverse proportion to the small cleanliness maintained in them ". At what precise moment any of the garments in process of being washed are *not* dirty " no one is able to say ; but an immense number are invariably put in the way of being dirtied over again . . . by being left in the passage for the mangling-woman who never seems to call for the clothes except when they are *not* ready ".

It is interesting to compare the second part of the following passage with that quoted earlier, in Chapter VIII, page 163, on the subject of " Conduct to Servants " :

> The servants are the *hands*, the mistress should be the *head* of the house. It is hers to think, to order, to arrange, to provide, to look, to over-look, to remember, to remind ; and she has no more *right* to *expect* these things from her servants than *they* have to demand from their mistress that she should get up first, light the fire, and take their place in the kitchen. . . . And let her not overlook the dignity and privilege of being thus wanted and called upon continually. The Almighty, who condescendingly chose the relations of human life as types of those which He desires should subsist between Him and His creatures, has, in ordaining that " the eyes of a maiden should look to the hand of her mistress ", hallowed the duty He appoints by making it illustrative of the bounteous Providence that upholds the Universe.

The lady thus invested with semi-divine attributes is strongly advised to attend to her marketing in person. Not only will she get better served by going herself ; as gossiping with the tradespeople will not be the same temptation to the mistress as it is to the maid, " the business will be much more speedily accomplished by her than by them ". Yet the author of *Home Truths for Home*

Peace shows a touch of kindly compunction, and even a gleam of humorous insight, when she suggests that the domestics should be sent on an *occasional* errand, " by means of which they, in their turn, may *inhale* a little fresh air and *exhale* some of the 'perilous stuff' which, if not communicated to our equals, is apt to prey upon the heart ". Such errands " are both unavoidable and desirable : but ", she adds gravely, " the temptation to *stay* out *when* out being one of the greatest to which they are liable they should not constantly be exposed to it ".

Though in the matter of costume and *décor* the early and mid-Victorian colour-scheme was every whit as strong and violent as the Regency colour-scheme had been, there were other fields in which a dulling and flattening influence seemed to be at work. The racy tang of idiosyncrasy, the rich bouquet of pomposity began to fail, and nowhere is this failure more conspicuous than in the phrasing of small advertisements. Here are a few specimens culled almost at random from *The Times* during the 1840's : it will be observed that the single gentleman has not ceased to attract — it is improbable that he ever will — and that ' respectable ' families still reside in the East End. The word had not yet taken on its later and narrower meaning, and though no longer used in the sense intended by Princess Mary when she alluded to George III as her " most valuable and respectable father ", it was still synonymous with ' superior ', or even ' distinguished '. The servant who would in these days be called a ' parlour-maid ' or a ' house-parlour-maid ' was still rather loosely labelled ' housemaid ', but we hear no more of ' chamber-maids ' until the word is revived to describe a housemaid in a hotel. Wages were more frequently mentioned in the 'forties, and were already rising, though the sum named in the following advertisement suggests an earlier and less liberal age :

> Wanted by female of high respectability and useful education, aged 35, a situation as Housekeeper to a single gentleman. The advertiser does not mind confinement, has no associates, and would accept any respectable situation where her services would be adequate to 8s. a week.

Wages range from £10 to £20, with or without tea and sugar, and often with " washing put out ". Sixteen pounds is offered in

1843 for a servant of all work in a respectable family in the East End of London. "None need apply who are not of a good disposition and a respectable and cleanly appearance", and those who fulfil these conditions should address themselves to Mr. Payne, Pastry Cook, Park Place, Mile End Road. "The small family of Mr. Tuck, Grocer, Tranquil Vale, Blackheath" wanted a respectable woman who thoroughly understood her business as cook. They offered £15 a year "and washing put out".

A serious family living ten miles from town near a railroad sought a young person of about twenty-five who understood dressmaking and was "willing to make herself generally useful" — a dangerously elastic clause. Some of the advertisers desire to cross the line between the kitchen and the parlour without having any particular qualifications to justify that promotion, as in the following :

> To the Aged or Invalid. A Young Person, respectably connected, wishes for a situation as companion or attendant on a Lady, or as a nursery governess where no accomplishments are required.

Families often proclaim their own seriousness or demand that quality in their employees ; but it is seldom now that any of the advertisements are either lyrical or ambiguous. There is none the less a faintly sinister element in the following :

> A Lady's Maid or Nurse needed to go abroad. A middle-aged person who speaks French, understands dressmaking and millinery and making children's clothes, is fond of children and strictly religious. Such a one may find a home for life. Widow or orphan preferred.

A middle-aged person would be likely to have lost both parents, and a person with a husband living might hesitate, however much she may have desired, to go abroad : but this preference for an applicant without family ties is, to say the least of it, curious.

A neat and even a pleasing appearance is sometimes specified, but excessively good looks were often a handicap, especially after 1849, when the comely and soft-spoken Mrs. Manning, murderess and ex-Abigail, suffered for her crime. Many ladies must then have viewed with even less enthusiasm than before any applicant of more than common attractions. This siren, in addition to a

mild and appealing type of beauty, is said to have had " a singularly musical and sympathetic voice which, with her gentle
manner, had made her the chosen distributor of alms to the poor
by the noble family whom she had served as Lady's Maid ". She
and her husband were tried for the murder of a wealthy fool
called O'Connor, who was infatuated by the woman, and whose
body was buried in quicklime under the paving-stones of
their kitchen floor by the precious pair. When the police came
to inspect the place, Mrs. Manning, observing that their eyes were
fixed upon the fresh cement and the discoloured flags, carelessly
and calmly drew her long skirts over the tell-tale patch — in vain.
" She drove out of use ", remarks a contemporary, " that previously indispensable part of a lady's wardrobe, a rich black satin
dress : for she insisted in wearing upon the scaffold one given to
her by a member of the noble family on whom she had waited."

Very different were the looks of the maid employed in the
'fifties of the century by the Academician, Edward Ward : the
first time he saw her he observed uncharitably, " If ever that
woman marries it will be a ticket-of-leave man " — a prophecy
fulfilled to the letter. It is Mrs. Ward who relates the story of
the eccentric Lord Crewe in whose country house no women-
servants were seen anywhere except at chapel, where a large
number would appear and then, at the conclusion of divine service,
mysteriously vanish away. It was explained to visitors by the
cousin who kept house for his lordship that he hated women, and
because he could not bear the sight of them himself, he thought
that everyone else must detest them too — so they were ordered,
under pain of instant dismissal, never to let themselves be seen.

Fiction in the early and mid-Victorian periods teems with
such a rich variety of Abigails that to choose those who are either
most typical or most unusual is a matter of no small difficulty.
Dickens, with his love for a crowded canvas and his flair for over-
statement, can be trusted to provide examples in either category.
His Abigails range from Mrs. Steerforth's prim, pretty parlour-
maid with the coloured ribbons in her cap to Peg Sliderskew,
deaf, draggled and depraved, simpering under the tipsy leer of
Wackford Squeers.

Pride of place must be given to that enchanting elf, " the

Marchioness ". Though there may be in her make-up certain remembered traits of Mrs. John Dickens's little workhouse waif (who also sat for the rough sketch of " the orfling " in *David Copperfield*), she cannot be ranked with the common run of mortals, and must surely have been discovered by Sally Brass cradled in an acorn. Acorns, it is true, were unlikely objects to be lying about in Bevis Marks : it may have been a cabbage-leaf. Some such theory is needed as an alternative to the suggestion that she was Sally Brass's illegitimate child and — still more repellant — that Daniel Quilp may have been her father.

The Victorian novelist, hurriedly scribbling his latest instalment with an inky boy waiting for it in the hall, can hardly be blamed for lapsing into inconsistencies and leaving unfollowed clues trailing about. Dickens never troubled — perhaps he did not choose — to elucidate his dark, reiterated hints that the origin of the Marchioness was a mystery of which the solution was known to Sally, suspected by Quilp and dimly divined by Dick Swiveller : but it is not an agreeable notion that he imagined either the dwarf or the virago, or both of them together, as responsible for her existence.

Another result of this helter-skelter method of composition was the strange variations in the looks, behaviour and personality of some of the characters as the narrative unrolled itself in weekly or monthly jerks. Dick Swiveller is an outstanding example of this. There is little to be found in common between the grubby, flashy, ill-spoken waster of chapter ii and the delightful, allusive, quixotic fellow who emerges by degrees, the champion of the oppressed, the avenger of the innocent, and finally the happy husband of " Sophronia Sphynx ".

The transformation dates from the period of his first contact with the Small Servant, and the operative influence was compassion. Almost from the moment that Dick Swiveller first looks down from his high office-stool and sees the " small, slip-shod girl in the dirty, coarse bib and apron which left nothing of her visible but her face and her feet ", the " Perpetual Grand of the Glorious Apollers " begins to fade out and the face and voice of the later and infinitely more likable Dick make themselves seen and heard. Writing from Broadstairs to John Forster in October

1840, Dickens, who had just issued those numbers containing the fifty-seventh and fifty-eighth chapters of *The Old Curiosity Shop*, declared " The way is clear for Kit now, and for a great effect at the last with the Marchioness ". No doubt the great effect, already shaping itself in that bubbling cauldron of a brain, was the episode in which the Marchioness, true to her fairy-tale character, cares for the helpless Dick in his fever and participates in the delights supplied (again in fairy-tale fashion) by the Garland family ; but novelists and their readers do not always see eye to eye in these matters, and to most people the peak of the story is reached in chapter lviii, when for the first time Dick and the Marchioness sit down to a game of cribbage in the dim and odorous vault that was Sally Brass's kitchen.

Susan Nipper's creator was undoubtedly right in relying upon her for " a strong character throughout the book ", and her excellent amalgam of devotion and asperity, so like that bestowed by Molière upon his Nicoles and Toinettes, illustrates yet again the curious Gallic quality in Dickens. As depicted by " Phiz ", she looks both smart and capable, with her neat little boots, trimly fitting dress and coy little cap.

The sycophantic " Phib " in *Nicholas Nickleby*, the feeble, afflicted " Guster " and the great-hearted Charley in *Bleak House*, the angular, amorous Miss Miggs in *Barnaby Rudge*, the casual Flopson in *Great Expectations*, all spring into reality as the spotlight of the novelist's fancy falls upon them ; Clara Peggotty Barkis is to many readers as convincing, and quite as dear, as if they, like David, had " looked perseveringly at her as she sat at work ; at the little bit of wax-candle she kept for her thread . . . at the little house with the thatched roof where the yard-measure lived : at her work-box with the sliding lid, with a view of St. Paul's Cathedral with a pink dome painted on it ; at the brass thimble on her finger ; at herself ", whom he " thought lovely ".

One of the earliest and most decorative of the Dickensian Abigails is surely " Mary, housemaid at Mr. Nupkins's, Ipswich ", the future Mrs. Sam Weller, the recipient of the Valentine that caused him such fierce throes of composition. Strict pedantry might demand that she should be placed in the pre-Victorian group, as the events in which she plays a part were supposed to occur ten years before the young Queen's accession : but Dickens is himself so ineluctably Victorian that it has seemed better to assemble all his characters in the same period.

Mary does not enter until chapter xxv, fifteen chapters later than Sam : she is the " very smart and pretty-faced servant-girl " who opens the green-painted door of Mr. Nupkins's house in Ipswich and holds up her hands in astonishment at the rebellious demeanour of the Pickwickians in the custody of Grummer and his special constables. When, after the *éclaircissement*, Sam was invited to dine in the magistrate's kitchen, he asked Muzzle, the man-servant, how many " ladies " there were in the household. " Only two in our kitchen," answered Muzzle. " Cook and 'ousemaid. We keep a boy to do the dirty work and a girl besides, but they dine in the washus." " Oh, they dines in the washus, do they ? " said Mr. Weller. " Yes," replied Muzzle. " We tried 'em at our table when they first come, but we couldn't keep 'em. The gal's manners is dreadful vulgar ; and the boy breathes so hard while he's eating that we found it impossible to sit at table with him." Later he explains to Sam that " that is the worst of country service . . . the juniors is always so very savage ".

Presumably the well-favoured Mary had once been a junior, but even the Chesterfieldian Muzzle could hardly at any time have called her 'savage'. Her gaiety, her good-humour and her good looks are all cleverly conveyed in the famous kitchen comedy scene which follows.

Mrs. Nupkins, though an alarming female, cannot have objected either to sandals or to side-curls, for in " Phiz "'s illustration Mary is seen wearing both, and a very fetching quilled cap with sprouting knots of ribbon into the bargain. The interior of the kitchen is interesting as showing what the background would be below-stairs in the year of grace 1827. Bunches of herbs and ropes of onions depend from the ceiling, flanked by three handsome hams — a fourth is being smoked over the open fire. An eight-day clock stands beside a dresser well garnished with plates, dishes and tureens, and a vasty frying-pan hangs — with a gridiron, a pair of tongs, a shovel and a poker — within the embrasure of the large and wide fireplace. Meat and drink obviously abound, but the four-legged wooden stools upon which the cook and Sam are perched could hardly be more uncompromisingly comfortless, and no easy-chair of any kind can be discerned.

When we — and Sam — meet the pretty housemaid again it is in a shady lane at Clifton, where he sees her shaking bedside carpets and gallantly goes to her aid before he realizes that " the very neat and pretty figure " belongs to his lady-love. In the meantime he had concocted, with much travail of mind and body, and with many interruptions from Mr. Weller, Senior, that celebrated Valentine of which the most celebrated passage runs :

> So I take the privilidge of the day, Mary my dear — as the gen'lemen in difficulties did, ven he valked out of a Sunday — to tell you that the first and only time I see you your likeness was took on my hart in much quicker time and brighter colours than ever a likeness was took by the profeel macheen (wich p'raps you may have heerd on, Mary my dear) although it *does* finish a portrait and put the frame and glass on complete with a hook at the end to hang it up by, and all in two minutes-and-a-quarter.

As attendant upon the charming Arabella Allen in her elopement with Mr. Nathaniel Winkle, Mary has an amiable part to play in the story of their wedding, their subsequent reconciliation with Winkle *père*, and their intervention in the romance of Mr. Snodgrass and Emily Wardle. " Phiz " shows us how attractive Mary looked when dressed for the road, with a tight-waisted, wide-sleeved gown and a large coal-scuttle bonnet ; and in the scene where, in cap and apron, she dines with the Fat Boy, we see that the visitors' servants' dining-room at Osborne's hotel, in the Adelphi, was furnished with Windsor chairs which, however austere, were an improvement upon the stools in the kitchen of the Ipswich magistrate.

In addition to taking us below-stairs in a variety of households and of houses, Dickens — in chapter xvi of *Nicholas Nickleby* — conducts us to that " temple of promise ", a registry office. There is no ambiguity about *this* establishment : all is decorous to the highest degree. " A genteel female in shepherd's plaid boots " is heard requesting Tom, the clerk, to " read out an easy place or two ". He obliges with particulars of Mrs. Wrymug's situation in Finsbury : "Wages, twelve guineas. No tea, no sugar. Serious family ".

"Ah, you needn't mind reading that," interrupted the client.

" ' Three serious footmen,' " said Tom, impressively.

"Three, did you say ? " asked the client, in an altered tone.

" ' Three serious footmen,' " replied Tom, " ' cook, housemaid, and nursemaid : each female servant required to join the Little Bethel Congregation three times every Sunday, with a serious footman.' . . ."

"I'll take the address of that place," said the client; "I don't know but what it mightn't suit me pretty well."

"If I leave this manuscript open on my table," wrote Thackeray in *Pendennis*, " I have not the slightest doubt Betty will read it, and they will talk it over in the lower regions to-night, and tomorrow she will bring in my breakfast with a face of such entire, imperturbable innocence that no mortal could suppose her guilty of playing the spy." He was, perhaps temperamentally, more interested in flunkeys than in women-servants, and when he descends to the kitchen quarters it is usually to draw a moral or point a satire, as in the *Vehmgericht* passage in *Vanity Fair*, chapter xliv. The same novel reveals the ugly, stunted figure of the little workhouse maid " on her promotion ", who fawns upon Betsy Horrocks, Sir Pitt Crawley's light o'-love, and then, as soon as a stroke deprives the old reprobate of speech and sense, rounds on Betsy and denounces her to Mrs. Bute Crawley. To balance her there is the less distinct but very different image of " honest Dolly ", the housemaid, who, when she heard Rawdon junior crying in the night, " took him out of his solitary nursery into her bed in the garret hard by and comforted him ".

When the footman, James de la Pluche, has made a fortune by gambling in railway shares, he thus takes leave of his former sweetheart, Mary Anne :

"Mary Hann," says I, " suckimstancies has haltered our rellatif positions in life. I quit the Servants' Hall for hever (for has for your marrying a person in my ranks, that, my dear, is hall gammin) and so I wish you a good by, my good gal, and if you want to better yourself, halways refer to me."

But Mary Ann did not answer : she looked Mr. de la Pluche in the face " quite wild-like, and bust into something betwigst a laugh and a cry, and fell down with her ed on the kitching dresser ". In the end, after the market in railway shares had collapsed, and James was lying, " a misrabble captif ", in the Queen's Bench prison, the faithful maiden returned to his side, " and there was sunlike in the dunjing of the pore prisoner ".

The Abigails depicted in *Punch* during its first two decades were of the pert and decorative rather than the shabby and down-trodden type : they are often seen sticking up for their rights and privileges, and not infrequently their comeliness is contrasted with their mistresses' lack of it. In a series called " Servant-Gallery " we get glimpses of life below-stairs which recall some of Swift's less savage touches in his *Directions to Servants* ; and it is made abundantly clear that any efforts on the part of the mistresses to deter their maids from following the fashions — even the most extreme fashions — have now been finally defeated.

The picture reproduced opposite page 182, and entitled " Protector and Protectee ", appeared in the same issue of *Punch* (April 14, 1866) that contained the cartoon celebrating Carlyle's Rectorial Address at Edinburgh. The enthusiasm of the maids at Chelsea on that occasion goes far to prove the assertion of the Sage's niece, Mrs. Alexander Carlyle, that he was the reverse of unpopular with his household ; and he was probably less exigent than Tennyson, whose deep-mouthed, long-sustained indignation because the housemaid at Farringford, one day in the 'fifties, had removed " a can of hot water which he had put out for his own shaving after breakfast ", is so amusingly described by Mr. Harold Nicolson in his *Life* of the poet. By growing a beard the Laureate relieved her of at least *that* part of her morning duty.

Whose shall be the last figure in this long, many-coloured pageant of English Abigails ? If we want one which will form a striking contrast to the " toylyng and slubberyng " damsel of the Prologue, why not Pretty Polly Perkins of Paddington Green ? She was, we know, " as beautiful as a butterfly and as proud as a Queen " ; and she cruelly jilted her milkman for the " bowlegged conductor of a twopenny bus ". Yet let us close the story with Martha, Miss Matty's maid in *Cranford* : Martha who, instructed to serve the ladies first at table, murmured, " I'll do as you tell me,

ma'am, but I like lads best " ; Martha who, when the Town and
County Bank stopped payment and Miss Matty was ruined,
fiercely refused to abandon her mistress, citing with scorn the
example of " Mrs. FitzAdam's Rosy ", who struck for higher
wages after living seven and a half years in one place ; Martha
who, disregarding Miss Matty's refusal to order a pudding,
declared, " I'll be up to her. Never you tell, but I'll make her a
pudding, and a pudding that she'll like, too, and I'll pay for it
myself. . . . Many a one has been comforted in their sorrow by
seeing a good dish come upon the table."

And so there was triumphantly set before dear Miss Matty
" the most wonderful representation of a lion couchant that
ever was moulded ". After Martha, tearful but exulting, had
rushed from the room, her mistress, nearly in tears herself,
turned to the teller of the story, Mary Smith. " I should like,"
she said, " to keep this pudding under a glass shade, dear."
The suggestion was received with gentle but irrepressible
laughter, " which rather surprised Miss Matty. ' I am sure,
dear, I have seen uglier things under a glass shade before now,'
said she." Yet in a sense her wish has been fulfilled ; for Martha's
lion, with its currant eyes and its mane of pudding, has not
perished, and may well outlast its bronze brethren in Trafalgar
Square.

INDEX

Index

Index

THE END

Printed in Great Britain by R. & R. CLARK, LIMITED, *Edinburgh*